Becoming American Jews

TEMPLE ISRAEL OF BOSTON

Meaghan Dwyer-Ryan
Susan L. Porter
Lisa Fagin Davis

BRANDEIS SERIES IN AMERICAN JEWISH HISTORY, CULTURE, AND LIFE

Jonathan D. Sarna, Editor

Sylvia Barack Fishman, Associate Editor

For a complete list of books that are available in the series, visit www.upne.com

MEAGHAN DWYER-RYAN, SUSAN L. PORTER, LISA FAGIN DAVIS

Becoming American Jews

TEMPLE ISRAEL OF BOSTON

BRANDEIS UNIVERSITY PRESS

Waltham, Massachusetts

PUBLISHED BY UNIVERSITY PRESS OF NEW ENGLAND

Hanover and London

Brandeis University Press
Published by University Press of New England,
One Court Street, Lebanon, NH 03766
www.upne.com

Library of Congress Cataloging-in-Publication Data
Dwyer-Ryan, Meaghan.
Becoming American Jews : Temple Israel of Boston /
Meaghan Dwyer-Ryan, Susan L. Porter, and Lisa Fagin Davis.
p.   cm. — (Brandeis series in American Jewish history, culture, and life)
Includes bibliographical references and index.
ISBN 978-1-58465-790-3 (pbk. : alk. paper)
1. Congregation Adath Israel (Boston, Mass.) — History.
2. Synagogues — Massachusetts — Boston — History.
3. Jews — Massachusetts — Boston — History.
4. Reform Judaism — Massachusetts — Boston — History.
I. Porter, Susan L. II. Davis, Lisa Fagin. III. Title.
BM225.B6D89   2009
296.09744'61 — dc22   2009018246

Cover image: Congregants leaving Commonwealth Avenue
Synagogue, 1908. (Courtesy of Temple Israel Archives)
Title page image: Confirmation class, on the steps of the Riverway
Meeting House, 1930. (Courtesy of Temple Israel Archives)

For our mothers:

Rosemary Twomey Dwyer,

Ruthe Orell Porter (1925–2004),

and Lois Levin Roisman (1938–2008)

and for the congregants of Temple Israel,

past, present, and future

CONTENTS

FOREWORD

The summer of 2004, the year of Temple Israel's sesquicentennial, brought the end of the stately Norway maple tree that had filled the frame of the window behind the ark since the construction of the sanctuary in 1973. That towering and majestic presence had provided us with moments of inspiration and contemplation, a vision of divine grandeur, a reflection of the seasons' alternation, juxtaposed against the human architectural inspirations of our worship space. Weddings and b'nai mitzvah celebrations that spilled onto the patio were graced by the dignity and beauty of that tree. The children of our Frances Jacobson Early Childhood Center played beneath its shade. It stood as a venerable tree of life, hovering protectively over the sanctity of our sacred space. After it was felled, the rings of the tree revealed that it had died at the age of 150.

If those rings could have spoken, they might have told us the story of the more than 150 years of Temple Israel's history. Instead, we have been blessed by an extraordinary team of coauthors: Temple archivist and historian Meaghan Dwyer-Ryan, historian Susan L. Porter, and bibliographer Lisa Fagin Davis (who spearheaded the research for our sesquicentennial historical exhibit). On behalf of the entire congregation, I express my gratitude to Meaghan, Susan, and Lisa, this talented trio, for their indefatigable investigation and their superb rendition of Temple Israel's history. They have used their collective expertise to probe the priceless documents in our temple archives (made accessible by the pioneering archival work of Rabbi Susan Abramson, Betsy Abrams, z.'l., Roberta Burstein, and others), research demographic data, conduct oral histories, and employ newly available outside sources to chronicle the complex stories of the people who were and are Temple Israel. Their insight informs not only our current reality: a "Beit Knesset" (a community of caring and action), a "Beit Tefillah" (a home for innovative ritual, prayer and spirituality), and a "Beit Midrash" (a Torah-centered space for Jewish learning), but also demonstrates that our history is inextricably intertwined with the stories of Boston and the larger American Reform movement.

This work was made possible by the continuing vision and generosity of Justin and Genevieve Wyner, who have supported, with their means and their spirit, this new historical study of our congregation. We, our children, and our children's children are in their debt.

As I read *Becoming American Jews*, I was reminded of William Wordsworth's "Intimations of Immortality" (1807):

> The thought of our past years in me doth breed
> Perpetual benediction: not indeed
> For that which is most worthy to be blessed —
> Delight and liberty . . .
> Not for these I raise
> The song of thanks and praise;
> But for those obstinate questionings
> Of sense and outward things
> Fallings from us, vanishings . . .
> But for those affections,
> Those shadowy recollections,
> Which, be they what they may,
> Are yet the fountain light of all our day
> Are yet a master light of all our seeing . . .

I pray that this book will always inspire both "perpetual benediction" and "obstinate questionings." May the Eternal Spirit of the Universe guide and bless Temple Israel and ensure that the past will be "a master light of all our seeing."

Rabbi Ronne Friedman
October 30, 2008

PREFACE

Congregation Adath Israel was founded in 1854 by a group of German-speaking immigrants from central Europe. Its story, however, began twelve years earlier, in 1842, when some of these newly arrived Jews gathered in Boston with others from different regions to celebrate a circumcision. At this event, they resolved to establish the city's first synagogue, Congregation Ohabei Shalom. The immigrants' desire to create a permanent institution where they could observe life-cycle events and worship, study, and socialize as a community in accord with Jewish law reflected age-old patterns. But, as these pioneers soon realized, the process of re-creating traditional Jewish communal life in the United States was complex due to several factors: the heterogeneity of the population, the expectation that individuals would want to make their own life choices, and, above all, the fact that religious institutions in America functioned as autonomous voluntary associations. As new immigrants from various regions joined Ohabei Shalom, their determination to worship according to their own customs led to conflict over ritual practices. The congregation divided, with many of the original members leaving to establish Congregation Adath Israel, Boston's second synagogue.

From its inception, Congregation Adath Israel took a forward-looking approach to religious practice. While the new synagogue retained the traditional German "minhag" (ritual) until the 1870s, its upwardly mobile members gradually began to question some customs as they adapted to their new cultural setting. In 1874, Adath Israel became the first synagogue in Boston to adopt some aspects of Reform; it has since become an innovator in religious practices, education, and social justice, as well as an important force in American Jewish life. At the same time, the synagogue continues to fulfill the deep, personal needs its founders expressed: to worship according to Jewish tradition, to encourage Jewish learning and fellowship, and to improve the moral and social condition of all Jews.

Becoming American Jews: Temple Israel of Boston tells the stories of the men and women who created and maintained the congregation from its beginning as a traditional German shul to its current status as the largest Reform synagogue in New England. The book demonstrates how Jews of various cultural backgrounds came together in the American setting, sought ways to maintain the equilibrium between their desire to practice their faith and their determination to be accepted as Americans, and tried to preserve Judaism as a living religion in a free society where acculturated Jews were tempted to intermarry, convert, or simply ignore their religion and ethnicity. Because this story is not unique to Temple Israel, *Becoming American Jews* is, in many ways, the narrative of American Reform Jewry in microcosm.

At Temple Israel, as elsewhere, congregants have regularly reformulated models of worship, education, and community in the context of their own cultural experiences and goals for the future. Generations of dedicated members have devoted themselves to enlivening, maintaining, and supporting the synagogue. They have hired an impressive roster of talented clergy and staff to inspire the congregation, serve as its public face, and secure its excellent reputation. Together, members, lay leaders, and clergy have engaged in regular debate and consensus-building to overcome the inevitable tensions over ritual practice and institutional governance that both maintain continuity and lead to change. Over time, the balance of power among these groups has frequently shifted and restabilized, often in response to larger cultural changes that have affected both the relationship between the synagogue and the larger Jewish community and the synagogue's role as a local religious and cultural institution. This book describes how these creative collaborations, dialogues, and, at times, conflicts between various constituencies have ultimately served to energize, strengthen, and diversify the temple community.

Becoming American Jews also demonstrates the striking continuities in the synagogue's long history. In addition to its primary function as a place of worship, Temple Israel has always provided opportunities for study, education, and communal service, and has continually worked to create an emotionally satisfying spiritual setting for Jewish life-cycle events. While these functions have adapted over time, the community that is Temple Israel has always provided a variety of ways for men, women, and children to affirm their Jewish identity and express Jewish values in a heterogeneous society.

Religious education has always been a central focus of the congregation. Over the years, most new members of Temple Israel (and other synagogues) have been parents of young children who were determined to have their offspring learn about their religion, experience such rites of passage as bar (and later bat) mitzvah and confirmation, and continue to practice and perpetuate Judaism as adults. As with worship, approaches to education have always reflected the changing values and concerns of the larger culture. Early on, children studied German and Hebrew—the languages the founders used in prayer—along with the Bible. Later, members and clergy came to view religious education as a lifelong endeavor to study Jewish history, culture, and the Bible (and, more recently, later rabbinic works), and focus on the meaning and the form of prayer.

This study also sheds new light on the roles that Jews have played in the history of greater Boston and elsewhere. Over the years, in their efforts to adapt Judaism to meet contemporary needs and pressures, Boston's Jews have striven to balance tradition and innovation, acculturation and distinctiveness. This process has resulted in a multiplicity of Jewish institutions that serve various communal purposes. In Boston, as in other urban areas, Jews used such organizations, in addition to synagogues, to build community, work toward self-improvement, and practice philanthropy. As Jews have become more integrated into mainstream American society, their position as an upwardly mobile minority seeking a better world has encouraged them to engage in "G'milut Chasadim" (deeds of loving kindness) in the larger community with the goal of reducing racial, religious, and class disparities. This process of imagining and re-imagining the personal and communal meaning of Judaism has been vital to the ongoing saga of "becoming American Jews."

Temple Israel early on assumed the mantle of Boston's "cathedral congregation"; as such, its members have long taken an interest in the world outside of the synagogue. They were determined to hire talented clergy who could perform important work in various public arenas along with their pastoral and congregational duties. Temple Israel's members and clergy have been disproportionately represented among the founders and leaders of New England's Jewish communal institutions; they have also served as activists and benefactors in other welfare and cultural organizations. Together, they have engaged in important political, legal, social, intellectual, and cultural work that has had significant local, national, and even international impact.

For more than 150 years, Temple Israel has helped Boston's Jews devise strategies for being Jewish in the United States that synthesize and balance Americanization and Judaism. The forms and accommodations that "synthesis" has taken have varied over the years as the challenges and environment have changed. The goals, however, have been consistent: to provide a welcoming community where Jews can find comfortable ways to practice

Judaism, find fellowship, seek inspiration, and work to repair the world. Today, Temple Israel is a "Beit Tefillah" (a house of worship and prayer), a "Beit Midrash" (a house of study and Torah), and a "Beit Knesset" (a house of gathering, caring, and action) for Boston's continually changing and evolving Jewish community.

ACKNOWLEDGMENTS

Becoming American Jews: Temple Israel of Boston was conceived almost a decade ago as part of the planning for Temple Israel's 2004–2005 sesquicentennial celebration. In part, it was designed to bring forward the story told in *Growth and Achievement*, the volume edited by historian Arthur Mann and published for the centennial in 1954. Because Mann's book focused almost entirely on the rabbis and our goal was to write a fuller history of the men, women, and children of the congregation — as well as the clergy — it was clear that we would need to start from the beginning.

Our methodology has been, as much as possible, to focus on primary sources, many of which have become accessible only recently in the Temple Israel Archives and elsewhere. As a result, this volume both builds on and revises previous studies of Temple Israel, including Stella Obst's *The Story of Temple Adath Israel* (1917), Susan Abramson's "The Social History of Temple Adath Israel, 1911–Present" (1973) and "The History of Temple Adath Israel As Seen Through the Evolution of the Worship Experience" (1976), Joseph Reimer's *Succeeding at Jewish Education* (1997), and Jeffrey Summit's *The Lord's Song in a Strange Land* (2000). Works about Boston's Jewish community such as Solomon Schindler's *Israelites in Boston* (1889), Albert Ehrenfried's *A Chronicle of Boston Jewry* (1963), William A. Braverman's "The Ascent of Boston's Jews, 1630–1918" (1990), and Jonathan Sarna, Ellen Smith, and Scott-Martin Kosofsky's *The Jews of Boston* (2005) were also very useful.

The process of researching and writing this book has been facilitated by many volunteers who, over the years, devoted themselves to collecting, preserving, and organizing materials in the Temple Israel Archives. We are particularly grateful to Betsy Abrams, z.'l., Roberta (Bobbie) Burstein, Rabbi Susan Abramson, and intern Rachel Wise. Monies allocated from the sesquicentennial budget and other special funds made it possible for the temple to hire Meaghan Dwyer as its first professional archivist in 2001. A generous gift from Justin and Genevieve Wyner provided funds for the writing, design, and publication of the book, as well as the distribution of a volume to each membership unit. In addition, a grant from Temple Israel's Clergy Discretionary Fund paid for a very useful trip to the American Jewish Archives in Cincinnati.

We are particularly grateful to those who read some or all of the manuscript: Barbara Burg, Rabbi Ronne Friedman, Frances (Fran) Godine, Dr. Karla Goldman, Carol Michael, Frances (Fran) Putnoi, Dr. Jonathan Sarna, Lesley Schoenfeld, Dr. Susan Walton, Genevieve Wyner, Justin Wyner, and Rabbi Elaine Zecher. Their comments and observations have greatly improved the final product. In the end, of course, all final editing and interpretative decisions, including any errors, are our responsibility.

We also thank those who shared their ideas, memories, and memorabilia or helped us with various aspects of the project, including Ann Abrams, Rabbi Susan Abramson, Ruth Aisner, Rabbi Ruth Alpers, Anita Bender, Bobbie Burstein, Helen Cohen, Sylvia Cooper, Cantor Roy Einhorn, Michele Fagin, Elly Finn, Fran Godine, Rabbi Albert Goldman, Edward Goldstein, Marvin Grossman, Samuel (Buster) Gutman, z.'l., Lois Isenman, Rabbi Bernard Mehlman, Emily Mehlman, z.'l., Susan (Sue) Misselbeck, Peggy Morrison, Cecily Morse, Ruth Nemzoff, Fran Putnoi, Irving Rabb, Shula Reinharz, Judy Rothman, Arthur Schatz, Andra Stein, Beverly Weiss, Henry Weiss, Genevieve Wyner, and Justin Wyner. Their advice and expertise, and, for many, their thoughtful accounts of their experiences, brought life to the documentary evidence, as did other previously collected oral histories of temple members. In addition, we acknowledge the many researchers who consulted materials in the Temple Israel Archives for various sesquicentennial exhibitions and programs, as well as other personal research projects; their questions, investigations, and findings have helped to shape ours.

People at many research institutions provided exceptional assistance on this project. We particularly wish to acknowledge Judi Garner of the American Jewish Historical Society; Lorna Condon and Emily Novak of the Historic New England Archives; the staff of the Louisiana and Special Collections Department, Earl K. Long Library, University of New Orleans; the staff of the Special Collections and Rare Book Room of the Boston Public Library; the staff of the Jacob Rader Marcus Center of the American Jewish Archives; the staff of the Howard Gotlieb Archival Research Center, Boston University; and the staff of the Robert D. Farber University Archives and Special Collections Department, Brandeis University.

We appreciate the support and encouragement of the editors and staff at the University Press of New England. Their assistance in helping us prepare the manuscript for publication in a timely manner has been invaluable. We found the comments of Jonathan Sarna, the editor of the Brandeis Series in American Jewish History, Culture, and Life, extremely insightful and very helpful.

Finally, we thank our families for their patience, kindness, and support throughout the research, writing, and production of this book.

Becoming American Jews

TEMPLE ISRAEL OF BOSTON

1842–1874

 The first Jews arrived in North America in 1654; even so, Boston, one of the continent's oldest cities, did not have a permanent Jewish community for nearly two centuries. Jews came to Boston as early as the mid-1600s, but, because the Puritans did not welcome outsiders to their "city on a hill," and other seaports offered better economic prospects, most Jewish immigrants settled in other trading centers such as New York, Philadelphia, and Newport, Rhode Island. The few Jews who lived in Boston in the eighteenth and early nineteenth centuries practiced their faith in private, joining synagogues elsewhere to maintain their Jewish connections and ensure that they would have Jewish burials. Some converted to Protestantism.[1]

In the early decades of the nineteenth century, Boston's successes in international trade and mechanized textile manufacturing led to an economic boom that, in turn, fueled other forms of industrial development and transformed the social, demographic, and physical landscape of the city. In the late 1830s, the region became a magnet for immigrants from Ireland, other parts of the British Isles, and Germany who hoped to fill the increasing demand for skilled and unskilled labor of all kinds. Among the influx of immigrants were Jews fleeing religious persecution and economic hardship in various German provinces. They, like other immigrants, hoped to take advantage of the new business opportunities in Boston's expanding consumer marketplace.[2]

BOSTON'S FIRST SYNAGOGUE

Two of the first Jews to settle in Boston in this period were William Goldschmidt (later Goldsmith) and Jacob Norton, who came via New York in 1842. Goldsmith, a thirty-two-year-old immigrant from Bavaria, a southwestern German province, was a jeweler who eventually became a successful

ISRAELITISH SYNAGOGUE,

WARREN STREET.

This building, which was erected in 1851, is a small wooden structure, tastefully decorated and pleasing in its appearance. It will seat about 500 persons, and has connected with it rooms for a school and for business meetings of the trustees of the society, and for other purposes. There are, also, in the rear, bathing rooms for the females of the society, after the ancient custom of the Israelites. The galleries of the church are set aside for the use of the females of the congregation, the body of the church being occupied exclusively by the males.

The Synagogue of Israelites were first organized in Boston in 1843, and consisted at that time of ten members with their families. There are at the present time belonging to the society about 120 families. The name which the Synagogue adopts and by which they are incorporated, is "Ohebei Shalom," which being interpreted is "Friends of Peace."

Connected with the church is a school for their children, where they are taught in the ancient Hebrew as well as in the English language.

There are, also, two charitable associations made up of members of this Synagogue, the one for males and the other for females.

The services in their church are all conducted in the Hebrew language and with all the ancient forms and ceremonies. They have the five books of Moses written on parchment, from which their Rabbi reads as part of their Sabbath service. At the present time the Rev. Joseph Sachs officiates as their religious instructor, and also as teacher of their children in the Hebrew tongue. They give him the ancient title of Rabbi. Their Sabbath commences on Friday at sundown, and ends at the corresponding hour on Saturday. Their numbers are quite rapidly increasing. They have a burial ground at East Boston.

Ohabei Shalom, Boston's first synagogue, in The Boston Almanac *for 1854. (Courtesy of Historic New England)*

real-estate trader in Roxbury. Norton, from Posen, a northeastern province, established himself as a furrier. In the fall of 1842, they, along with several other new arrivals, gathered at the Fort Hill home of Peter Spitz, a cap maker from Posen, to celebrate the Jewish New Year. The following May, when almost twenty Jews assembled to circumcise Spitz's firstborn son, George, they decided to establish a permanent religious community where they could worship according to their customs and establish the proper arrangements for living, and dying, in accordance with Jewish law. They named the new congregation, chartered in 1845, Kahal Kadosh Ohabei Shalom (Holy Community Lovers of Peace). They elected Goldsmith as president and hired a "hazan" (reader), who also served as "shohet" (ritual slaughterer) and "mohel" (circumciser). In the same year, they established a mutual aid and burial society, the Chevra Ahabas Achim (Society of Brotherly Love). In 1847, the congregation purchased land for a cemetery in East Boston. By 1852, the members had raised enough funds to build a small two-story synagogue on Warren (now Warrenton) Street in the South End.[3]

The Jewish community consisted mainly of young families and single men in sibling groups. Because Boston was often the second or third stop for Jewish immigrants, most arrived speaking some English and having some familiarity with American culture. They worked as peddlers, shopkeepers, merchants, opticians, tailors, and other skilled craftsmen, and lived near their workplaces in the crowded, low-rent, immigrant neighborhoods of the South or North End. Like most of Boston's other working-class residents, Jews were highly mobile, moving frequently and often leaving the city entirely.[4]

In 1850, many of Ohabei Shalom's members were married men in their thirties with young children. Many were related to other members through kin or marriage, and the same names — Goldsmith, Strauss, Heineman, Spier, Wolf, and others — appeared in multiple households. For example, Moses Ehrlich, the synagogue president, was a dry goods dealer who lived on Pleasant Street, in the South End, with his wife Henrietta, five children under the age of six, and four sets of boarders: two young couples, a single woman, and a single man who may have worked with Ehrlich in his business. Brothers Bernard and David Heineman were jewelers; Bernard lived near Beacon Hill on Blossom Street, while David lived on Madison Place, around the corner from the Ehrlichs. David and his wife, Henrietta, had two toddlers and two boarders: Samuel Strauss, a young dry goods dealer, and his wife, Betsy. Charles Hyneman, a synagogue trustee, was a clothing dealer who lived on Eliot Street, just off Pleasant Street, with his wife, Bertha. Nathan and Leon Strauss were watchmakers and traders who lived on Fayette Street, which also ran off Pleasant, near Henry Waterman, a tailor. Julius Wolf was a watchmaker and jeweler who lived one block away, on Marion Street.[5]

The small group of Jewish settlers did not face serious discrimination from native-born Protestants, who viewed them as a curiosity rather than a threat; Bostonians were more concerned about the hordes of Irish Catholic immigrants swarming into the city in these years. The Jewish community would, however, soon experience internal strife over religious, cultural, and economic differences. In Boston, the two major Jewish immigrant groups were "Bayers," from the southwestern German territories, and "Polanders," from the northeast. By the 1850s, the two groups exhibited differential geographic, residential, and work patterns; most of the Bayers resided in the South End, while many of the Polanders worked and lived near each other in the North End.[6]

European Jewish communities worshipped according to age-old, locally based rituals; as a result, when Jews from different regions with disparate religious and cultural traditions came together to worship in America, tensions frequently emerged. While synagogues in Europe were arms of an established religious hierarchy maintained by rabbinic leaders who oversaw ritual practices and settled disputes, the United States had few rabbis and no such structure. American synagogues were voluntary associations founded and run by lay leaders, and congregants who failed to find common ground simply left and organized new institutions.[7]

At Ohabei Shalom, where ritual practices had been determined by the Bayers, tensions over cultural traditions came to a head when the "Polanders" became a majority and rejected the reappointment of Joseph Sachs, the Bayer hazan.[8] In early 1854, a contingent of twenty-five southwestern German families, led by synagogue president Moses Ehrlich, seceded, taking Sachs, the congregational "shofar" (ram's horn), and a Torah scroll donated by Bertha Hyneman with them. The dissenters made no claims to congregational funds or the cemetery, but, as the founders of the original synagogue, they asserted their right to the name "Ohabei Shalom"—at least in part because they wished to stake their claim to a recent bequest.[9]

By March, the new congregation, led by President Ehrlich, had applied to the Massachusetts Legislature for a charter and elected a board of trustees that included several officers of the old temple: Nathan Strauss, Julius Wolf, Charles Hyneman, Leon Strauss, Samuel Wolf, Henry Waterman, and recording secretary David Samuelson (who had lived with the Ehrlichs). The board leased "a long, narrow frame structure" for fifty-eight dollars a month on nearby Pleasant Street (now Charles Street South) to serve as a synagogue. After $4,000 was spent on improvements, the synagogue was dedicated on September 15, 1854. Affirming its cultural background, the congregation invited noted Bavarian rabbi Max Lilienthal of New York to

Consecration of the Pleasant Street shul, in the Daily Evening Traveler, *September 16, 1854. (Courtesy of Temple Israel Archives)*

(*Daily Evening Traveler, Saturday, September 16, 1854*)

CONSECRATION OF A JEWISH SYNAGOGUE

YESTERDAY afternoon a small but very neat looking church or synagogue, erected by Messrs. Powell & McNutt for the German Jews in Pleasant near Marion Street and named the "Ohabei Shalom," was duly consecrated according to the peculiar and interesting ceremonies of that remarkable nation. The church sits a little back from the street and is capable of accommodating some two hundred persons. It is so constructed that the worshiper sits facing toward the East, the direction of Jerusalem. The females are seated in a gallery surrounding three sides of the church, being scrupulously separated from the males. On both sides of the only aisle are lamps which are kept burning during the services. The singers stand in front of the minister with their hats on, and neither the minister nor the congregation are uncovered during the ceremonies.

The church was crowded, a mayor and other prominent citizens being present. The order of the service was as follows:

1. Singing of psalm, "Lift Up Your Heads, O Ye Gates."

2. Mr. Moses Ehrlich, President, opens the doors for the taking of the scrolls.

3. Procession. Rev. Dr. Lilienthal of New York, then the minister, Rev. J. Sachs, while the choir sings "How Beautiful are Thy Tents, O Jacob."

4. "Hear, O Israel" by choir, and the scrolls are returned.

5. Prayer and sermon by Rev. Dr. Lilienthal. (Spoken in broken English but fully understood).

6. Closing benediction by Rev. Sachs in German.

The congregation consists of about sixty persons. They are mostly, as was stated to us, seceders from the first Jewish Synagogue established in this city, in which as they say the Polish Jews (whose ceremonies are somewhat different from theirs) obtained the preponderance. Since the secession they have forbidden the executors of the will of the late Judah Touro to pay over the sum of $5,000 left by him to the Jewish Synagogue in the City of Boston, until it can be ascertained which society can legally claim it. They are about to build in the rear of their church a schoolhouse for their children.

deliver a sermon on education; many city dignitaries, local Protestant ministers, and important Jewish leaders also attended.[10]

KEHILLAH KEDOSHA ADATH ISRAEL

The tensions between the "Polanders" and "Bayers" did not end with establishment of the new synagogue; in fact, they were exacerbated by a contentious lawsuit. When prominent New Orleans philanthropist Judah Touro

died in January 1854, his many bequests included $5,000 for "the Hebrew
Congregation of Oharbay Shalom of Boston." The executors of Touro's estate
awarded the money to the Warren Street synagogue, but the Bayer contingent also laid claim to it. On March 20, 1855, Moses Ehrlich filed a lawsuit
in the Superior District Court of New Orleans to claim Touro's bequest on
behalf of the Pleasant Street congregation.[11]

The records of the suit reveal the animosity engendered by the complex
politics of religious practice in a small but culturally diverse community.
The plaintiffs argued that, in the early 1850s, "Polanders came flocking in
five or six every month" and, without warning or discussion, "claimed to
be members and controlled the affairs of the Society." The German-style
liturgy was discarded in favor of Polish-style prayers, and, the plaintiffs
averred, the Polanders "laughed at us when we stood still [during the ser-
vice], not understanding" Bayer customs. One member testified that the
leadership was scheming to replace Joseph Sachs, "a good man, and one of
the best scholars I ever knew," with Max Wolf, a "Polish reader," who, the
deponent claimed, "was no scholar either in German, English, or Hebrew,
in fact he had no learning at all." Revealing their ethnic prejudices, the
Bayers declared that the Polish mode of ritual could not "be justified by
any grammarian." Arguing that they wanted their children "properly educated," the Bayers "engaged the Rev. Mr. Sax [*sic*] and with him . . . left the
Congregation."[12]

The lead defendant, Prussian-born merchant Alexander Saroni, had a different perspective. He observed that Congregation Ohabei Shalom included
members from many countries, including England and Holland, as well as
various German regions. Joseph Sachs had tendered his resignation in June
1854, Saroni stated; there was no plot to take over the temple, just a search
for a replacement. "A reader of Polish descent [Max Wolf], who happened
to be here a few days afterward, was invited to officiate the next Sabbath," he
explained. "Certain German members of the congregation insisted that no
Polish reader should be elected in the Congregation." After an "angry controversy, Mr. Ehrlich and his associates withdrew from the worship of the
synagogue and, not paying their dues for the space of twelve months, they
ceased to be members, according to our Constitution."[13]

In the end, the case would hinge on establishing who was the legal president of the incorporated entity known as Ohabei Shalom. Moses Ehrlich
asserted that, as he had been the president of Ohabei Shalom at the time
of the schism, his group had sole claim to the name. Saroni, for the other

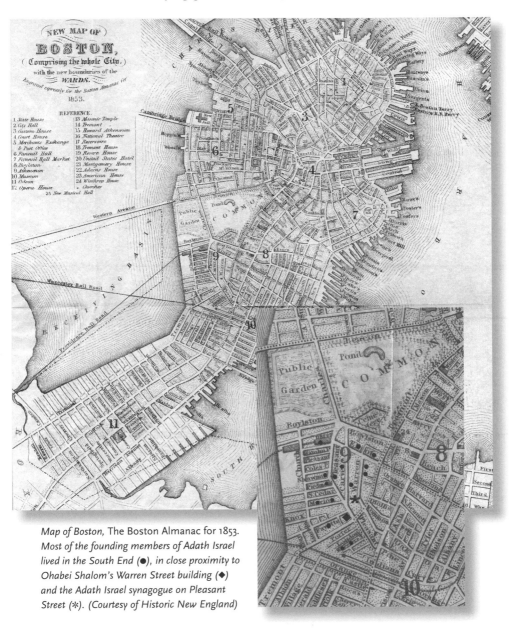

Map of Boston, The Boston Almanac for 1853.
Most of the founding members of Adath Israel
lived in the South End (●), in close proximity to
Ohabei Shalom's Warren Street building (◆)
and the Adath Israel synagogue on Pleasant
Street (✳). (Courtesy of Historic New England)

side, produced Sachs's letter of resignation and the temple's original bylaws
as part of a complicated legal argument regarding incorporation based
on Massachusetts case law. After two years of depositions and briefs that
included virulent attacks from both parties, the Louisiana State Supreme
Court ruled in favor of Saroni and his supporters. The judges argued that,

by calling themselves the "new congregation" when they filed their case, the Bayers implied a clear distinction between their group and the original organization. In February 1856, the new synagogue, forced to concede both Touro's bequest and the name, "Ohabei Shalom," became "Kehillah Kedosha Adath Israel" (the Holy Community of the Tribe of Israel), commonly known as Congregation Adath Israel.[14]

Adath Israel's members continued to practice traditional German-style Jewish rites for almost two more decades: the hazan, who also served as teacher and shohet, led services in Hebrew and German; men covered their heads; and women sat separately in the balcony gallery. Because people typically worked six days per week, and Massachusetts's strict "blue laws," designed to propagate morality by enforcing Sabbath adherence, barred businesses from opening on Sunday, it was difficult for people in business to choose between their livelihoods and religious observance. Despite the congregation's small size (Ohabei Shalom would remain Boston's largest synagogue until the early 1880s), and the demands of work, members were able to ensure a daily minyan by dividing the men into groups and scheduling times for each to attend services.[15]

As was typical in American synagogues, the board and its committees maintained control over all aspects of the institution's services, cemetery, and religious school. The president and treasurer divided the recordkeeping responsibilities; the vice president served as superintendent of the religious school. The "shamas" (sexton) was the only paid administrator, serving as reader during services, clerk to the board, and caretaker of the building.[16]

The hazan, unlike later rabbis, had little congregational authority. Any changes in ritual practice were the province of the board; this right was later safeguarded in the congregation's bylaws. The hazan's primary responsibilities were to lead services and to educate children, and he preached only when authorized by the board. He also served as the congregation's secretary, taking notes during board meetings and sending notices and minutes to members. When Joseph Sachs left in 1856, the congregation chose Joseph Shoninger, who had earlier served as Sachs's assistant, to replace him. Shoninger would stay for twenty years; under his quiet stewardship, the congregation would gradually expand and the Pleasant Street shul would achieve stability, relative solvency, and significant standing in the community.[17]

The new congregation recognized that its future depended on its ability to provide services to families who wished to educate their children in Jewish practices and bury their dead in consecrated ground. With a

Joseph Sachs

As a young man, Joseph Sachs (1816–1869), the "scholarly son of a poor Bavarian saddlemaker," had been hired to tutor Sophia Baer, the daughter of a wealthy goldsmith. When Sachs and Sophia decided to marry, her parents did not approve, and the couple eloped to Rotterdam. From there, they immigrated to New York, arriving in 1847. Sachs worked as a schoolteacher until he was hired by Boston's Ohabei Shalom as "hazan" and teacher in early 1853. In 1854, he left with the Bayer contingent to become the hazan at Adath Israel. Known as a serious scholar and dedicated teacher, Sachs's responsibilities included leading traditional services in German and Hebrew, running the religious school, and serving as the synagogue's secretary.

The Sachs family left Boston in 1856 for New York, where Sachs established a private school for boys and girls that would become a famous training ground for the scions of elite Jewish families. The Sachses had six children; when Joseph died in 1869, his son Julius, who had earned a Ph.D. in 1867, took over the school and renamed it the Sachs Collegiate Institute for Boys. Julius and his brother Samuel married two daughters of Marcus and Bertha Goldman, old family friends who had relocated to New York from Philadelphia. Samuel and his father-in-law, a successful merchant, would found Goldman Sachs, the investment banking firm.

Hazan Joseph Sachs
(Courtesy of Temple Israel Archives)

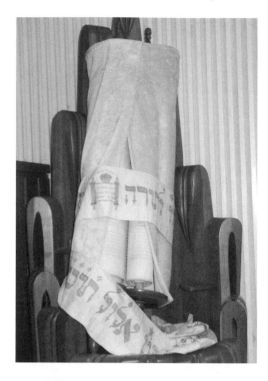

professional teacher as hazan, the congregation could tout its educational programs from its inception. Influenced by the Sunday School movement initiated in 1838 by Rebecca Gratz, the noted Philadelphia educator and philanthropist, many American Jews in this period saw Jewish education as the best means of fulfilling Israel's mission, guarding against Protestant proselytizing, and promoting "Americanization within a Jewish setting." As Sachs noted at Michael Bayersdorfer's bar mitzvah ceremony in 1856, "Let us educate our youth in true religion, let us teach them the acts and works done by our fathers, and every one of them will resemble a Maccabeus — he will live and die for his religion."[18]

While boys received bar mitzvah instruction at the home of the hazan, Sachs, and later Shoninger, taught both boys and girls in the synagogue school three days per week. The curriculum included German, as well as Hebrew scripture and Jewish history (taught in English and German) — subjects commonly taught in Jewish religious schools. The School Committee's most pressing concerns included discipline, order, class size, and finances. Its June 1862 report, for example, noted that "the performance of teacher and pupils [eighteen boys and twenty-eight girls] were delight-

ful and praiseworthy. However the discipline and order is far from satis-
factory." The committee proposed that the board grant the hazan "more
power in order to punish bad and unorderly children and by so doing create more respect."[19]

The death of a member in 1858 prompted the board of trustees to purchase land for a congregational burial ground. Adath Israel acquired a site
in South Reading (now Wakefield), about ten miles from Boston, the next
year. The new cemetery was key to the institution's growth; with no independent Jewish cemeteries in mid-nineteenth-century America, many Jews
saw burial privileges as a strong incentive to join a synagogue. As a later
rabbi recalled, "The enterprising Jewish trader—having left Europe in the
hope of finding greater freedom . . . cared little about social attractions such
as a congregation could offer him, neither did he care much for synagogical
devotion, but he did care to be buried among his brethren."[20]

For the first few decades, the board devoted much energy to cemetery
business. The trustees' approval was required for burial even though the sexton handled all administrative details. Fees ranged from one to twenty dollars based on the applicant's financial circumstances. Minyans were assigned
to attend each funeral, and the board levied a two-dollar fine for truancy. In
1876, the board would establish a standing cemetery committee to oversee
the sale of plots (a much-needed source of synagogue income), coordinate
burials, and ensure perpetual care. The committee also ruled on religious
issues, such as burial privileges for non-Jewish family members. Some petitions were summarily denied (such as burials for children of intermarriage);
others were taken under advisement. When complex issues arose, the board
consulted well-known rabbis for advice; in 1863, for example, when the trustees were unclear about the propriety of saying Kaddish for the "yahrzeit" of
a member buried in a Christian cemetery, they sent letters to Rabbi Lilienthal, Rabbi Isaac Mayer Wise of Cincinnati, and a third unnamed rabbi.[21]

The cemetery and the religious school both proved successful in attracting potential members. Candidates were interviewed, asked to present two
references, and voted on by the board, largely to ensure that they would be
able to pay their dues. In 1859, fifteen families belonged; by 1870, the number had expanded to forty-five, leading to proportionate increases in income
and expenses, as well as concerns about space. In the 1870s, it became clear
that dues, religious school tuitions, and burial fees would not provide
enough income to balance the budget or cover building repairs, especially
during economic downturns, when many members could not afford to pay.

Located next to Wakefield's Lake Quannapowitt,
Adath Israel's cemetery reflects the Victorian
ideal of tranquil, gardenlike burial grounds. Louis
Rosenfeld, who died in February 1860 at the age
of fifteen, was the first person interred. Of the
seventy-nine members buried there between 1860
and 1880, more than 40 percent were under the
age of ten. (Courtesy of Temple Israel Archives)

In November 1875, the women of Adath Israel raised almost five thousand
dollars for the synagogue by holding Boston's first Jewish "benevolent fair"
at Horticultural Hall. Such fairs, where women sold handmade products
and other goods to raise funds for charitable causes, were common in the
nineteenth century, and the Adath Israel fair demonstrated Jewish wom-
en's evolving Americanization as well as their fund-raising skills. In 1877,

the board ruled that the charter allowed solicitations, and the congregation raised $464 during its first recorded "fund drive." Despite such measures, however, the synagogue's financial condition would remain precarious into the 1880s.[22]

"CHARITIES OF THE ISRAELITISH PERSUASION"

Adath Israel's growth reflected that of the larger Jewish community; by the beginning of the Civil War in 1861, nearly a thousand Jews lived in Boston. A number of them had become successful merchants and entrepreneurs. While they earned the respect of Yankee businessmen, they associated with non-Jews only during working hours, and their lives were divided into "distinct social and business spheres."[23]

Successful Jews, including many Adath Israel members, also engaged in philanthropic activities, especially those designed to serve newer Jewish immigrants. By the 1860s, it was clear that the needs of Boston's Jewish poor could no longer be met solely by the city's three synagogues (Mishkan Israel, a second offshoot of Ohabei Shalom, had been founded in 1858). In this case, cultural, social, and economic differences within the Jewish community were less important than the fact that "to natives, Jews formed only one group." Although Boston, like other cities, already had dozens of philanthropic and other voluntary associations, Jews established their own citywide organizations to ensure that their co-religionists would be aided rather than converted.[24]

In 1864, twenty-six "financially responsible" men—mainly dry goods merchants, shoe and leather manufacturers, and wool brokers who had prospered as a result of an increased demand for ready-made clothing and other apparel during the Civil War—met at the Pleasant Street synagogue to establish the United Hebrew Benevolent Association (UHBA). Led by Adath Israel member Nathan Strauss, a mortgage broker, the association proposed "to dispense the charities of the Israelitish persuasion with a greater degree of system and effectiveness than has heretofore prevailed." Like their Protestant neighbors, the UHBA founders tried to adopt "modern" methods of helping the "worthy poor," but they also replicated approaches used by traditional immigrant aid societies. The UHBA raised money from direct donations as well as fund-raising activities such as an annual Horticultural Ball and picnic. Those in need applied directly to the president, who considered each case and recommended action to the membership at monthly meetings.[25]

When President Abraham Lincoln was assassinated in 1865, Adath Israel congregants demonstrated their patriotism by participating "as equals in the rites of national mourning." As these board minutes attest, they, like their Christian neighbors, draped their house of worship in black crepe, closed their businesses, and held a memorial service (at which Joseph Shoninger delivered his first eulogy in English). They also said Kaddish for thirty days. (Courtesy of Temple Israel Archives)

Five years later, Boston's Jewish women came together at Adath Israel to establish their own philanthropic organization, the Hebrew Ladies' Sewing Circle. The founding president, Sonia Einstein, the wife of prominent businessman and philanthropist Abraham Einstein, was a woman in her early thirties who had recently lost three young sons. Einstein's experience may have made her particularly sympathetic to the vicissitudes of other, less financially secure, women. Modeled after similar local Protestant organizations, the Sewing Circle purchased cloth and hired poor women to make garments to be distributed in immigrant neighborhoods. Although its membership soon dwindled, the organization would be revitalized in 1878 under the leadership of well-known philanthropist Lina Hecht (see chapter 2).[26]

SEEDS OF REFORM

The Jewish Reform movement had originated in Germany in the early nineteenth century, but it developed in a "uniquely American" way in the United States. Jews who came to America looked for ways to ensure the survival of Judaism in a heterogeneous, secular state. Because the American Constitution forbade any established state religion, religious practice was voluntary, and synagogues, like churches, had to find a means of attracting members.

Joseph Shoninger

Joseph Shoninger (1829–1910) was educated in Würzburg, Bavaria. After he and his wife, Lizette, immigrated to New York, Shoninger, a talented musician, worked as a violinist at the Bowery Theatre and searched for a position as a hazan. In 1854, Shoninger became Joseph Sachs's assistant at Congregation Adath Israel. He returned to New York a year later, but when Sachs resigned in 1856, Shoninger took his place. During his nearly twenty-year tenure, Adath Israel began to consider "contemporary reforms" that would make services more orderly and harmonious. Shoninger was ambivalent about these changes, and he left in 1874.

The Shoningers remained active in Boston's Jewish community. Shoninger continued to work as a minister and teacher for the next twenty-five years, while Lizette was active in the Naomi Lodge of the United Order of True Sisters, an early Jewish women's philanthropic organization. The Shoningers had a total of seven children; their two surviving sons founded a successful dry goods firm in Boston and their two daughters married prominent Jewish businessmen. The Shoningers eventually retired to New York, where Joseph died at his daughter's home in 1910 at the age of eighty.

Hazan Joseph Shoninger
(Courtesy of Temple Israel Archives)

Some advocated for strict adherence to traditional practices, while others argued that rituals should be adapted to meet changing needs. Many affiliated Jews feared that their more Americanized children might convert or intermarry, and they looked for ways to retain them and bring in new members by making the Jewish religious experience seem less foreign. Their solution was to emulate some of the features of Protestant churches: formalizing services through the addition of English-language sermons, Bibles, prayer books, and musical innovations like organs and choirs.[27]

By the end of the Civil War, Jewish Bostonians who had observed Reform temples in other American cities began to "feel that they had remained behind the time, and that 'something' ought to be done to catch up." While the immigrant generation had only business associations with non-Jews, their American-born children, especially those who became financially successful, began "a co-mingling of the Jewish and non-Jewish world." They, and others like them, hoped to institute new rituals that would help the synagogue, as board members later recalled, "elevate the social as well as the moral standing of our race."[28]

In 1863, the congregation first expressed interest in "contemporary reforms" when the board established a committee to look into "forming a Choir for Sabbaths and Holidays." For Jews who were used to praying out loud at their own pace, a choir that would formalize the tempo of prayer and set standards of musicality was a major departure. Some members were enthusiastic, claiming that a chorus could lead to "a better order during the services" that might encourage more members, including children, to attend. Others resisted, however, and a choir was not established until 1871. As Solomon Schindler, who would replace Shoninger in 1874, later observed in a timeless comment, older members "resented attempts to wean them from usages to which they were accustomed since childhood."[29]

These issues were cultural as well as religious, and they were particularly significant for the immigrant generation, no matter how upwardly mobile. Thus, even when changes were instituted, cultural concerns continued to matter. In 1866, for example, when the board voted to have the Haftarah read in both Hebrew and in translation on the Sabbath and holidays, the language of choice was German, as it would continue to be for at least another decade. The minutes of the synagogue board meetings would be kept in German until the late 1870s.[30]

Even so, most members of Congregation Adath Israel agreed that the worship experience should be more orderly and appealing. In 1870, the

Michael and Teresa Rosenfeld were typical mid-nineteenth-century German Jewish immigrants. Married by Joseph Shoninger in 1862, the Rosenfelds lived in the South End near the Pleasant Street shul. Michael, a twenty-nine-year-old "trader," later became a grocer. Like many of her peers, Teresa gave birth to many children, but only seven of the fifteen Rosenfeld offspring survived to adulthood. The children attended Adath Israel's religious school; this 1879 report notes the good deportment of daughters Clara, Minnie, and Rachel. (Courtesy of Temple Israel Archives)

board agreed to advertise for a new hazan with "a good and agreeable voice" who could "install the services in moderate reform" and direct a chorus, but it would take four more years to obtain the majority required to make this happen. In the meantime, Shoninger, who was clearly reluctant to institute reforms, continued to be rehired from year to year. The board's committee on reform continued to explore various options and, in May 1873, it concluded that "we consider it in the interest of the congregation . . . to introduce an appropriate moderate reform fitting the spirit of the time." The committee recommended hiring "a preacher at a fixed salary," renovating the synagogue's interior and installing "family seats," and, to "help in edifying and solemnifying the services," procuring a chorus, an organ, and a conductor. Mixed seating would highlight the new image of the synagogue as a family space shared by men and women, where children would attend services with their parents; the choir and organ would bring order and harmony to the worship experience.[31]

But reaching consensus was a long and trying process. In September 1873, when Shoninger was again rehired, the frustrated outgoing president of the board, John Phillips (1872–1873), wished the incoming one, John H. Bendix (1866–1869; 1873–1876), more success in bringing the congregation to "present times." Finally, in March 1874, the board proposed a plan to "put the Synagogue in good condition, divide it up in family seats, and upholster the seats" for $500, and to hire a "preacher who at the same time would be a teacher" as well as a hazan. After much debate at a special meeting in May, the congregation unanimously decided to move forward with the renovations and to "advertize for a reader who could deliver a Sermon, and give lectures."[32]

By the summer of 1874, the members of Congregation Adath Israel had concluded that their future was with the "spirit of the time" rather than their immigrant past. In keeping with the committee's desire to become more "contemporary," the proposed changes included adopting Protestant terms for offices and functions, as well as those most visible symbols of the American Jewish Reform movement — "family" (mixed) seating, a chorus, and an organ. Finally, instead of a hazan who "davened" (prayed) in the midst of a noisy sanctuary, the congregation looked for a reader and "preacher" to lead orderly prayers and deliver illuminating sermons and lectures from the front of a quiet room.

1874–1911

The decision to hire a "Reader, Preacher, and Teacher" confirmed Congregation Adath Israel's commitment to meeting the evolving needs of its members. By 1874, most were upwardly mobile immigrants living in relative prosperity, with native-born children who attended public school with their non-Jewish neighbors. While congregants wished to continue to honor the traditions of their youth, they were determined to create a religious setting that would feel less "foreign" to their children and reflect their growing social aspirations. The first step was to remodel the shul to incorporate a cabinet organ and family pews. The new preacher they advertised for would, they hoped, propose other appropriate changes and address the congregation's most fundamental challenge—attracting new members and convincing current ones to actively participate by attending services, sending their children to the religious school, and supporting the synagogue financially.[1]

In July 1874, the board hired thirty-two-year-old Solomon Schindler, who had been leading a small shul in Hoboken, New Jersey. The Prussian-born son of a cantor, Schindler had grown up during the turbulent years of European nationalism. As a young man, he had rejected the teachings of traditional Judaism in favor of modern science, rational thinking, and democratic ideals. Like other immigrants, he believed that the United States was a land of religious, as well as social and economic, opportunity. He was convinced that American Jews could establish "the religion of the future," a modern faith based on "Jewish theories, Jewish doctrines, Jewish morals, [and] Jewish ethics." This new, "pure" Judaism would no longer "cling" to the "ceremonies" that encouraged "Israel to exclude itself from society"; rather, it would promote religious life in a secular state while "keeping the religion of our ancestors intact and delivering it immaculate to our children." This vision would guide Schindler's approach to reforms at Congregation Adath

Israel; during his tenure, he and the congregation would reinvent the identity of the synagogue by altering the rituals, tone, and content of religious services. In the process, Adath Israel would become the most influential synagogue in Boston.[2]

Schindler arrived in late July, and, in early September, the congregation celebrated "the consecration of our temple." The use of the word "temple" reflected Reform Judaism's rejection of "messianic redemption" and the desire to reconstruct the Temple in Jerusalem. The Reform synagogue "was to be a temple unto itself." While members liked this concept, they disagreed over the nature, extent, and shape of other reforms. Some simply wished to make their temple feel more "American" by introducing order, harmony, and decorum into the worship service; others were eager to institute comprehensive theological reforms.[3]

The Reform Committee had been considering the central question of adopting a new "minhag," or ritual, for some time. Schindler favored Dr. Adolph Huebsch's *Seder Tfilah*, the German-language minhag written for Congregation Anshe Cheset in New York. While some members would have preferred a moderate Reform prayer book available in English, such as the new edition of Rabbi Isaac Mayer Wise's *Minhag Amerika*, the board agreed to follow Schindler's recommendation. Other long-anticipated ritual changes included the addition of weekly sermons and a trained choir with organ accompaniment.[4]

The board soon realized that hiring a preacher and instituting reforms had ongoing budget implications; it would also be more difficult to maintain control over ritual change. Schindler, who was "nothing if not frank and fearless," was quick to make his opinions known and to make demands upon the trustees. Within two months of his arrival, Schindler had decided that he would need "better singers" than the children and adults who had volunteered for the choir and he recommended engaging a quartet of Christian performers at $600 per year — a figure that represented more than a third of his $1,500 salary. He would spend another $2,000 having music copied in the next year. The board was frustrated by the burden on the budget and by Schindler's penchant for implementing changes without prior consultation. Six months after his arrival, for example, when Schindler made the executive decision to discontinue the practice of bar mitzvah, the board notified him that, before "departing in any way of the ritual, custom or ceremony as

Solomon Schindler

Solomon Schindler (1842–1915), the son of a cantor, was born in Neisse, Silesia, a Prussian province. He enrolled in the rabbinic school and gymnasium in Breslau but left to earn a teaching diploma. Schindler and Henriette Scholz married in 1868 and opened a school. In 1871, after publicly speaking out against Prussia's annexation of Alsace-Lorraine, he fled with his family to New York to escape arrest. Schindler tried to support his wife and two children, Otto and Paul (two more, Charles and Clara, would be born in America), by peddling shoelaces, but financial exigency led him to take a position at Congregation Adath Emunoh, a traditional shul in Hoboken, New Jersey.

In 1874, Schindler was hired by Adath Israel. During his tenure, the congregation adopted many Reform practices, built an impressive new building, and became the preeminent Reform synagogue in Boston. In the 1880s, Schindler became a popular lecturer, author, and newspaper editor. He served on the Boston School Committee from 1888 to 1894.

In 1894, Schindler's contract was not renewed because the congregation had become uncomfortable with his confrontational style and increasingly radical views. He had been a director of the Hebrew Benevolent Association since 1881, and for the rest of his life he headed organizations that served Boston's impoverished Jewish immigrants. By 1908, Schindler had returned to more traditional Jewish beliefs, and he was appointed Adath Israel's first rabbi emeritus. Upon his death in 1915, Schindler became the first rabbi interred in the temple's Wakefield cemetery.

Rabbi Solomon Schindler
(Courtesy of Temple Israel Archives)

well as in extra ordinary cases in the services, confirmations or Bar Mitz-vahs" he must "inform Mr. President and . . . follow his judgment." The alter-ation was made nevertheless, and, a few months later, Schindler conducted Adath Israel's first confirmation service with a class of four thirteen-year-olds: Samuel Hirschfield, Louis Morse, Emma Morse, and Cora Stern.[5]

Such tensions between the board and the "preacher" would continue throughout Schindler's two decades at Adath Israel. He later asserted that "even the very first steps, the introduction of family pews, of an organ and a choir, of a new prayer-book, met with displeasure; and of the forty members that composed the congregation, fifteen" resigned. Those who remained also rejected some of his proposed innovations. When Schindler recommended removing head coverings in the synagogue, for example, the congregation refused. When, in 1877, he encouraged the temple to join the four-year-old Union of American Hebrew Congregations (UAHC), the board demurred, as it would throughout his tenure, unwilling to pay the one dollar per capita yearly membership fee, and, perhaps, fearing a potential loss of autonomy. Schindler's fiery sermons undoubtedly fanned the flames of friction. He regularly chastised his congregants for their "indifference" to religion, espe-cially in regard to observing the Sabbath and other holidays; their "slavery" to business and the credo that "riches are the highest good"; and their fail-ure to take the necessary steps to preserve Judaism for future generations. These critiques of the congregation's priorities rankled, especially given Schindler's repeated requests for money.[6]

Nevertheless, some traditional practices, such as two-day observances of holidays, were abandoned, and the rumble of davening men was slowly replaced by an orderly congregation that would listen to the choir sing and Schindler preach. These adjustments took time, and, as late as December 1875, the board was addressing complaints that "some members do not rise when told to do so and are lax when asked to sit down." The congregation also experienced another transition, as English slowly replaced German in the synagogue. In the mid-1870s, Schindler began to preach sermons alter-nately in both languages; by 1880, English had become the standard for all of the synagogue's business.[7]

These changes attracted new members, many of whom were new to Boston or had previously been unaffiliated. By 1880, fifty-seven families belonged to the synagogue, only eighteen of whom had been members in 1870. In 1875, the building was so overcrowded that religious school classes were moved to a rented storefront on Berkeley Street for two years while, despite a budget shortfall exacerbated by a serious economic downturn, the congregation spent almost $4,000 to enlarge the building.[8]

As new members joined, the congregational desire for cultural assimilation encouraged the proliferation of mainstream American practices. In 1876, in honor of the nation's centennial, the synagogue arranged a religious service and fireworks display that became the first of many congregational celebrations of secular American holidays. Thanksgiving, which had become a national "feast day" in 1863 as a means of promoting unity during the Civil War, was also first celebrated at Adath Israel that year. The service included a sermon by Rabbi Schindler and a reading of the annual presidential proclamation (the Massachusetts governor's proclamation, too Christian in tone, was rejected by the board as "against us"). In 1876 the board president, clothing wholesaler Charles Morse (1870–1872; 1876–1883), also proposed that the Wakefield cemetery be divided into the family plots typically found in Protestant garden cemeteries of the period.[9]

The temple's religious school program also came under scrutiny. An experienced teacher, Schindler proposed updating the curriculum and extending the length of the program. "The school system of today," he declared in April 1877, "according to which children five or six years old learn religion by heart . . . and study Hebrew and German and I know not what else . . . and ends with the confirmation . . . is more pernicious than salutary," especially as many parents "do not send them at all or very irregularly." Jewish education was vital to the preservation of Judaism in America, Schindler argued, and he exhorted his congregants to "strengthen religious feeling in the rising generation. . . . You have your children confirmed but after confirmation, just in the very time when their mind is ripe and open for religious truth, and able to comprehend its teachings, they neglect with your consent all that might lead to a more religious life." To combat this neglect, he instituted a post-confirmation class designed to encourage students to study religious philosophy and Jewish history. Many members disagreed with Schindler's approach, however, viewing the temple's educational program more as a means of preserving cultural heritage than of strengthening religious knowledge and devotion. In 1877, despite Schindler's opposition, the school committee, responding to "a general desire that German be introduced as a specialty," voted to purchase textbooks and hire an assistant teacher. By the late 1870s, almost sixty students attended the Sabbath school, studying German, Hebrew, religion, the Bible, and singing on Saturday afternoons and Sunday mornings.[10]

Theatralische Abendunterhaltung

gegeben von den Schülern

der Sabbathschule des Tempels Adath Israel,

zur Feier des Purimfestes, 5642 (1882).

PROGRAMM.

SEPPI.

Ein Alpenmärchen in 4 Acten, für die Jugendbühne gearbeitet von
S. SCHINDLER.

PERSONEN.

Vater Walter	Otto Schindler.
Mutter Anna	Bella Morse.
....mi, ihre Tochter	Grace Alexander.
Suessholz, ein Kaufmann	Moses Mayer.
Herr von Rataplan, ein Lieutenant	
Seppi	
Kunz	
Klaus } Hirten	
Veit	
Liese	
Triene } Mægde	
Grete	
Parlez-vous, Berichterstatter des " Moniteur "	
Kræuterliese	
Frigor, der Eiskœnig	
Frigida, seine Tochter	
Zephira	
Pluvia } Elfen	
Borcalia	
	Chor der Elfen.

Kassenœffnung 7 Uhr.   Anfang des The...

Die Mitglieder des PROGRESS-CLUB haben es freundlic...
nommen als " Ushers " zu fungiren.

Der Ball wird beginnen, sobald die Sitze aus der Ha...
werden. — Ein Abendbrot, wird im Laufe des Abends...
Halle bereitet werden.

Jewish Watchman Print, 9 Bromfield Street, Boston.

Chanuka - Festival.
celebrated
December 22. 1878 (5639) at the Temple
"Adath Israel"
Boston, Mass.

Programme.

I.	Choral,	by the	A. I. M. S
II.	Introduct. Address	" "	Rev. Sol. Schindler.
III.	Song	" "	Pupils of the Sabb. School.
IV.	Prayer	by	Miss Fennie Cohen.
V.	Song	" "	Pupils of the Sabb. School.
VI.	The Menorah.	" "	
	Schamas		Miss H. Weinberg.
	1. Candle		Master Ive. Hecht.
	2. "		Miss Minnie Hecht.
	3. "		Master Sam. Ehrenreich.
	4. "		Miss Fannie Frank.
	5. "		Master A.B. Benari.
	6. "		Miss Rose Benari.
	7. "		Master Moses Morse.
	8. "		Miss Lottie Lyons.
VII.	Chanuka Hymne	by the	Pupils of the Sabb. School.
VIII.	Prayer	"	Miss Frances Cohen.
IX.	Choral	" "	A. I. M. S.
X.	Addresses	" "	Board of School Com.
XI.	Song	" "	Pupils of the Sabb. School.
XII.	Distribution of presents.		

L.

Electric - Pen - Print.

Rabbi Schindler wrote annual holiday
entertainments performed by students to
promote the "new and novel reformed
way of celebrating" Jewish festivals and
provide alternatives to "the growing allure
of Christmas" and other Christian holidays.
He later recalled that the first Chanukah
celebration (in 1876) "delighted both old
and young, particularly the young, because
I had added one more attractive feature to
it: each child received a toy." (Courtesy of
Temple Israel Archives)

Schindler also endeavored to excite students about Jewish holidays, especially Chanukah and Purim, two minor feasts that the Reform movement promoted. In 1876, he and the children held a theatrical performance (in German), honoring and explaining Chanukah, "to the great pleasure and gratification" of all present. The next year, he introduced an annual Purim play, also in German, that became a "recognized Boston feature" and raised hundreds of dollars for the school every year, eventually making it self-supporting.[11]

The board, committees, and members all took an active role in fostering and promoting religious education. In 1877, Edward S. Goulston, Sr., chair of the Education Committee, proposed the policy, still in effect, that members pay no additional surcharge for religious education. "The school is fully if not more important than any branch of the Temple," Goulston argued, "and should be fostered and encouraged by the members and officers."[12]

In 1879, the board codified the changes of the previous five years by formally reincorporating Congregation Kehillah Kedosha Adath Israel as Congregation Adath Israel, with new bylaws that reflected the temple's evolving vision of itself as a modern, communal, businesslike institution. Policy was to be set by the officers (a president, vice president, treasurer, and secretary [or clerk]) and six trustees, who were elected for two-year terms, as well as three standing committees (the Finance Committee, Sabbath School Committee, and Cemetery Committee) on which both trustees and general members served. Each male head of household had one vote at annual and special congregational meetings. Women could not apply for membership, but widows could inherit their husbands' status. The bylaws referred to the "preacher" as "rabbi" for the first time, and, in 1880, the congregation, reflecting a sense of permanence and perhaps increasing comfort with their new leader, granted Schindler the temple's first two-year contract.[13]

AMBITIOUS ENTREPRENEURS:
BOSTON'S CHANGING JEWISH COMMUNITY

The reforms at Temple Adath Israel reflected economic, social, and demographic changes in the lives of its members in the decades after the Civil War, a period of "confident optimism" for American Jewry. In Boston, upward mobility was accelerated by the close occupational, social, and familial ties among Central European Jews. Many of the earlier arrivals who started out as peddlers and grocery clerks achieved success as clothing retailers, tobacconists, and shoe manufacturers in the 1870s and 1880s. A few entered the world of finance.[14]

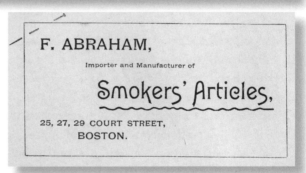

Advertisements for congregant-owned businesses, in Solomon Schindler's Israelites of Boston. *(Courtesy of Temple Israel Archives)*

Most Jews continued to live near each other, working together in overlapping circles of commerce. Men and women married within the community, often with "an eye toward consolidating business interests," and loans between neighbors were common. Boys entered family businesses as apprentices to their fathers, uncles, or brothers. Women often worked alongside their husbands and male relatives, helping customers, managing stock, inventories, and accounts in the backroom, and taking care of boarders and young relatives in their homes. Family labor reduced costs and allowed business owners to invest their profits in expansion or related enterprises that would provide additional employment opportunities. These factors may have helped Jews advance faster than other immigrant groups; by the early 1880s, Boston's Jewish community included a stable working-class population as well as a number of well-established businessmen.[15]

By this time, most of the long-standing members of Adath Israel were now part of the Jewish business elite—including Abraham Shuman, who became an influential clothing wholesaler and retailer; two of the Morse brothers, peddlers who prospered in the post–Civil War clothing boom; and Jacob Hecht, a prominent shoe merchant and banker. They may have attracted other successful businessmen, as more than three-quarters of the temple's members in 1880 operated retail establishments, while another ten percent were manufacturers. The men were generally immigrants in their mid-forties who had come to Boston as youths and delayed marriage until they could afford to support a family. Their wives tended to be a decade younger, mostly in their mid-thirties; a quarter had been born in the United States. Most families included several children.[16]

The ambitious entrepreneurs at Adath Israel adopted lifestyles that reflected their new economic position. By 1880, most had moved from the crowded, working-class neighborhoods of the "inner" South End and the North End to the handsome brownstone row houses of the "new" South End, a middle-class, residential, tree-lined district. Others had settled in the Back Bay and the nearby suburb of Roxbury. Most occupied, and at least ten owned, single-family homes that they, like their non-Jewish neighbors, maintained with the help of Irish servants.[17]

Most upwardly mobile Jews in Boston belonged to either Temple Adath Israel or Ohabei Shalom, which had also adopted some reforms. Over time, elite members of these congregations established a variety of voluntary associations, generally modeled after Protestant organizations, that would demonstrate the rewards of hard work in the "land of opportunity" and reflect their "continuing desire to associate among themselves as Jews." Some Jewish organizations focused on self-improvement; others, like the Young Men's Hebrew Association, founded in 1875, and the Hebrew Ladies Sewing Society, revived by Lina Hecht in 1878, incorporated both social and philanthropic goals. Eventually, exclusive male social clubs like the Elysium Club and the Comus Club, modeled after elite Protestant societies that excluded Jews, were also established.[18]

BUILDING PRESTIGE, VISIBILITY, AND THE "TRUE SPIRIT OF REFORM"

By 1880, Congregation Adath Israel had outgrown the small wooden structure on Pleasant Street. The board began to envision a larger, more imposing synagogue that would attract other upwardly mobile Jews and be located in the "new" South End, where the majority now lived. To fund the new enterprise, the board solicited donations from members and auctioned off lots in the Wakefield cemetery. The women of the synagogue also raised significant sums, and by 1883, the board had enough cash to purchase a plot on the corner of Columbus Avenue and Northampton Street. It hired the architectural firm of Weissbein and Jones, which designed a towering, church-like

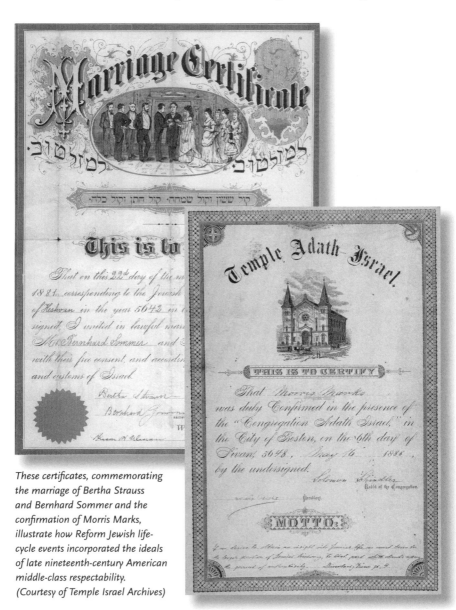

These certificates, commemorating the marriage of Bertha Strauss and Bernhard Sommer and the confirmation of Morris Marks, illustrate how Reform Jewish life-cycle events incorporated the ideals of late nineteenth-century American middle-class respectability. (Courtesy of Temple Israel Archives)

The Columbus Avenue synagogue, with its Stars of David and tablets of the Ten Commandments, was the first visibly Jewish synagogue in Boston. The building incorporated Romanesque revival elements of Bavarian synagogues familiar to many of its members, but also local features such as the steepled stair towers common in Boston's immigrant Catholic churches. (Courtesy of Temple Israel Archives)

edifice of Philadelphia brick with brownstone and terracotta trim. The new synagogue would be a modern facility complete with steam heat and electricity, a built-in organ, and an entire floor devoted to religious school and committee meeting rooms. With a seating capacity of 850, the sanctuary would provide permanent mixed seating in family-owned pews and space for hundreds of guests.[19]

Completed in 1885, the new building cemented Temple Adath Israel's position as the most influential Jewish institution in Boston. The dedication ceremony connected the congregation's traditional past with its Reform future and commitment to ecumenical cooperation. Rabbi Schindler co-officiated with retired hazan Joseph Shoninger and Rabbi Raphael Lasker of Ohabei Shalom, while Isaac Mayer Wise, president of Hebrew Union College (HUC), the new Reform seminary in Cincinnati, Ohio, delivered the principal address. The mayor and several public officials and prominent ministers also participated. Expressing the congregation's intent, Board President Goulston (1883–1885) observed, "We have built this temple . . . that its products shall be good and true men and women, imbued with reverence and loyalty to God, and with patriotism and loyalty to the country we live in."[20]

In 1884, Schindler had predicted that, with the new temple, the congregation "will and must increase in membership and take a higher stand in usefulness and activity. The present indifference will and must give way to religious enthusiasm and enterprise." The impressive structure, along with the congregation's outspoken rabbi, did attract additional members and, by the end of 1885, ninety-nine families belonged. Like their predecessors, the new congregants were generally retailers and manufacturers in their thirties and forties. Many may have joined because they saw the Columbus Avenue synagogue as a more appropriate worship space than the Pleasant Street shul. A number, like clothing merchant Leopold Morse, who had served as Massachusetts's first Jewish congressman from 1876 to 1885, were related to other members. The new members were also slightly more diverse; many were born in the United States or in European countries other than Germany and Poland. Most lived in the South End and a few of the more affluent lived in the Back Bay.[21]

Even as many Central European Jews displayed their new affluence by joining Adath Israel and Jewish social clubs, the composition of Boston's Jewish community was rapidly changing. By the 1880s, thousands of Eastern European Jews had begun to pour into Boston. The earlier arrivals had been part of a larger migrant group of skilled tradesmen who chose to leave the German-speaking provinces of central Europe during a time of political instability in search of economic opportunity. In contrast, the newcomers, who spoke primarily Yiddish, were refugees with no resources and few applicable skills who fled poverty and the increasingly antisemitic policies of the Russian empire. "German" Jews regarded the "greenhorns" with disdain, but they soon learned that non-Jews made little distinction between the small number of Americanized Jews and the thousands of Eastern European foreigners who crowded into the tenement slums of the North, South, and West Ends.[22]

Concerned about losing their hard-won status and worried about burgeoning antisemitism, Temple Adath Israel leaders like Jacob and Lina Hecht, Edward and Theresa Goulston, and Rabbi Schindler took responsibility for aiding their co-religionists. Many saw philanthropy as a way of training immigrants to become "proper" American Jews while demonstrating their ability to care for their own. Yet despite their genuine concern for the poor, the Jewish elite's means of practicing charity were often ineffective because they did not understand or appreciate the new immigrants' culture and their attachment to traditional Jewish practices.[23]

One Neighborhood's Story: Holyoke Street

In 1885, six Temple Adath Israel families lived on Holyoke Street, a short dead-end street off Columbus Avenue about ten blocks from the new synagogue. Four of the families had moved to this attractive street, lined with bowfront brick rowhouses, since 1880, and all but one were relatively new synagogue members. The Goulston, Beckhard, Weil, Fuchs, Hirshberg, and Frank families each had several children — at least twenty in all (ten boys and ten girls) — ranging in age from two to twenty-one. Two of the families were missing a parent; Athalia Frank was a widow and Meyer Hirshberg a widower.

The five men were merchants, selling tobacco, "gentleman's furnishings," cigars, liquor, and shoes, respectively. They were representative of the congregation's membership, as were the women, aged 30 to 45, two of whom were born in the United States. Each family occupied a full rowhouse, but only one couple, the Beckhards, owned their property.

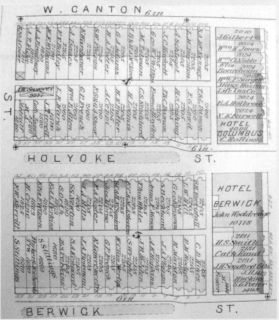

G. W. Bromley,
Atlas of the City of
Boston, 1883.
(Courtesy of Historic
New England)

Philanthropy: Jacob and Lina Hecht

Jacob H. Hecht (1834–1903), a Baden-born entrepreneur, married Baltimore-born Caroline (Lina) Frank (1848–1920), in Maryland. By 1870, the Hechts had moved to Boston and joined Temple Adath Israel. The Hechts were childless, but they took in various relatives, including Lina's brothers, Daniel and Abe Frank, who worked with Jacob in the shoe business, and Jacob's nieces, Sophie and Rose Liebmann (who later married Daniel). They mentored "rising stars" in Boston's Jewish community including future Supreme Court Justice Louis D. Brandeis and writer Mary Antin. They were among the few Jews invited to join elite Protestant organizations in Boston.

The Hechts tirelessly engaged in social service, and, together, they established a high standard for Jewish philanthropy in Boston. Lina, known as "Lady Bountiful," raised money for various charitable causes by organizing lavish benefit events. In 1878, Lina annexed the Ladies Hebrew Sewing Society to the United Hebrew Benevolent Association (UHBA). When Jacob became president in 1881, he reorganized the "Benevolent" and adopted modern casework principles. He became founding president of the Federation of Jewish Charities in 1895; Lina later served as a vice president. Both were devoted to improving the plight of immigrants. Jacob became the founding president of the Boston branch of the American Committee Ameliorating the Condition of the Russian Refugees, and also opened a Free Employment Bureau for newcomers. Lina was a trustee of the Leopold Morse Home and established the Hebrew Industrial School in 1890.

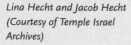

Lina Hecht and Jacob Hecht (Courtesy of Temple Israel Archives)

In 1883, Rabbi Schindler had proposed coordinating the various organizations' efforts through "a union . . . of the Benevolent, the Ladies' Sewing Society, and the different lodges." From this time forward, the rabbi would devote much of his prodigious energy to charitable activities. Twelve years later, when the Federation of Jewish Charities (today called the Combined Jewish Philanthropies) was finally established as a consortium of Central European Jewish philanthropic organizations, it would attempt to "avoid duplication and fraud" while respecting the autonomy of the individual organizations. Influenced by new post–Civil War methodologies embraced by Protestant charities, especially the Associated Charities of Boston (founded in 1879), the Federation would ally Jewish leaders more closely with other social and intellectual reformers. Establishing guidelines for granting aid to the "deserving poor," it sought to "bring the foreigner into touch with our American institutions in the shortest possible space of time," and stressed the importance of citizenship. The Federation was also determined to protect newcomers from Christian "proselytizing." By the 1890s, these organizations, and the environment that spawned them, would have a significant effect on organized Jewish life in Boston as even the most Americanized Jews began to debate the relative values of acculturation and particularism in an increasingly antisemitic environment.[24]

At Adath Israel, the changing environment, the synagogue's expansive space, and its growing membership encouraged a number of new initiatives that reflected the congregation's willingness to institute more comprehensive reforms. In 1885, the board voted to adopt the English translation of Rabbi David Einhorn's *Olath Tamid*, the "radical" Reform prayer book that would later become a model for the *Union Prayer Book* (1895). The trustees established a library and purchased new books with the proceeds of the religious school's annual Purim plays; by 1891 it contained more than 1,000 volumes.[25]

The Religious School Committee also instituted long-needed curricular changes. In the past, language instruction had taken precedence over religious education, but Schindler believed that the "first and foremost duty" of the congregation was to "instruct the rising generation in the tenets of Judaism" and help the children become "familiar with the history of our [Jewish] nation and the moral and ethical laws prescribed by our religion." The school offered three classes on religion and biblical history on weekend mornings. Schindler taught the confirmation class; six "young ladies of the Congregation" who volunteered as assistant teachers led the younger classes according to his "prescribed plan." In 1885, sixty-nine students attended these classes, while fifty-eight also studied German on Tuesday afternoons with Schindler, his son Paul, and volunteer teacher Lottie Rosenfeld. Few, however, attended the rabbi's Hebrew class on Thursday afternoons, as their parents apparently did not consider Hebrew instruction a priority. The changes were considered successful, although, as the school committee noted, conduct remained a problem.[26]

Rabbi Schindler's growing reputation as a thinker, writer, and orator may also have attracted new members. Like other religious reformers of his time, Schindler derived his belief system from contemporary philosophy and science, as well as theology, and Boston, where Unitarianism was the dominant Christian denomination, was fertile soil for intellectuals with advanced ideas. Like them, he espoused a popular social ideology called "liberalism" that emphasized "freedom and altruism, a strong foundation in social ethics and moral imperatives, an obvious removal from many traditional dogmas and rituals, and an optimism about human destiny."[27]

Liberalism was a good fit for Schindler's theology. He believed that Judaism, the "mother" of all religions, was the only religion that could stand up to rational inquiry. All faiths, he argued, including Judaism, were shaped by the historical conditions of their time, and they all evolved as civilization progressed. But the core principles of Judaism, "that there is but one God, and none besides him, and the ten commandments, which are the consequence of it," he claimed, "have remained unchanged, and will remain unchanged forever, until the whole human race shall have adopted them." Schindler admired the Unitarians because they recognized that "the trinitarian idea was no improvement on monotheism" and had come to embrace a more "Jewish" conception of God; he hoped that, ultimately, all Christians would follow their enlightened example.[28]

Although this utopian vision of religious unity set him apart from most mainstream American Reform Jews, Schindler's concept of Judaism aligned with the principles of the UAHC, adopted in the Pittsburgh Platform of 1885. These principles reimagined Judaism as a progressive religion "ever striving to be in accord with the postulates of reason"; they rejected ceremonies "not adapted to the views and habits of modern civilization," as well as Messianism and Zionism. Schindler saw no need to wish for a savior or yearn for a Jewish homeland. "In the United States," he argued, "the Hebrews had freedom of religion and speech, enjoyed the ballot, could aspire to political office, and enjoyed the privileges of citizenship. Why then return to Palestine?" In addition, he expressed sympathy for two other principles that the UAHC did not endorse: abandoning the "historical Sabbath" (because he believed that one should call "that day your Sabbath on which you in reality abstain from labor") and the rite of circumcision (because he believed that it was a "custom," not a rite, and that the surgery was dangerous).[29]

Schindler disseminated these ideas, and many others on a variety of historical, social, and political topics, in his temple sermons (two volumes of which were published in 1886 and 1888), his two newspapers, the *Boston Hebrew Observer* (1883–1886), and the *Jewish Chronicle* (1890–1893), and many public lectures. By the 1880s, Schindler had entered a circle of liberal intellectuals that included Unitarian clergymen, literary figures, and even an Irish Catholic editor. His essays frequently appeared in various journals, his sermons were reported in the daily press, and he was a popular lecturer. As an immigrant, he valued the American system of participatory government and his potential, as a citizen, to have an impact on public policy. In 1888, for example, he was elected to Boston's School Committee, where he served for six years. As a result, Schindler, and the temple, became recognized in the wider Boston community as "a bridge between the Jewish middle classes and their non-Jewish neighbors."[30]

Even so, the growth of the congregation, the expanded religious school program, the new space, and Schindler's reputation failed to increase attendance at the 10 A.M. Sabbath service. Many of Adath Israel's members were merchants and manufacturers who catered to a broad clientele and could not afford to close their businesses on Saturday, and even wealthy financiers like Jacob Hecht found it difficult to keep the Sabbath. Generally, it was women, children, and elderly men who went to services while their husbands, fathers, and sons went to work. In the summer, services were discontinued due to "the intervention of the vacation season."[31]

The board had attempted to address this issue as early as 1879 by legislating a rotating, mandatory monthly attendance policy, but many members refused to comply, preferring to risk being assessed a two-dollar fine. In 1884, Schindler predicted that "besides the regular Sabbath service, services for the benefit of those who can not attend at that day will become a necessity" in the new building. In the mid-1880s, Adath Israel, following the lead of other Reform congregations, instituted Friday night services. In the winter of 1885, these services featured a "Lecture Course" whose speakers included "liberal Unitarian Ministers" addressing "prominent and worldly topics." Some members, including Board President Goulston, a strong

Schindler supporter, believed that this experiment "produced great good in our community." Others, however, disliked the idea of Christian ministers preaching from the synagogue pulpit, and the lectures were discontinued. Similarly, while Friday night services were initially popular, "by degrees the attendance fell off" due to competition from concerts, other amusements, and bad winter weather.[32]

In 1888, Schindler, fearful that "the beautiful temple on which so much money had been spent was to remain unoccupied . . . excepting a few holidays," determined to take "the so much dreaded step of introducing Sunday services." Contending that "no matter how much [Jews] were justified in clinging to the historical Sabbath . . . hardly any person could withstand the drift of the time, and keep that day conscientiously, as a day of rest and spiritual edification." Sunday services, he argued, had been successfully adopted at other American synagogues and would actually strengthen Judaism. But many American Jews flatly opposed Sunday services as the "initial step toward the complete assimilation of the Jew," and the Adath Israel board agreed. The trustees did, however, permit Schindler to supplement the regular Saturday and Friday night services with a Sunday morning lecture series. Six months later, a musical component was added.[33]

Schindler saw his lectures as an opportunity to keep the congregation "abreast with the time and to win for it the respect of the Gentile world." Reprinted in the local press, the lectures, which addressed such topics as education, immigration, prohibition, socialism, race relations, and Christian theology, affirmed Schindler's position as *the* Jewish voice in non-Jewish Boston—and Temple Adath Israel as the most progressive institution in the Jewish community. Liberal Christians flocked to Schindler's lectures, generally outnumbering the Jews present. Flattered by their admiration, he increasingly implied that most differences between liberal Jews and Unitarians were cultural rather than theological. Traditional Jews and observant Christians, on the other hand, objected to this evolving "universalist" theology because they felt it demeaned the value, importance, and distinctiveness of each religion.[34]

From the congregation's perspective, the Sunday morning lectures were of mixed value because few members attended. In 1890, they were moved to the evening with no better result, and in 1891, a board committee approached Schindler about canceling them entirely. The rabbi was furious. Issuing an "urgent invitation" for the congregation to attend the Sunday lecture on December 21, he proclaimed to those assembled that the religious

Communal Service:
Edward S. and Theresa Goulston

Edward S. Goulston (1847–1898), an English-born tobacconist, and his Prussian-born wife Theresa (1848–1931), a talented pianist, were life-long community leaders. Married in the late 1860s, they had six children between 1869 and 1884, four of whom survived to adulthood. Like other upwardly mobile Jews, the Goulstons had high expectations for their children, and they encouraged them to enter the professions rather than business; two became attorneys, founding the well-known Boston firm of Goulston and Storrs in 1900.

The Goulstons joined the synagogue in the 1870s. A strong advocate for radical Reform, Edward, as chairperson of the Education Committee, advocated for tuition-free education in 1877; as president of the board from 1883 to 1885, he led the building campaign for the Columbus Avenue synagogue. Theresa organized bazaars and an annual Succoth Harvest Festival to raise funds for the religious school and the new sanctuary. Her leadership skills were recognized when she became president of the temple's first auxiliary in 1894, vice president of the Woman's Society in 1903, and one of the first two female trustees in 1923.

Edward S. Goulston (Courtesy of Temple Israel Archives)

The Goulstons also led social service initiatives outside of Temple Adath Israel. "We have to take care of the thousands coming to our shores," Edward declared at an 1891 UHBA meeting. "We must help them to become good citizens" and treat them "with kindness and toleration." Edward died in 1898, but Theresa remained an active community organizer throughout her life; in 1918, on her seventieth birthday, some five hundred people gathered at the temple to honor her. Theresa was also involved in various charitable and reform organizations, including the Council of Jewish Women (founded in 1897), which aided delinquent girls and unmarried women. This work introduced her to Jewish prisoners, and, in 1913, she founded the Jewish Prisoners' Aid Society.

Theresa Goulston (Jewish Advocate, February 14, 1918)

indifference and "intellectual apathy of this congregation against which I have fought in vain for 18 years has now reached its utmost limits . . . the congregational life we are leading has grown worse than a mockery of religion." Despite his efforts to introduce reforms (including Friday evening services and the "last resort" of Sunday lectures), Schindler continued, he found himself preaching to an almost empty synagogue on Saturdays and to "strangers" on Sundays who "express their delight with my lectures" but wonder "why the members of my congregation shine so brightly by their absence." Discontinuing the evening lectures, he argued, would "be equivalent to the closing of the temple because people do not go on the Sabbath, as they are determined to work, and their social and charitable lives are centered elsewhere." The temple was more than a place to educate their children and ensure a Jewish burial, he declared. Because members are only expected "to come, to sit down, and to be prayed and preached at," they do not take an active role in the important work of ending prejudice against Jews—a goal, Schindler argued, that had become even more important with the influx of "Russian Israelites" who needed help, not only from their co-religionists, but also from the "public at large."[35]

This diatribe preserved the Sunday lectures, but it did not appease Schindler's congregants, who were tired of his complaints, resentful about the activities that took him away from his pastoral duties, and outraged by his recent remarks condoning intermarriage between liberal Jews and Unitarians. As the rabbi and a recognized public figure, Schindler wielded more power in the temple than his predecessors, but American synagogues were voluntary associations run by lay boards; as an employee, Schindler had "neither seat nor voice" in the official meetings where proposed changes were discussed and voted upon. He had always chafed under the board's authority and he had become increasingly frustrated by the fact that he was more appreciated by liberal Christians than his own community. Schindler concluded his December lecture by offering to "sacrifice" himself (by resigning), but the reality was that he had just agreed to a new three-year contract, and he could not afford to leave.[36]

When Schindler failed to convince the congregation to adopt a new prayer book in early 1893, the situation deteriorated even further. In September, the trustees agreed that a change was "highly necessary" for the "good and welfare" of the congregation; Rabbi Schindler's contract would not be renewed. The rabbi was unrepentant. "It is a grievous fault of yours," he reproved members, "that you have not caught the true spirit of reform." Two

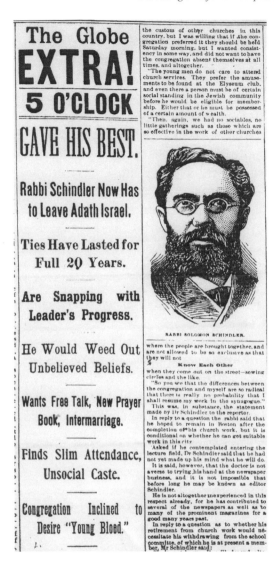

The Globe
EXTRA!
5 O'CLOCK
GAVE HIS BEST.

Rabbi Schindler Now Has to Leave Adath Israel.

Ties Have Lasted for Full 20 Years.

Are Snapping with Leader's Progress.

He Would Weed Out Unbelieved Beliefs.

Wants Free Talk, New Prayer Book, Intermarriage.

Finds Slim Attendance, Unsocial Caste.

Congregation Inclined to Desire "Young Blood."

the custom of other churches in this country, but I was willing that if the congregation preferred it they should be held Saturday morning, but I wanted consistency in some way, and did not want to have the congregation absent themselves at all times, and altogether.

"The young men do not care to attend church services. They prefer the amusements to be found at the Elyseum club, and even there a person must be of certain social standing in the Jewish community before he would be eligible for membership. Either that or he must be possessed of a certain amount of wealth.

"Then, again, we had no sociables, no little gatherings such as those which are so effective in the work of other churches

RABBI SOLOMON SCHINDLER.

where the people are brought together, and are not allowed to be so exclusive as that they will not

Know Each Other

when they come out on the street—sowing circles and the like.

"So you see that the differences between the congregation and myself are so radical that there is really no probability that I shall resume my work in the synagogue." This was, in substance, the statement made by Dr Schindler to the reporter.

In reply to a question the rabbi said that he hoped to remain in Boston after the completion of his church work, but it is conditional on whether he can get suitable work in this city.

Asked if he contemplated entering the lecture field, Dr Schindler said that he had not yet made up his mind what he will do.

It is said, however, that the doctor is not averse to trying his hand at the newspaper business, and it is not impossible that before long he may be known as editor Schindler.

He is not altogether inexperienced in this respect already, for he has contributed to several of the newspapers as well as to many of the prominent magazines for a good many years past.

In reply to a question as to whether his retirement from church work would necessitate his withdrawing from the school committee, of which he is at present a member, Mr Schindler said:

The Boston Globe *announced Rabbi Schindler's "retirement" in an extra edition. (Boston Globe, October 25, 1893)*

weeks later, he added, "the true prosperity of a congregation" did not consist in the "wealth of its members" or the "magnificence of its synagogue."[37]

Schindler's "retirement" was front-page news in several Boston newspapers, as reporters speculated about his departure. After leaving Adath Israel in June 1894, Schindler completed a sequel to Edward Bellamy's *Looking Backward* (*Young West*, 1894). Active in charitable work in Boston for many years, he had become the director of the Leopold Morse Home for Aged and Infirm Hebrews and Orphans in 1889. In 1895, he was appointed

as the founding director of Boston's Federation of Jewish Charities, serving
at the Federation until 1899 and the Morse Home until 1909.[38]

"THE HIGHEST LEVEL OF USEFULNESS"

In the wake of Solomon Schindler's stormy tenure, Temple Adath Israel
sought a rabbi who would embrace mainstream Reform Judaism and attend
to his pastoral duties. By 1893, the members of the UAHC had codified the
basic principles that would identify "classical" Reform Judaism for many
years in the Pittsburgh Platform (1885), opened Hebrew Union College
(1875), which had already ordained more than twenty rabbis, and established a professional organization for them (the Central Conference of
American Rabbis [CCAR], 1889). The Adath Israel board asked for recommendations from Rabbi Wise, CCAR president, and determined to interview only HUC graduates. After five candidates came to Boston to "lecture
on trial," the board offered the job to twenty-three-year-old Charles Fleischer, a "brilliant young preacher" who had recently earned both rabbinical
and literature degrees.[39]

Adath Israel's first ordained rabbi, Fleischer was a staunch proponent of
the Pittsburgh Platform. Soon after his arrival, as "a fitting announcement to
the Jews of America that we are one with them in all that pertains to the welfare of Judaism," he convinced the temple trustees to join the UAHC for the
first time. He also persuaded them to adopt the Reform movement's forthcoming *Union Prayer Book*, a largely English-language liturgy that opened
from left to right and included poetic translations of prayers and responsive readings designed to encourage participation. The board celebrated the
arrival of their magnetic new rabbi with a two-day installation.[40]

Rabbi Fleischer threw himself into his duties. Like his predecessors, the
new rabbi believed that the "hope of the people as a congregation . . . lay in
the Jewish Sunday School," and he repeatedly encouraged members to enroll
their children. Committed to bringing "our little school to the highest level
of usefulness in making of the growing generation a set of intelligent loyal
and reverent Jews," Fleischer reorganized the confirmation program and
raised the age of confirmation. Under his tutelage the school thrived and
the School Committee expanded the program to non-members. During the
"depression times" of the mid-1890s, the school opened its doors to the children of poor parents, "the only requirement being good behavior and clean
in person"; later, those who could afford to pay were assessed tuition on a
sliding scale. In 1897, two of the fourteen confirmands were orphans from

Charles Fleischer

Charles Fleischer (1871–1942), born in Breslau, Silesia, immigrated to New York with his widowed mother and three brothers at the age of nine. He earned a degree in Hebrew Letters and a rabbinic degree from Hebrew Union College in 1887 and 1893, respectively, as well as a literature degree from the University of Cincinnati. He worked for a year as assistant to Rabbi Henry Berkowitz of Philadelphia, founder of the Jewish Chautauqua Society, before being hired at Temple Adath Israel at the age of twenty-three.

Once called the "Beau Brummel of the Back Bay," Rabbi Fleischer's handsome appearance, youth, and intelligence captured the attention of political and social reformers, religious liberals, philosophers, and artists, including John Singer Sargent. Fleischer believed in the power of enlightened citizenship and sought to make Adath Israel a center of education and intellectual dialogue. He served on the Boston School Committee from 1896 to 1900.

Ultimately, Fleischer rejected Judaism in favor of an inclusive humanist theology. He left Temple Adath Israel in 1911 to establish the Sunday Commons, a nonsectarian church that promoted common American values rather than specific religious principles. In 1919, he married Mabel R. Leslie, a Presbyterian lawyer from Vermont. Three years later, they moved to New York, where she practiced law and he became the editor of the editorial page of William Randolph Hearst's *New York American* and the first commentator on the CBS radio network. He remained a well-known lecturer and writer until his death in 1942.

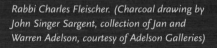

Rabbi Charles Fleischer. (Charcoal drawing by John Singer Sargent, collection of Jan and Warren Adelson, courtesy of Adelson Galleries)

PURIM BALL A BRILLIANT SPECTACLE.

Festivities Enjoyed by 1500 Persons and Large Sum Realized for Charity.

Temple Adath Israel congregants joined other like-minded Boston Jews in activities that combined charitable and social goals. In 1896, the women of the Purim Association held the first of many "brilliant" annual balls to raise funds for Jewish charities.
(Boston Globe, February 9, 1900)

the Morse Home. Fleischer supported other educational opportunities as well, including a "Young Folks" reading circle, and, later, a series of Sunday night "Young Folks Meetings" for Jews and Christians, organized by the congregation, that proved extremely popular with young immigrants in the North and West Ends.[41]

Rabbi Fleischer hoped to engage members intellectually, politically, and culturally. In 1895, he instituted the popular practice of pulpit exchange, in which various rabbis, sometimes from distant cities, would speak at each other's services. In 1896, in an effort to foster patriotism, he introduced an annual Memorial Day service in which local veterans groups participated. When Fleischer succeeded Theresa Goulston as president of the auxiliary society established to promote "sociability" in 1894, he encouraged it to become a literary society and social service organization of the kind then popular in Boston. It met monthly to discuss the Bible, debate current

issues, hold musical recitals, and mete out financial assistance to congregational families in need.[42]

An intellectual with a philosophical bent, Fleischer was deeply interested
in the myriad ideas, issues, and causes of the period. He was convinced that
Jews could both "retain a certain amount of their individuality" and "be
as broad as humanity." Young, attractive, charming, intelligent, and articulate, the new rabbi of the city's largest Reform synagogue quickly became
an ambassador for liberal Judaism in Boston and beyond. Even so, he occupied a complicated position as a Reform rabbi, a reformer, and an immigrant eager for acceptance in his adopted country. Proud to have "achieved"
American citizenship, he was a staunch Americanist and a committed progressive in a time of international unrest. He believed that citizens had
a duty to study issues and question policies, and he gave lectures across
New England on political and social subjects, whether they were related
to Judaism or not. Fleischer opposed capital punishment and immigration restriction; he advocated for women's rights, "family limitation," and
thoughtful urban planning. In 1894, he criticized the French for their persecution of Alfred Dreyfus, the Jewish army officer accused of treason; later,
he inveighed against President Theodore Roosevelt, calling him an impe-
rialist warmonger who had betrayed America's principles by maintaining
the Philippines as a "colony" after the Spanish-American War. Like Rabbi
Schindler, he also demonstrated civic engagement by serving on the Boston
School Committee from 1897 to 1900.[43]

By the late 1890s, Fleischer's wide-ranging interests, his growing reputation as a radical thinker, and his burgeoning hubris were beginning to
create tension between him and the congregation. He was a popular lecturer outside the synagogue, and, as early as 1896, the board chided him for
accepting engagements that took him away from his duties at the temple or
the school. Determined to spend his time where he felt most appreciated,
he, like his predecessor, became fixated on the issue of low attendance at
religious services, especially on the Sabbath. In 1898, he began a campaign
to decrease the number of Saturday services "to save our money and our
self-respect" in favor of special Sunday services for occasions like Memorial
Day, and monthly pulpit exchanges on Friday evenings, that would draw
bigger crowds. Fleischer also complained about spending "too much time
doing funerals and weddings for non-members, for 'paltry fees,'" when
he felt he had more important work to do elsewhere. Determined to gain
"sympathetic support" for his public activities, Fleischer tried, and failed,

Rabbi Fleischer was passionate
about many "American" activities,
including baseball. Writing in
Baseball Magazine, he recalled
a sermon in which he "meant
to plead for the empire of
righteousness" but instead "waxed
enthusiastic about the 'umpire of
righteousness!'" In 1903, when the
opening game of the first World
Series took place in Boston on Yom
Kippur, Fleischer and a number of
congregants attended the second
game as guests of Barney Dreyfuss,
the Jewish owner of the Pittsburgh
Pirates. (Undated mockup, courtesy
of Tamara P. Miller)

to convince the board that "in such broader devotion of my energies I feel
that I make the best use of myself not only for the greater work of humanity and for the particular cause of Judaism at large but also for the increased
glory and success of our own 'Adath Israel,' to which I have more specially
consecrated myself."[44]

In 1900, Fleischer began to advocate for replacing both the Sunday evening lectures and the traditional Saturday morning services with a religious
service held on Sunday mornings. A year later, when the lectures were sus-
pended due to "lack of patronage" — despite the fact that "non-Jews, appre-
ciating his liberalism, flocked" to them — Fleischer publicly announced his
support for the Sunday Sabbath. Maintaining the "historical Sabbath," he
argued, was impractical and futile when the business world ran on a Christian calendar. With the Sunday Sabbath, Reform Jews could have "the sanc-
tification of a day by public worship and aspiration." This "next step," he

proclaimed, "is plainly indicated, and yet we take it not, because fear and stubbornness, indifference and a sentimental loyalty . . . prevent." (Using the same logic, he opposed a proposed Jewish Saturday Sabbath bill in the Massachusetts legislature that would have permitted Jews to open their businesses on Sunday, thereby infuriating many of his co-religionists in Boston.) The board agreed to hold Sunday morning "meetings" and to extend the practice of pulpit exchange to "local liberal ministers" who were Christian, but also repeatedly reaffirmed the "historical Sabbath" and the continuance of the Saturday services. Determined to turn the Sunday meetings into "modern" Sunday services, Fleischer slowly began to incorporate liturgical and musical elements, to the trustees' consternation. In 1903, when he asked to celebrate the confirmation service on a Sunday morning, the board insisted that it be held, as always, on Shavuoth.[45]

Even so, the congregation continued to support its young rabbi because the synagogue was thriving in other ways. The school was successful, the congregation was growing, and, although many of the men in the congregation paid more attention to business than religion, their wives and daughters devoted themselves to maintaining the spiritual and communal life of the temple. In 1903, for example, the women established a society "to develop the solidarity of the congregation, to co-operate with the pulpit in every way, and to stress the study and fostering of Jewish ideals." The first president, forty-year-old Rose Liebmann Frank, was the wife of Board President Daniel Frank (1904–1911), a wealthy cigar merchant, and the mother of fourteen-year-old Fannie. The Woman's Society built on the proven record of women's fund-raising at the temple, provided formal hospitality for all congregational functions, and, beginning in 1907, published a monthly temple bulletin. The society also supported youth programs by organizing annual festival celebrations for the religious school at Purim and Chanukah. In 1906, it held a conference for Jewish Sunday school teachers designed to improve religious education. In 1908, the society initiated a series of dances, meetings, and other activities for Jewish students attending Wellesley, Simmons, and Radcliffe.[46]

THE "BROTHERHOOD OF MAN" AND
THE "FATHERHOOD OF GOD"

By the turn of the twentieth century, the Columbus Avenue synagogue was becoming inconvenient for members who had abandoned the increasingly immigrant-filled South End for Brookline and other, more suburban,

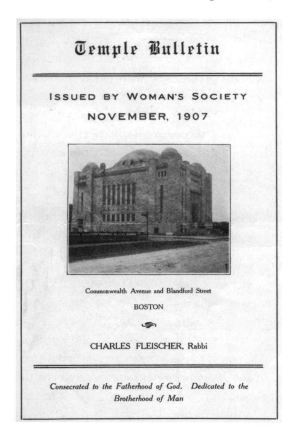

Monthly Temple Bulletin, *first
issued by the Woman's Society in
1907. (Courtesy of Temple Israel
Archives)*

neighborhoods. In November 1902, when the North Russell Street African Methodist Episcopal Zion Church offered $45,000 for the building, the board enthusiastically accepted. The next year, the temple purchased land on the corner of Commonwealth Avenue and Blandford Street, an undeveloped area near Kenmore Square. The new Woman's Society spearheaded an extremely successful capital campaign with the slogan "The Temple Must Be Built!"[47]

Designed by Clarence Blackall, one of Boston's premier architects, the Commonwealth Avenue synagogue illustrated the congregation's changing perception of American Judaism. The imposing white marble structure, described by the press as "Solomon's Temple," incorporated Byzantine design elements symbolizing "the religion which has come to us from the most ancient time." The facade inscription, however, "Dedicated to the Brotherhood of Man. Consecrated to the Fatherhood of God," clearly expressed American ideals.[48]

During the years of construction, services were held in various rented halls and in the New Century Building (now the Huntington Avenue Theater), while religious school classes took place on the second floor of the New England Women's Club on Park Street, near the State House, and elsewhere. The temple continued to offer a variety of programs and to participate in community activities. In 1905, for example, Adath Israel was part of a citywide commemoration of the 250th anniversary of Jewish settlement in America; the celebration was organized by member Lee M. Friedman, an attorney who was the son of the nation's largest shoe and boot wholesaler.[49]

Hoping to create the decorous atmosphere that marked classical Reform Judaism and emulated American churches in their splendid new building, the board and women's auxiliary met in 1906 to discuss ritual issues and appropriate behavior. Soon thereafter, the Temple Committee established "rules" that included, among other things, prohibitions against smoking and "loud conversation in the corridors or in any part of the temple building."

Designed by architect Clarence Blackall, the Commonwealth Avenue temple incorporated "exotic" Byzantine and Egyptian motifs. The impressive interior included a magnificent onyx and marble ark and an organ topped with large, trumpet-shaped pipes, arrayed in a semicircle, symbolizing "the confident world-outlook of the Jewish faith." (Courtesy of Temple Israel Archives)

Children under ten could not "enter the property" without an adult, nor could anyone "enter or leave the Auditorium during Service." Members also occasionally proposed ritual changes, such as when one trustee suggested adopting "the custom practiced elsewhere that the entire Congregation rise while the Kaddish prayer is read at all services."[50]

Such rules of behavior, and the new building's elegance, reflected the congregation's growing size, wealth, and prominence. By the time the Commonwealth Avenue structure opened in 1907, its membership included 135 families. The 1907 dedication, like that of the Columbus Avenue temple in 1885, attracted local officials, national Jewish leaders, and other guests who filled the nine hundred–seat sanctuary to capacity. Rabbi Fleischer was joined on the bima by his predecessors Joseph Shoninger and Solomon Schindler in a symbolic demonstration of continuity. The important contributions of the synagogue's women were recognized when the board gave Lina Hecht the honor of kindling the Ner Tamid.[51]

As the congregation prepared to move to its new home, Fleischer renewed his case for Sunday services; this time, he convinced the board to try the experiment of substituting a "religious service" for the Sunday morning meeting, while continuing to hold Saturday services. In December, triumphant over the positive response, Fleischer proposed making the Sunday services permanent, designing "a suitable ritual," and adding "adequate music" via a paid, professional quartet and organist. Once again, he proposed eliminating the Saturday services or holding them, "modestly but appropriately," in the vestry with "volunteered music—if we want any at all." He also asked for control over pulpit exchanges and a raise "commensurate with the dignity of his position and his standing in the community." The board, forced to admit the success of the Sunday services, agreed to continue them, and asked Fleischer to prepare a "ritual" for its approval. But the trustees also insisted that Saturday services continue to be held—in the auditorium, with a soloist.[52]

This confrontation made it clear that the board had become as uncomfortable with Fleischer as the trustees had earlier been with Schindler, and for similar reasons. Fleischer's dynamism, energy, and progressive ideas had brought him, and Adath Israel, recognition, but trustees felt that he devoted more attention to his public persona than to temple business, and they frequently disliked what he said outside the synagogue. By this time, Fleischer was considered "one of the most intellectual and radical Jews in America." Although he had rarely discussed his evolving beliefs from the pulpit dur-

Congregants leaving Commonwealth Avenue synagogue, 1908. (Courtesy of Temple Israel Archives)

ing his first decade in Boston, he had come to embrace a universalist theology based on the idea that "religious organization is valuable mainly to give organized force to the embodied ideals of persons and peoples"; what really mattered, he believed, was "the essential spirituality of our human nature." When Fleischer began to preach this new doctrine openly at Adath Israel and elsewhere, the board tried to limit his speaking engagements, admonishing him for traveling out of town without permission and for lecturing about controversial subjects, such as divorce.[53]

The trustees' response to Fleischer's new contract demands reflected these concerns. They agreed to a raise in his next three-year contract, but restated their policy of board approval for all pulpit exchanges. They also added provisions that the rabbi must follow the ritual established "by the constituted authorities of the congregation" and that his discourses must remain "within the limits of the Jewish religion." At the same time, not coincidentally, the board appointed Rabbi Schindler, who by this time had begun to rethink his earlier theological views, as rabbi emeritus of the congregation.[54]

Rabbi Fleischer agreed to the contract, but nonetheless continued to push for discontinuance of the Saturday service. On April 26, 1908, after a board conference on this subject, Fleischer, feeling "a sense of assault upon the dignity of the position and the freedom of the pulpit," delivered an impassioned Sunday morning address in which he declared himself "unwilling to preach to a congregation which will not accept his teachings and ideas." He stated that he intended "to preach what he denominates the 'Universal Religion' under Jewish auspices if he may but under non-Jewish auspices if he must." At the same time, he announced that he would "not accept a re-election at the end of the term of three years which I had just accepted." In response, the board issued an ultimatum: Fleischer must agree to either abide by the terms he had agreed upon and recognize that "the congregation exists as a distinctively and exclusively Jewish religious organization," or resign immediately.[55]

Fleischer reluctantly assented, and his contract was renewed. Ultimately, however, the controversy took a toll on the congregation. At the end of 1908, attendance at the Saturday service was sparse, with thirty to fifty members present, and very few men at Sunday services. Convinced that the membership at large would respond to his appeal to their "honesty and moral sense" and override the board's decision to maintain Saturday services, Fleischer requested a general meeting in April 1909. "The now established Sunday service," he argued, would allow the congregation to "rightly continue the historic career of the Jew as a prophetic leader of the religious life of the western world," and permit him to become "the voice of a congregation whose sentiment I represent." In the end, the members concurred with the board, deciding by a vote of 49 to 2 to retain the traditional Sabbath ritual, "a fundamental feature of Jewish identity that could not — should not — be given up," along with the Sunday service, and to support the board's determination to remain in control of ritual practices.[56]

For several months after this drama, the relationship between the mercurial rabbi and the congregation was stable. Although the regular services continued to be poorly attended, a number of pulpit exchanges and a special Thanksgiving service held jointly with the New Old South Church were very popular. These events made Fleischer feel more optimistic about his situation, and in January 1910 he averred that the temple stood for "the type of religion which not only expresses honestly the belief and aspiration of our times, but also undertakes to influence, vitally and for good, the complex life of our day." He even announced: "I am privileged to carry our message of sane spirituality and militant goodwill to all kinds of bodies of our fellow men. This fulfills my ideal of making Judaism not merely a reminiscent cult, but the 'light to the peoples' which our prophets meant it to be."[57]

Pleased by this praise, the board proposed to extend Fleischer's contract, due to expire in 1911, and the rabbi agreed to stay on. Then, in May, the board was stunned to hear a report that Fleischer intended to marry a woman who, presumably, was not Jewish. After a committee conferred with the rabbi, the trustees voted that Fleischer should take a leave of absence at half-pay for the remaining year of his current contract, and then leave Adath Israel. The marriage did not take place, however, and, in June, the rabbi decided to work full-time until the end of his contract. Yet, almost immediately thereafter, Fleischer shocked the congregation — and all of Jewish Boston — when, despite his promise to keep his sermons "within the limits of the Jewish religion," he announced from the Adath Israel pulpit his intent to establish a "new religion" that would amalgamate progressive Christianity and Judaism.[58]

The trustees immediately initiated a search for a new rabbi "of sterling character, [and] splendid attainments," who was "an able speaker and of a religious nature." Congregants wanted to maintain the temple's stature as the preeminent Reform synagogue in Boston; above all, they were determined to preserve their religious and cultural identity as Jews. They therefore looked for a rabbi who could achieve that balance while recognizing that his primary responsibility was to serve his congregation. Their ideal spiritual guide, Board President Daniel Frank stated, would be able to attract people to services and activities, demonstrate "ability as a teacher of our children," be a "leader in communal work," and exhibit an "active interest in our Charities." By February, they had found their man: Rabbi Harry Levi of Wheeling, West Virginia. Levi would assume his position in September 1911.[59]

By the beginning of March, Temple Adath Israel's future path was set, but a more ironic denouement would unfold later that month. On March 26th, Rabbi Emeritus Schindler publicly apologized from the temple's bima for "Some Mistakes I Have Made." Looking back on his time at Adath Israel after twenty years of experience working with Boston's impoverished Eastern European Jewish immigrant families, Rabbi Schindler admitted that he had ignored his congregants' needs because he had been too intent on filling the pews and obtaining the good opinion of gentiles. He had relied too much on rationalism, forgetting that people become "good member[s] of religious society not due to reason but emotion." Ever the iconoclast, Schindler was now as passionate about his errors as he had been about his original convictions. "Assimilation," he declared, "in which I believed and of

MAY FOUND NEW CHURCH

"Quite Possible," Says Rabbi Fleischer.

Reiterates His Decision to Leave Temple Israel.

Aim is to Universalize the Jewish Religion.

Rabbi Charles Fleischer of the congregation Adath Israel, who notified the trustees two years ago of his intention to sever his connection with the congregation at the close of his term, which ends a little more than a year hence, sent the trustees yesterday a second letter, assuring them that he remains of the same mind today, and that he will certainly retire in August next year.

RABBI CHARLES FLEISCHER,
Who Says He May Found New Church After Leaving Congregation Adath Israel.

He intimated to a Globe reporter that he might organize a new church

In explanation of his proposed retirement and of his latest letter to the trustees, Rabbi Fleischer explained last evening that his original resolution to leave the congregation of Adath Israel was due to his conviction that it was too conservative for his idea of a modern church.

"I do not mean to say," he continued, "that it is orthodox in the ordinary sense of the word, but that it is as orthodox as a conservative Unitarian church would be. I wish it to become as progressive and liberal as a radical Unitarian church.

Reforms Not Radical Enough.

"I have felt that the younger Jewish element, born in this country, is likely

---

Rabbi Fleischer ultimately left Temple Israel to establish a new "church" designed to "universalize the Jewish religion so that it may be applicable everywhere and to all sorts of people." (Boston Globe, June 15, 1910)

which I was an upholder, is a failure." A Jew "must be, in his religion, a different person . . . and proud of it."[60]

Fleischer's freethinking had led him down a different path. In his public response to Schindler and the congregation, a sermon entitled "Some Seeming Mistakes I Have Gladly Made," Fleischer acknowledged that he no longer considered himself a Jew. "While it is obvious that no one can force the Jew out of existence," he observed, "I believe it is a pious duty for every one who loves mankind more than his own particular element, to foster every movement that makes towards the union of the human family on an increasingly inclusive basis." Fleischer's last sermon, in June 1911, advocated for "unbounded non-Sectarianism" and a new religion based on "the creative power and the creative energy of man," truth, progress, character, and love. Soon after leaving Adath Israel, he established the Sunday Commons, a humanist congregation focused on "enlightened citizenship"; in 1919, he married Mabel R. Leslie, a Presbyterian lawyer.[61]

Rabbi Fleischer's departure, and Rabbi Schindler's reversal, reflected two different responses to a world where Jews flooding into the United States in record numbers (1911 was the peak year of immigration) encountered economic hardship, discrimination, and increasingly shrill demands for immigration restriction. Successful Jews, such as the members of Temple Adath Israel, viewed themselves as fully American, yet they now understood, as never before, that even in the United States they would always be seen as Jews first — whether they liked it or not. Over the next three decades, the congregation and its new rabbi would devote themselves to negotiating this complex balance.[62]

1911–1928

In Rabbi Harry Levi, Temple Adath Israel's members found a leader with whom they could be in greater "mental accord." Levi described himself as a "middle of the road man" belonging to the "modern school of moderate reformers." The first American-born rabbi of a Boston synagogue, Levi felt comfortable with both his American and his Jewish identities. He believed that Reform practices like Sunday services, vernacular prayers, and an organ and choir expressed a "sane and safe philosophy" that helped Jews to "blend without reaching after any sort of extreme ideas." At the same time, "emotional" and "poetic" Jewish rituals helped maintain the time-honored traditions that defined Judaism.[1]

Rabbi Levi saw himself primarily as a pastor, and he focused on creating a well-run institution that would meet the spiritual, as well as the social and intellectual, needs of his new congregation. Like his prosperous constituents, he was optimistic and pragmatic about the future of Reform Judaism in America, but he was also a seasoned administrator and a wise adjudicator. After Levi's arrival in September 1911, the synagogue (by this time commonly known as Temple Israel) and its rabbi would, in keeping with classical Reform Judaism, focus on Jewish ethical teachings and moral values such as tolerance and goodwill. This approach, along with the new rabbi's compassion, serene confidence in rationality and progress, and ecumenical attitude—"it takes all kinds of people and all kinds of religions to make a world"—would make Rabbi Levi beloved in Boston for more than thirty years and solidify Temple Israel's position as the most influential Reform synagogue in New England.[2]

"THE HUB OF LOCAL JEWISH LIFE"

By the early twentieth century, Jews no longer needed to join synagogues to obtain burial privileges or participate in Jewish activities, as burial societies and other organizations served these functions. In addition, there were a burgeoning number of Reform, Conservative, and Orthodox synagogues in Boston. As a result, Temple Israel's future hinged on its ability to offer services that would attract and keep dues-paying members. The "basic function of the synagogue," Rabbi Levi stated in his inaugural sermon, was to "make good Jews." Hoping to find new ways to appeal to the unaffiliated, he planned to make the temple "the hub of local Jewish life," a center of education, fellowship, and sociability. Levi also promoted interfaith understanding, welcoming "strangers" to congregational events and encouraging members to become involved in civic activities.[3]

Rabbi Levi was received with enthusiasm in Boston. Not only Temple Israel members, but many other Jews, as well as the press, responded positively to his moderate message and engaging style. In the fall of 1911, the temple's High Holy Day services had more attendees than ever before, including a large number from a new constituency: area college students. Five months after Rabbi Levi's arrival, the average attendance at Saturday services had tripled to about one hundred (with increasing numbers of men present), while Sunday services were filled to overflowing. Membership also increased dramatically; by the end of Levi's first year, 266 families belonged. By 1920, the number would increase to 430. Many new members were the relatives, friends, and adult children of long-standing congregants, but others made the community more diverse. Half of the men, and even more of the women, were born in America, with more than 65 percent of German parentage. But more than a quarter of the newcomers were Russian-born (17 percent) or of at least partial Russian extraction (9 percent). Like their predecessors, the new members were financially comfortable; almost two-thirds of the men were engaged in mercantile activities, manufacturing, or finance. Most were families with school-aged children. Almost a third owned their homes, and almost half could afford to employ at least one servant.[4]

In the early years of Rabbi Levi's tenure, the congregation made important modifications to ritual practices, the educational program, and various cultural, social service, and interfaith initiatives. In 1912, at Levi's urging, the board voted to rejoin the Union of American Hebrew Congregations (UAHC), this time for good, and to adopt a new "Sunday ritual." The music committee, along with organist/choirmaster Henry L. Gideon, who had been hired in 1907 (and would serve until 1938), hoped to beautify the services, reinvigorate festival celebrations, and encourage congregational

Harry Levi

Harry Levi (1875–1944) was born in Cincinnati to Orthodox Polish immigrants. He graduated from Hebrew Union College in 1892 and earned degrees in divinity and the arts from the University of Cincinnati in 1896. A leader of the Jewish Chautauqua Society and author of *Jewish Characters in English Fiction* (1903), Levi became the rabbi at Congregation Leshem Shomayim (commonly known as the Eoff Street Reform Congregation; now Temple Shalom), in Wheeling, West Virginia, in 1897 and stayed for fourteen years. He married Ruth Wolf in 1908; they had two sons, Robert and Harry, Jr.

Rabbi Levi came to Temple Israel in 1911 and served for twenty-eight years. During his tenure, the congregation attracted a broad spectrum of new members, dramatically increased in size, and became a temple center that offered programs for all ages. He was revered for his administrative and pastoral skills, his eloquence and even-tempered optimism, and his devotion to social service and religious tolerance. Levi became the temple's first "Radio Rabbi" in 1924, and broadcast sermons across New England for almost twenty years. He published two volumes of these sermons, *The Great Adventure* (1929) and *A Rabbi Speaks* (1930). Often described as a "saintly man," Levi was the first rabbi to be granted life tenure at Temple Israel. He retired in 1939 due to ill health, but continued as the temple's second rabbi emeritus until his death in 1944 of Parkinson's disease. In 1947, the Rabbi Harry Levi Auditorium at the Riverway Meeting House was named in his honor.

Rabbi Harry Levi
(Courtesy of Temple Israel Archives)

For many years, this cornet was thought to be the "shofar" purchased by Ohabei Shalom and brought to Adath Israel in 1854. However, the company that manufactured it was not founded until 1869. Its original owner was merchant Jacob R. Morse, board president from 1915 to 1922, who was, according to Rabbi Schindler, a cornet "virtuoso." (Portrait courtesy of Alan and Cecily Morse)

(Cornet courtesy of Wyner Museum, Temple Israel)

singing. Like other committees, it struggled to balance tradition and innovation; some members found modern music more "entertaining" while others were more "impressed" by "old Jewish music." As one congregant insisted in 1916, "Our children should hear ['Ein Kelohenu'] every Sabbath so they may know it as well as they know 'America.'"[5]

Recognizing that the educational program was a significant draw for families with school-aged children (more than 40 percent of new members), the temple's school committee, led by Lee M. Friedman, worked with Rabbi Levi to reorganize and professionalize the religious school to make it more like the children's secular schools. The committee divided classes into grade levels for the first time and replaced the volunteer instructors with paid teachers trained in the public schools. The religious school curriculum focused on Jewish history, ethics, and traditions. Children were encouraged to engage in social service by hosting parties for needy children and collecting pennies for the poor. Although the fifth and sixth graders were given the option of studying Hebrew, few participated. Students aged seven to fourteen attended on Sunday mornings while the confirmation class studied with Rabbi Levi on Tuesday afternoons. In 1913, Levi established a monthly post-confirmation seminar on Jewish issues for young adults aged sixteen to twenty. Several extracurricular activities were also introduced, including a dramatic club, two monthly school magazines (*The School Record* and *The Temple-ite*), and a teen group (the Jewish Juniors).[6]

Convinced that religious enthusiasm among the students would spread to the rest of the congregation, Levi, the board, and the auxiliaries estab-

(Courtesy of Temple Israel Archives)

lished community-building events that became long-standing traditions, including a popular monthly children's service. The new rabbi's first confirmation ceremony was a congregational affair designed to impress young and old with the significance of Jewish education. Board members led the five confirmands into the sanctuary (a tradition still in effect) and the Woman's Society feted them and their families with a grand reception.[7]

Other congregational initiatives were designed to encourage members to practice Jewish rituals in their homes. The first congregational seder in 1912, for example, run by the rabbi and the Woman's Society, introduced families to the "interesting and impressive" ceremonies associated with Passover. For several years, the society gave children copies of the "haggadah," hoping that parents would hold their own family seders. Thinking its work done, the society discontinued the seder in 1921, but members mourned the loss of the popular event and it was reinstated in 1929.[8]

These initiatives paid off. One hundred children between the ages of seven and fourteen (including those of some non-members) had attended religious school in 1911; by 1917, the school had 250 students. The confirmation class also ballooned, with 22 confirmands in 1915 and 60 by 1928. In 1919, the post-confirmation class included 110 students.[9]

The congregation's efforts to make the synagogue the focus of Jewish life extended to young adults as well. In 1912, Rabbi Levi and Board President Louis Strauss (1911–1915), a clothing merchant, established a new, inexpensive class of membership for recently confirmed young men — a group that synagogues generally found difficult to retain. Three years later, congregants established the Young People's Society of Temple Adath Israel (YPSOTAI) for unmarried young adults sixteen and over, which sponsored dances, plays, and other social and charitable activities. Temple leaders encouraged these and other community organizations that promoted Jewish fellowship, including the intercollegiate Menorah Society and the Young Men's Hebrew Association (YMHA), because they benefited the congregation's young people and Jewish students at local universities. Levi spoke at club meetings; the board sponsored "YMHA" days at the temple and set aside seats at High Holy Day services; the Woman's Society organized dances and sent the temple bulletin to area universities.[10]

Rabbi Levi's knowledge of Jewish history and ethics spurred adults to request additional educational opportunities. Soon after his arrival, Levi established biweekly classes on the Bible and "Jews in Many Lands." In 1914, he instituted a study class for the Woman's Society's weekly Sewing Circle

Confirmation classes, 1895, 1918, 1928. (Courtesy of Temple Israel Archives)

(founded two years earlier), that lasted for several decades. As some one hundred women sat in the vestry sewing clothing for needy and hospitalized children, Levi "read to them or told them Bible stories or discussed things with them," one member later recalled. Eventually, the Sewing Circle also organized lectures, concerts, and sales of handmade items to fund their charitable activities.[11]

In 1913, the Woman's Society became a founding member of the National Federation of Temple Sisterhoods. The Temple Israel Sisterhood, as it was now called, organized social service and cultural activities for the community to further its goals—extending hospitality to strangers and making "our Religion a living force in the community." In addition to their efforts on behalf of college students, the religious school, and the temple's coffers, the women arranged flowers for the pulpit, visited the congregation's sick, provided social services to impoverished Jews, gave money to charitable causes, and ran social activities, including an annual Chanukah luncheon. In 1914, the board acknowledged the Sisterhood's vital contributions by inviting female members to participate in the annual meeting for the first time.[12]

Inspired by the Sisterhood and the efforts of other Reform synagogues, male leaders organized the Temple Israel Brotherhood in November 1913 to encourage men to take a more active role in the life of the temple and the

YPSOTAI.

You are earnestly requested by above society.
Particularly members, quite a crowd we'd like to see.
So please attend, and bring a friend, remember without fail.
On MONDAY EVE., DECEMBER 10, at TEMPLE ISRAEL.
This DANCE will be informal, now start the season right.
And show the proper spirit, please be present on that night.
If you've paid your dues, there'll be no charge, so send your dollar now.

A friend's expense is fifty cents.
   RESERVE THIS DATE SOMEHOW:
                    President: WARREN BLOOM.

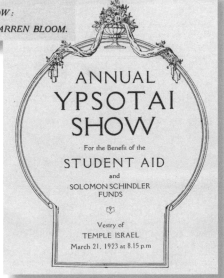

ANNUAL
YPSOTAI
SHOW
For the Benefit of the
STUDENT AID
and
SOLOMON SCHINDLER
FUNDS

Vestry of
TEMPLE ISRAEL
March 21, 1923 at 8.15 p.m

The Young People's Society of Temple Adath Israel (YPSOTAI) was established in 1912 for unmarried men and women aged sixteen and older. In the early 1920s, two-thirds of the forty-one who belonged were the children of members; almost half had been confirmed at the temple. Sixty percent were women, and most were in their late teens and early twenties. Many were students; others worked as clerks and teachers. Most lived near the temple and two-thirds were third-generation Americans. However, as in the congregation as a whole, about a quarter had parents born in Russia. (Courtesy of Temple Israel Archives)

TENTH ANNIVERSARY

Temple Israel Sisterhood

NOVEMBER 30, 1913

1 PRELUDE — "Lohengrin"   .   .   .   .   Wagner

2 INVOCATION — Dr. Abram Simon
        of Washington, D.C.

3 GREETING — Jacob R. Morse
        Vice-President of Temple Israel

4 VOCAL SOLO — "Die Allmacht"   .   .   .   Shubert
        Mrs. Edwin J. Dreyfus

5. ADDRESS — Mrs. Daniel Frank

6 ADDRESS — Mrs. Abram Simon
        Pres. of National Federation Temple Sisterhood

7 VIOLIN SOLO — Air from Violin Concerto   .   .   Goldmark
        Mr. Alexander Ribarsch

8 ADDRESS — Pres. of Temple Brotherhood

9 BENEDICTION — Rabbi Harry Levi

10 POSTLUDE — "I Believe"   .   .   .   Gideon
        Mr. Henry L. Gideon, Organist

An informal reception to Dr. and Mrs. Simon will be held in the Vestry immediately following the exercises, which you are cordially requested to attend.

The Sisterhood gave women the opportunity to play a more equal role in the congregation. As President Rose Frank observed at the group's tenth anniversary celebration in 1913, "Woman has always addressed herself to the maintenance of religion in the Home," but the Sisterhood allowed her "to take her place side by side with man in the direction of congregational affairs." (Courtesy of Temple Israel Archives)

larger Jewish community. With trustee Lee M. Friedman as its first president, the Brotherhood, like the Sisterhood, chose to extend membership to Jews who were not members of Temple Israel. The organization grew quickly; by 1917, it had 168 members. Intended as a social service, educational, and cultural society, the Brotherhood organized a variety of programs for the Jewish community, including a speakers' forum (established in 1917). As Levi had hoped, all this congregational activity led to better attendance at services, especially among men and young people. The sanctuary was often full to capacity, and people were frequently turned away.[13]

"A BENEFIT TO THE COMMUNITY AT LARGE"

By 1915, Temple Israel had become "the center of Jewish communal activities" in the city and one of the largest synagogues in the eastern United States. The congregation and Rabbi Levi worked hard to demonstrate to their "fellow-citizens" of all faiths that Temple Israel stood for "good practical endeavor that will be a benefit to the community at large." Like his predecessors, Levi was an eloquent orator who was regularly sought out by both religious and secular organizations; he delivered more than thirty lectures in his first year alone. His unflaggingly optimistic speeches and sermons focused on Jewish values in relation to various social justice issues, including child labor, immigration restriction, racism, women's suffrage, and war. Preaching "a strongly patriotic Judaism" and the efficacy of the ballot and social service, Levi urged his listeners to give "the best that in you lies to the city, the state, the country in which you live."[14]

Temple Israel members embraced Rabbi Levi's message. Many had worked for years to provide basic services and education to the expanding Eastern European population, to promote Americanization and citizenship, and to foster Jewish unity through organizations like the Federated Jewish Charities and the Council of Jewish Women. Earlier efforts had sometimes been ineffective, but with Boston's Jewish population swelling to nearly 65,000 by 1910, the elite Jews who ran these organizations finally learned to listen to and work with Eastern European Jews so that they could better meet the needs of the entire community.[15]

The Hebrew Industrial School, founded in Boston's West End by Lina Hecht in 1890, offered vocational programs to Jewish immigrant children in a kosher environment. It eventually became the Hecht Neighborhood House, a settlement house that was later renamed the West End House. (Boston Globe, January 28, 1900)

"Model" American Citizens

In the early twentieth century, Boston's Jewish leaders served as "model" American citizens for young Jewish men — American and foreign-born. Temple Israel trustees Abraham C. Ratshesky and Felix Vorenberg (board president, 1922–1927) combined business acumen and social ideals to establish institutions and support policies that would help immigrants of all backgrounds to get ahead.

Boston native A. C. "Cap" Ratshesky (1866–1943) was an entrepreneur and philanthropist who believed that everyone deserved the chance to "acquire the skills necessary to become full participants in our democratic society." A committed Republican, he served as a city councilman (1889–1891), state senator (1892–1894), and later, ambassador to Czechoslovakia (1930–1932). In 1895, he and his brother Israel established the United States Trust Company, which provided loans and banking services to the city's immigrant communities. Well known for his disaster relief efforts and civic work, including serving in the Massachusetts food and public safety administrations during World War I, Ratshesky was also president of the Federated Jewish Charities (1909–1918) and a founder of Beth Israel Hospital in 1916. He established a family foundation in the same year to combat social and economic injustice. He and his wife Edith were directors of the Red Cross, and they founded a Jewish boys' summer camp on Essex's Chebacco Lake in 1929.

German-born Felix Vorenberg (1868–1943) was an advocate of "economic democracy." A merchant who became the president and owner of Gilchrist Department Stores and the founder of National Retailers, Inc., Vorenberg was one of the first proprietors in Boston to hire African Americans for sales positions. In 1914, he helped department store owner and progressive reformer Edward A. Filene establish the Massachusetts Credit Union — the first in America — to provide employees with low-interest loans.

Left: *Abraham C. Ratshesky*
(Boston Globe, *January 1, 1892*)

Right: *Felix Vorenberg*
(Jewish Advocate, *December 18, 1922*)

Temple Israel's congregational efforts also focused on immigrant children. In 1912, the board had permitted the Boston Section of the Council of Jewish Women, most of whose leaders were Temple Israel members, to conduct a religious education class for immigrant women and children in the temple vestry. Two years later, the Sisterhood established a branch religious school at the Orthodox Congregation Beth Israel (commonly known as the Baldwin Place Synagogue) in the North End to educate Jewish immigrant children in Reform practices and help them adjust to American life. Financed by the Sisterhood and the Brotherhood and supervised by Rabbi Levi and a Sisterhood committee, the school employed a superintendent and six teachers who taught the same curriculum offered to children at Temple Israel. Sisterhood President Rose Frank's hope that the school would "become a medium for moral uplift in a much needed district" was soon realized. Sixty-four students attended the first year, and by 1917, there were 110.[16]

Cross-class religious education was becoming a trend by the early twentieth century. In 1916, three thousand Jewish children, including those from Temple Israel's religious schools, participated in a community-wide Purim celebration "to revive the old Purim spirit, to afford the Jewish public of Boston an exhibition of the educational work carried on in the Religious Schools of this city" and demonstrate "communal solidarity and union." By the late 1920s, Temple Israel operated five additional branch schools—in the West End, Hyde Park, Mattapan, Roxbury, and Brookline. In the 1930s,

Baldwin Place School, 1916–1917. The Sisterhood-sponsored program for immigrant children in the North End offered a full curriculum, including confirmation. (Courtesy of Temple Israel Archives)

the program expanded to various suburbs and more than three hundred students attended schools in Waltham, Watertown-Belmont, Stoughton, and Everett.[17]

Because the influx of immigrants highlighted the continued social prejudice that even prominent Jews experienced in Boston, community leaders worked to increase civic and political participation as a means of promoting the interests of the entire Jewish population. Lawyer David A. Ellis, Temple Israel trustee and religious school chair, was a member of the Boston School Committee (1903–1913; chair, 1909–1913). Esther Meyer Andrews, Sisterhood member, businesswoman, and the first woman to serve on the Governor's Council (1927–1934), was president of the Boston Section of the Council of Jewish Women (1902–1907, 1910–1915). They and others worked with Jewish immigrants to improve their quality of life through social service and political activism.[18]

Even so, Boston's Jews continued to disagree about other important issues, including the establishment of a Jewish state in Palestine. As Zionism gained momentum, many joined the movement, but the Reform community was deeply divided. The majority of Temple Israel's leaders believed that the future of Judaism was in America, not Palestine, and their rabbi agreed. While Levi understood the appeal of such a movement, a tour of the Holy Land had convinced Rabbi Levi that Zionism was "impracticable," and he maintained that "loyalty to America" should come before "every other loyalty."[19]

Some temple members, however, were active in local Zionist organizations, hoping that a Jewish state would become a refuge for persecuted Eastern European Jews and improve Jewish standing everywhere. As Louis D. Brandeis, a progressive lawyer, president of the Federation of American Zionists, and future Supreme Court Justice, argued in 1914, "To be better Americans we must be better Jews; and to become better Jews we all must become Zionists." The eruption of World War I in Europe intensified concerns about the fate of Jews in war-torn regions. As many Americans called for immigration restrictions, American Jews set up relief organizations like the Jewish War Relief Committee to aid their co-religionists overseas. In response to worldwide pressure, the British government pledged support for a Jewish homeland in Palestine in the Balfour Declaration (1917). These events convinced more of Temple Israel's members to become Zionists, but the synagogue would not officially endorse the concept of a Jewish homeland for many years.[20]

NATIONAL FLAGS UNFURLED BEFORE TEMPLE ISRAEL

Rabbi Levi Tells Patriotic Audience the Better Americans They Are, the Better Jews They Will Be

FLAG-RAISING EXERCISES AT TEMPLE ISRAEL, COMMONWEALTH AVENUE.
Two large flags were unfurled from sides of the edifice, while 200 children sang "America."

Flag-raising at Temple Israel, April 1, 1917. (Unidentified, undated clipping, courtesy of Temple Israel Archives)

When the United States entered the war in April 1917, Boston's Jews—secular, religious, English-speaking, and immigrant alike—were eager to dispel charges of "hyphenated Americanism." Temple Israel, with its German roots, quickly arranged a flag-raising ceremony, described by the press as an "impressive" display of "Jewish loyalty." Standing on the steps of the Commonwealth Avenue temple, Rabbi Levi declared, "We are Jews, but also we are Americans. . . . The better Jews we are the more American we shall be, and the better Americans, the better Jews. We love our faith, but also we love the land it bids us love." Throughout the war he encouraged members to maintain a positive attitude. "Let us . . . fight to win," he exhorted, "but let us fight with vision and with justice. . . . God is still the father of all and men are still brothers."[21]

Congregants threw themselves wholeheartedly into the war effort. Fifty male and two female members served in the armed forces. Only one, Private Paul Francis Andrews of Brookline, perished—with the "Lost Battalion" in Germany's Argonne Forest. Early in the war, the congregation subscribed $2,500 in Liberty Bonds; many members also subscribed individually. Concerned about rationing, the Sisterhood hosted a food conservation exhibit in June 1917 attended by more than eight hundred women. Speakers included Temple Israel member and nutritionist Frances Stern of the Bureau of Labor and Industry, who, with fellow member and social worker Gertrude Spitz, later published *Food for the Worker* (1919), a guide to healthy, economical eating. The Sisterhood, Brotherhood, and youth groups participated in Red Cross activities, hosted outings and other entertainments for soldiers, and raised money for Liberty Loan drives. Reviewing the temple's multitudinous wartime activities in 1918, Board President Jacob R. Morse (1915–1922) noted with satisfaction, "no one can doubt our loyalty, either as good Americans or good Jews."[22]

A GOLDEN AGE

The spirit of goodwill that propelled the congregation through World War I lasted well into the 1920s. Members would later remember that decade as a "golden age" when Temple Israel and Rabbi Levi had "a power and an influence" in New England. Over the years, Levi had become increasingly focused on his pastoral role; at Temple Israel and in the larger community he was seen as a wise counselor and a "bridge" for individuals from traditional homes who sought a balance between modernity and Jewishness. While many such Jews became part of the burgeoning Conservative synagogue movement, others, who preferred to focus on Jewish values rather than traditional ritual practice, chose to join Temple Israel.

Rabbi Levi sought to capture this balance by maintaining the Saturday service and establishing a new ritual for Sunday mornings. In 1919, he published a very brief Sunday morning liturgy focused on Jewish continuity and values that included only four Hebrew prayers: the Barechu, Shema, Kaddish, and the Va'anachnu portion of the Aleinu. The new service particularly appealed to college students and young professionals who wanted to practice a more "modern" Judaism.[23]

The Sunday service had become a formal, church-like event that attracted large numbers and displayed the congregation's middle-class respectability and status. The Brotherhood ushers, in dark suits and kid gloves, greeted

THIRD SERVICE

HYMN

OPENING PRAYER

FATHER, we have gathered here this morning to commune with Thee, to thank Thee for the many blessings Thou hast vouchsafed us, to ask that Thou make us worthy of them, and to beseech a continuance of Thy favor. We know that Thou art everywhere, that the Psalmist voiced the eternal truth when he asked "Whither shall I go from Thy spirit, whither shall I flee from Thy presence." The heaven of heavens cannot contain Thee, how much less this house which we have builded? Always art Thou near us, wherever we go and whatever we do, so that if we but seek Thee we may find Thee. Thy goodness is all-embracing, and Thy grace reaches and affects all. Yet we humbly confess that we feel Thy presence most deeply here in this house of worship dedicated to Thy glory and consecrated to the service of Thy people. Here Thy children have come week in and week out to sing Thy praises, to witness to Thy truth, to find comfort in their trials and sorrows, and encouragement with which to face

[22]

their daily tasks. Be with us as Thou hast been with them. Help us as we pour out our hearts to Thee. By way of this service bless us, with the vision that will give us clean hands and pure hearts, and with that deep and abiding peace that is virtue's sure reward.

CONGREGATION RISES

RABBI

בָּרְכוּ אֶת יְיָ הַמְבֹרָךְ׃

Praise God Who is Worthy of Praise

CHOIR

בָּרוּךְ יְיָ הַמְבֹרָךְ לְעוֹלָם וָעֶר׃

Praise God Who is Worthy of Praise Forever and Ever

CONGREGATION SEATED

WE look forward, trying to pierce the veil of the days that are still to come. We know not what the future holds in store for us, but we know that we can trust Thee, even when mystery envelops us. We look back upon the history of Israel since first Thou didst appoint it to teach the truth of Thee to the world. To that mission Thy people have been loyal thru the ages. As the descendants of those who first received

[23]

Sunday Service, *Rabbi Harry Levi, 1919. (Courtesy of Temple Israel Archives)*

members at the entrance to the impressive sanctuary and escorted them to their family pews. After the service began, as one congregant recalled, the usher patrolled the aisles "like a beadle out of Dickens, hushing the children and pointing a warning finger if they made a single sound." In 1919, Levi and the ritual committee also initiated a series of smaller, more personal Sunday afternoon services for specific groups, including adolescents, young men and women, fathers and sons, and mothers and daughters.[24]

Membership continued to surge; between 1920 and 1923, the congregation grew from 433 to 652 families. Many of the younger members were of Eastern European parentage, including businessman Joseph H. Cohen, who would become the temple's first Russian-born board president (1942–1954), and his wife Rose. Temple Israel's rapidly expanding school became a model for educators across the country and attracted new members who wanted their children to have a religious, but not an Orthodox, education. Some had rejected their traditional Orthodox background; others had grown up in secular or Reform households; some had one parent from each. Anna

Segal Castleman, who grew up in Winthrop, recalled that her mother was "highly spiritual," while her father, born into an Orthodox family, was raised as a socialist.[25]

The religious school also attracted students from a wide geographical area that encompassed immigrant communities like Winthrop and Chelsea, as well as several Boston suburbs. "Many of our children and our members, almost 50% of them," Levi noted in 1920, "take a triple change of cars to reach the Temple and ride at least an hour"; others attended branch schools in their own neighborhoods. As Anna's sister, Harriet Segal Cohn, observed, children who made the trip could meet other Jewish boys and girls and learn about Reform Judaism at the same time. In 1917, the temple had instituted a second session on Sunday afternoons to accommodate more children. In 1924, when Saturday morning classes were added, more than two hundred students registered. By the end of the decade, the confirmation class alone included between fifty and sixty children.[26]

The Brotherhood, Sisterhood, and Parent-Teacher Association (founded in 1922) found ways to encourage young people of all ages to spend more time at the temple. They organized Boy Scout (1925) and Girl Scout (1929) troops for children. In 1920, a new College Club attracted 480 students in its first year. The Sisterhood had hosted a popular annual college dance since 1908; in 1922, when it decided to add monthly teas, 150 out-of-town students attended the inaugural event; two years later, 450 came. Hirsh Sharf, board president from 1958 to 1961, recalled that Temple Israel "was a wonderful place to go" while he was a student at Harvard because it offered spiritual, intellectual, and social refreshment — from Rabbi Levi's Sunday sermons to the opportunity to meet "nice young ladies" at the free dances.[27]

Membership in the adult auxiliaries also soared. The Brotherhood and Sisterhood numbered 550 and 615 respectively in 1927 and new organizations that addressed a variety of interests sprang up throughout the decade. In 1920, librarian Fanny Goldstein and playwright and religious school teacher Fannie Barnett Linsky formed a dramatic club that became a "Little Theatre" in 1929; in 1923, they helped a small group of women establish a Booklovers Society to review Jewish works of literature and assemble a library of Judaica for the congregation and community. By 1930, the society had more than two hundred members.[28]

In the 1920s, the congregation and Rabbi Levi also engaged in activities that would foster interfaith understanding in Boston. Convinced that the war had "brought Jew and non-Jew so much nearer each other," the

Anna and Harriet Segal, circa 1920. The Segal sisters traveled by streetcar from Winthrop to attend religious school at Temple Israel. Harriet recalled her mother admonishing her to "remember your manners, because they're going to judge all Jewish children by you." (Courtesy of Temple Israel Archives and Wyner Museum)

ever-optimistic rabbi encouraged the temple to join the Greater Boston Federation of Churches in 1921. The "true test of religion, Americanism and education," Levi believed, was "respect for one another's opinion." In 1924, Morris Morse, a hotel proprietor, recommended that the Brotherhood finance the radio broadcast of Rabbi Levi's Sunday sermons, renowned throughout greater Boston for their "spiritual and humanitarian value."[29]

Rabbi Levi embraced the idea of radio sermons as "an opportunity and a responsibility" and "a way to overcome prejudice." The "reason why Christians and Jews do not understand each other," he observed, "is that they do not know each other." Given the mounting antisemitism in America, as demonstrated by Harvard's 1922 Jewish quota scandal, automaker Henry Ford's widely quoted antisemitic diatribes, and the passage of the 1924 Johnson-Reed Immigration Restriction Act, Jews sought to defend Judaism and its place in American society. Levi was an articulate weapon. "Let us live so that no matter what the world says of us," he declared, "it can justly find no fault with us, live so as to refute the charges made against us, live so as to shame our detractors."[30]

Levi spoke to a New England audience on radio station WNAC every third Sunday on a program sponsored by Shepard Department Stores and the New England Telephone Company. After his first sermon, entitled "Law and Life," was broadcast in January 1924, he received more than 150 letters, "almost all . . . from Christians." Many listeners confessed prior ignorance or dislike of Jews; as one writer remarked, "I could not believe the Synagogue could offer so appealing a program. The Jews cannot be as bad as they are painted." Another commented, "I am happy to know that your ideas of God, of fellowship and of brotherhood are identical" to those invoked by "our dear old priest at St. Mary's Roman Catholic Church." Pleased by the response, Levi declared, "I know nothing which Temple Israel has ever done which so definitely is bound to serve the cause of the Jew." The broadcasts became so popular over the next decade that Harry Levi became known as the "Radio Rabbi," and two books of his radio sermons, *The Great Adventure* (1929) and *A Rabbi Speaks* (1930), were published. The broadcasts also attracted thousands of visitors to Sunday services, which some members, concerned about overcrowding and less "desirable" attendees, saw as a mixed blessing.[31]

BUILDING A "TEMPLE CENTRE"

In the 1920s, the temple's ever-burgeoning size — 650 families by 1924—and programming prompted several administrative proposals. In 1919, Rabbi Levi had noted that many were forced to stand at Sunday services while the pews of long-standing members remained empty or half-full. The next year, after the UAHC endorsed the unassigned pew system, the temple board raised this issue, hoping to "place our congregation on a democratic plan." As Board President Felix Vorenberg (1922–1927) declared, "In our place of worship . . . the rich and poor [should] be considered alike." The congregation decided in 1921 to institute free pews as a two-year experiment. In the end, however, the majority of pew owners rejected the plan, and the pew system remained intact until the mid-1950s.[32]

Although women had always played a key role in the temple through the auxiliaries and committees, married women could not own pews and women could not serve as trustees. In response to the 1922 recommendation of a joint committee of men and women, Vorenberg proposed changing the bylaws to permit women to be elected to the board. "We need them," he argued. "I know that the Congregation will be helped in many ways by having the advantage of their advice." After the required bylaw amendment was passed in 1923, two long-standing members, Theresa Goulston and Hennie F. Liebmann, were elected as the temple's first female trustees. Even so, the board remained a largely male bastion for many years, with only two seats "reserved" for women, and most female members continued to devote their energy to the Sisterhood and other Jewish communal organizations.[33]

The increased size of the congregation also required staffing changes to provide Rabbi Levi with much-needed assistance. By the second decade of the twentieth century, the board had granted him permission to hire a secretary. When she left in 1921, he hired Bessie Berman, a young woman from an Orthodox background — largely, she recalled, because she was the only candidate who "interviewed him." Berman became an institution at Temple Israel, working for Levi and his successors for fifty-six years, until 1977. In 1923, the board voted to hire its first assistant rabbi, Samuel Wolk, to help officiate at services and life-cycle events, teach religious school classes, and organize auxiliary activities. During his six years at Temple Israel, Rabbi Wolk (1923–1929) took responsibility for mentoring the Young People's Society and worked closely with the Sisterhood to organize the religious school library and run the branch schools.[34]

In accordance with contemporary theories of scientific management, the board also assigned greater responsibility for daily administration of the synagogue to the sexton and the clerk. Louis Selig, the sexton from 1918 to 1942, was responsible for the maintenance of the temple buildings. Journalist Leo J. Lyons, who was the part-time clerk from 1899 to 1930, took notes at board meetings and handled membership, cemetery maintenance, and accounting functions.[35]

By this time, the Commonwealth Avenue synagogue, just seventeen years old, was bursting at its marble seams. Twelve to fourteen hundred people regularly crowded into the 1,052-seat sanctuary on Sunday mornings and 455 students attended the religious school in shifts. More than thirty children were packed into classrooms built for twenty, perching on fire escapes and leaning against doors during classes. After several committees looked into renting additional school space or building an addition, the board approved a more ambitious plan — a "Temple Centre" with a "Community House," a religious school, and a sanctuary — that would give physical form to the image of the synagogue the community had endorsed.[36]

Rabbi Levi and the congregation had been working toward making Temple Israel a "temple centre" since his arrival in 1911. He was intrigued by Rabbi Mordecai Kaplan's proposal that Conservative synagogues add study opportunities, drama, sports, and various social activities to their programs, and the success of that movement. By 1923, the national synagogue

Women and Jewish Culture

In the 1920s, many female members, including religious school educators Fanny Goldstein (1895–1961) and Fannie Barnett Linsky (1885–
1950), creatively used their experiences at Temple Israel to promote
and elevate Jewish culture in Boston. Fanny Goldstein had immigrated
to Boston from Russia as a child in 1900. After taking courses at Simmons College, Boston University, and Radcliffe College, she worked
as a librarian at the Boston Public Library's North End branch, where
she ran programs for immigrant girls and edited the Saturday Evening
Girls Club newsletter. She was appointed the first woman director of
the West End Branch Library in 1922 and the city's first female Judaica
librarian in 1954. Goldstein became a teacher at Temple Israel's religious
school in the late 1910s, and in 1920, the temple's first librarian, helping
to transform the library into the "heart of our educational endeavors."
Her "Miss Goldstein Recommends" column in the *Temple Israel Bulletin*, programs at the West End library, and published bibliographies all

*Saturday Evening Girls, circa 1914. Fanny Goldstein, Temple Israel secretary Bessie Berman
and her sister Sarah, and Sadie and Jesse Guttentag were all members of the Saturday
Evening Girls, a North End literary and social club for young girls from immigrant familes.
Goldstein also edited the club's newsletter. (Courtesy of Temple Israel Archives and Wyner
Museum)*

THREE SCORE YEARS and TEN.

by

FANNIE BARNETT LINSKY.

- - - - - - - - - - - - - - - - - -

CHRONICLER: ----

    Friends, we're gathered in this way
    To commemorate the day
    Of our birth, exactly seventy years ago;
    And with tableau, music, song,
    We would have you come along
    Down the span of years through scenes you little know.
    In the olden days were found
    As Time's circling hand swung round,
    Problems difficult, and changing points of view;
    Careful planning--vision clear--
    Men to counsel without fear--

Temple Israel's Seventieth Anniversary Pageant in 1924 was written by Fannie Barnett Linsky and performed by more than 160 men, women, and children. (Courtesy of Temple Israel Archives)

promoted Jewish history and culture. In 1925, she founded Jewish Book Week, which later became Jewish Book Month.

The daughter of German-born cigarmaker Ellis Barnett and his wife Pauline, Fannie Barnett grew up at Temple Israel. As a teenager, she became an assistant teacher in the religious school. After her marriage to Polish-born tailor Joseph H. Linsky in 1912, she taught primary school at Temple Israel and at Ohabei Shalom, her husband's congregation, for decades. A published playwright, Linsky combined her love of theater and Judaism in a number of pageants, including several Temple Israel productions, including "America and the Jew" (1922) and "Three Score Years and Ten" (1924).

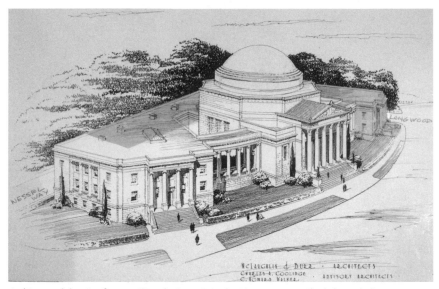

Architectural drawing for new "Temple Centre" on the Riverway, 1924. Shaded area indicates structures completed in 1928. (Courtesy of Temple Israel Archives)

center movement was in full swing; that year the UAHC annual meeting, with its "Back to the Synagog" theme, exhorted congregations to "bring all aspects of Jewish activity, prayer, assembly, and learning under one roof." Other synagogues, including several local temples, were also embarking on ambitious building campaigns, and Board President Vorenberg and Building Committee chair Abraham C. Ratshesky, an influential banker and politician, argued that a new building would secure Temple Israel's position as the "leading congregation of Boston" and put it on the national map.[37]

The building committee organized a fund-raising drive to purchase a "suitable" plot of land on which to build the new Temple Centre, and, in 1924, the congregation bought a 65,000 square foot lot at the corner of the Riverway and Longwood Avenue. Committee members visited synagogue centers across the country for design ideas before hiring McLaughlin & Burr, architects of the nearby Harvard Medical School. Their classically inspired design for Temple Israel's campus included a grand sanctuary flanked by wings on either side for offices, an auditorium, and meeting spaces for temple staff, committees, and auxiliary clubs, as well as a large educational building with classrooms designed to accommodate one thousand pupils.[38]

Meeting House as built, 1928. (Courtesy of Temple Israel Archives)

Given the grand scale of the project, it would be built in phases. Priority was given to the administrative wing and religious school, as these spaces were most overcrowded at Commonwealth Avenue. Ground was broken in 1926, and the "Meeting House," as it was called, was dedicated in October 1928. As built, its columned west-wing facade opened to an elaborate vestibule, with marble staircases leading up to a balcony and down to a coatroom and social hall. The education wing was connected to the auditorium at the far end. The beautiful new building was highly praised, and members looked forward to completing the campus.[39]

The new Meeting House fulfilled Rabbi Levi's dream of making Temple Israel the "hub of Jewish life" in Boston. It also symbolized the economic success and status of the synagogue and its members. After almost twenty years of prosperity and diversification, the congregants seemed comfortable as Americans and as Jews, and they looked forward to a secure and expansive future in their grand new Temple Centre.

1928–1953

The 1928 completion of the Meeting House and religious school wing poised Temple Israel to embark on a new era of growth and achievement. Rabbi Levi's radio programs had brought the temple widespread recognition and the congregation had grown to more than seven hundred families. In 1930, after nineteen years of service, Harry Levi became the first Temple Israel rabbi to be granted life tenure. The Sisterhood continued its successful activities for members and college students, and the Brotherhood expanded its popular "Lyceum" lecture series. By 1929, the school had primary, intermediate, and high school departments, each with an age-specific curriculum. That year, the "most wonderful year that our Religious Schools ever had," 917 children were enrolled (703 children at the temple and 214 at the branch schools).[1]

The new building was an exciting symbol of congregational success, but it also engendered serious financial problems. Nearly $600,000 had been borrowed for the construction project, and the maintenance costs for the additional structure nearly doubled the annual budget. In 1930, the board was forced to increase dues just as the Great Depression took hold. With many congregants unable to pay dues or fulfill their pledges to the Land and Building Fund, Temple Israel, for the first time in decades, faced a budget crisis, a loss in membership, and a steep decline in morale. As Rabbi Levi observed in 1931, "The most tragic thing about economic depression is that it robs us of spiritual vision."[2]

By November 1932, the temple had lost so much revenue that the board began to implement unprecedented economies, including limiting use of the Meeting House and opening the synagogue only for the High Holy Days and consecration services. Between 1932 and 1934, the trustees repeatedly slashed the budget, reducing committee expenses and salaries for the rabbis, choir director, and professional choir members by fifteen to twenty per-

Meeting House auditorium (named for Rabbi Levi in 1947) and chapel (near current Nessel Way entrance). (Courtesy of Temple Israel Archives)

cent. In 1938, still struggling to pay the Meeting House mortgage, the board abandoned any plans for further construction on the Temple Centre.[3]

"OUR RELIGIOUS PROGRAM MARCHES ON UNIMPAIRED"

Despite its financial woes, the congregation tried to address new concerns while remaining a center of worship, study, and social service. The temple's new Committee on Unemployment attempted to aid those affected by the Great Depression. Rabbi Levi's reassuring sermons continued to attract large crowds and the religious school and auxiliaries worked to meet members' spiritual needs.[4]

The Education Committee, working with Assistant Rabbi Beryl D. Cohon (1930–1939), remained committed to providing religious education for all children, convinced that the program would help students deal with the "vicissitudes of their personal lives" and develop pride in their Jewish identity. Despite perennial concerns — inexperienced teachers without "a rich Jewish background," inadequate textbooks, issues of discipline, and occasional complaints that the material was "not interesting" — the school continued to serve many students with its staff of twenty-one teachers, a librarian, a dramatic coach, and two volunteers. Because of budget shortfalls, the Sunday morning school was restricted to the children of temple members and non-members who paid tuition, but the Education Committee also established scholarships for non-members' children who demonstrated "outstanding character and ability." Others could attend either the Sunday afternoon religious school, supported by the Sisterhood, or the branch schools, for a small fee. As a result, the overall number of school attendees remained stable, but the Sunday morning program suffered a significant enrollment decline.[5]

The school maintained extracurricular activities for children and teenagers in both the morning and afternoon sessions: a debating team, dramatic

Religious school children on the bima under the sukkah, 1936. (Courtesy of Temple Israel Archives)

*Tableau from Fannie
Barnett Linsky's 1932
Chanukah pageant,
"Through the Ages."
(Courtesy of Temple
Israel Archives)*

club, children's choir, and glee club. The Temple Israel Juniors, reorganized
in 1928, offered opportunities for teenagers and their non-Jewish friends to
participate in drama, music, debate, and social service. In 1934, recent graduates organized a separate Young People's Congregation affiliated with the
temple to maintain interest in synagogue life.[6]

Adult programs like Rabbi Levi's popular Bible class, a fifty-member
Choral Society, Sunday morning study group, Tuesday luncheon group,
Booklovers program, and Little Theatre, as well as many Sisterhood and
Brotherhood activities, continued to thrive in the 1930s. In 1932, the Brotherhood and the Education Committee created a dedicated adult education
program for the many members who had "little opportunity to learn and
appraise the elements of Jewish culture." Such courses, they hoped, would
bring "home and school into closer harmony," especially for the parents of
religious school students, and "recreate a wholesome respect for the religious values that the Synagogue seeks to preserve." "The Philosophy of
Judaism," and "The History and Social Idealism of the Jew" soon joined
courses on the bible as standards.[7]

The by now well-established Brotherhood and Sisterhood had hundreds of members. Open to the wider Jewish community, the templé auxiliaries served as great equalizers that offered "democratic social contact as well as enjoyable and instructive entertainment" in a synagogue where class status and background still mattered. The Brotherhood, in particular, experienced tremendous vitality in the interwar years; in 1938, it was the largest in the country. One member recalled its guiding principle: "If you have been lucky enough to have been well brought up, well educated, and have done well economically so that you're comfortable, you carry with that a real obligation to do for other people." Intent on offering its members opportunities for community service as well as fellowship, the Brotherhood established initiatives like the Prisoner Rehabilitation Committee, led by dentist Julius Aisner for more than thirty years, which provided assistance to Jews who had been incarcerated.[8]

Sisterhood members also engaged in community work, sponsored luncheons, teas, plays, and educational events, and provided much-needed funding for temple programming. As Board President Lee M. Friedman (1931–1942) observed in 1938, "Judaism owes more and more to its women," who have become leaders "in every new path of progress." The women initiated mostly "feminine" activities; in 1930, for example, they established the Woman's Exchange in the Sisterhood Room at the new Meeting House, where members and other local Jewish women sold home-cooked food as a way of generating income for themselves and the Sisterhood (which kept a share of the proceeds).[9]

Temple Israel's ongoing educational, religious, and social service programs also helped members unite against the rising tide of antisemitism in Europe and America. While Jews had always experienced prejudice, the assimilated, successful members of Temple Israel were generally less exposed than more recent arrivals and those who were less financially secure. By the mid-1930s, however, Boston, with its ethnically segregated neighborhoods, had become a center of anti-Jewish sentiment. Cultural differences within Boston's working-class population were exacerbated by worldwide and national issues, including the Great Depression, the spread of fascism and communism abroad, resentment against Jewish New Deal leaders, and the popularity of bigoted demagogue Charles E. Coughlin, the famous "Radio Priest." As the Irish Catholic mayor, James Michael Curley, observed, Boston was "the strongest Coughlin city in the world," and while he, William Cardinal O'Connell, and others eventually denounced Father

Posters for Sisterhood summer outings, 1931, 1933, 1934. (Courtesy of Temple Israel Archives)

Coughlin's rhetoric, many of the city's Catholic leaders did little to prevent the frequent outbreaks of antisemitic street violence that lasted well into the 1940s. "In these sad days," Lee Friedman declared in 1936, "we must accept the challenge of the world and justify our Judaism by a knowledge-able understanding of our religion."[10]

Rabbi Levi and a number of members worked with other religious insti-tutions locally and nationally to promote greater interfaith understanding. Levi, dubbed "Jewry's good-will ambassador to Christendom" by the *Boston Evening Traveler*, continued to emphasize "genuine belief in the goodness of man" in his speeches and radio sermons. Over time, however, he began to highlight Jewish uniqueness rather than commonalities with other faiths. Eventually, world events even changed his position on the need for a Jewish state. "We American Jews of course will not go to live in Palestine," he had declared in 1930, "but thousands in various parts of the world, living hopeless lives . . . will go if they can find the way to do so. We must help them find the way [by] joining the larger Zionist cause." By the mid-1930s, as violence against Jews began to spread, even the ever-optimistic Rabbi Levi became discouraged by world events. In November 1938, with his health failing, the sixty-three-year-old rabbi announced his decision to retire.[11]

As the board searched for his replacement, most of Rabbi Levi's administrative and rabbinical duties fell to Beryl Cohon, who had been promoted to associate rabbi in 1937. In his eight years in Boston, Cohon had earned acclaim for his accomplishments in the field of education. In 1932, he had founded a joint program of religious education and social service at Boston University that took the temple's message of religious values to a broader community; six years later, he helped to establish a three-year normal school at Temple Israel to train Boston-area teachers in religion and pedagogy. While Cohon recognized that the board was not committed "in any way in regard to succession of the pulpit," he hoped to impress the trustees with his leadership potential. In various memos cataloging the temple's "weaknesses," he outlined ways to attract younger members with "no roots in Temple Israel" (especially those from Orthodox homes) to synagogue

Notice for meeting to discuss implications for German Jews of Adolf Hitler's appointment as German chancellor in January, 1933. (Brotherhood News, April 1933, courtesy of Temple Israel Archives)

Waterman Memorial Library stained-glass window and bookplate. Library Committee chair Dr. Albert Ehrenfried, author of The Chronicle of Boston Jewry *(1968), and his wife Grace donated funds to expand the collections and create a new library space in the Riverway Meeting House. Dedicated in 1938, the Julius and Rosa Waterman Memorial Library was named in honor of Grace's parents. (Courtesy of Temple Israel Archives and Waterman Library)*

committees and educational programs, including the reinstatement of Friday night services and bar mitzvah.[12]

To Cohon's dismay, the board refused to institute costly changes that might later be reversed by a new senior rabbi. In addition, because Rabbi Levi continued to perform his most visible functions, including broadcasting his radio sermons, Cohon felt that he was "not free to assume any initiative in any direction, except the educational department." He had many supporters, including a number of trustees, who felt that he was being unfairly disregarded as a candidate. Citing his "rare spirituality, scholarly intellect, initiative and executive and administrative ability," they asked that Cohon be named the acting senior rabbi.[13]

In the end, however, the congregation, determined to hire "a man of Jewish scholarship" who would "carry on the traditions which Rabbi Levi had so ardently fostered," voted overwhelmingly to hire Joshua Loth Liebman, the thirty-two-year-old rabbi of Chicago's K.A.M. Congregation. After Rabbi Liebman was hired, Rabbi Cohon resigned, unwilling to serve as associate rabbi under a younger, and in his eyes, less accomplished man. Along with a third of the Temple Israel congregation, he established Temple Sinai in Brighton (now Brookline), a new Reform synagogue.[14]

"AWAKENING A DEEPER JEWISH CONSCIOUSNESS"

The decision to hire Joshua Loth Liebman in 1939 may have reflected the congregation's changing worldview. Rabbi Levi's ideology, style, and pastoral concerns had matched the optimism of the Progressive Era and the 1920s; Rabbi Liebman's approach and vision mirrored the turbulence of the 1930s and its impact on the psyche. A scholar of ancient philosophy and contemporary psychology, as well as Judaism, Liebman created an intellectual framework for religion that incorporated elements of all three disciplines. Judaism was "more than an expression of ethical monotheism," Liebman believed. "It was the rallying point of the Jewish people, a bed rock of spiritual comfort at a time when the very survival of this people was being radically called into question." He saw the synagogue as the link between all Jews. In this time of "world-wide struggle," he argued, "no Jew who is aware of his historic responsibility should weaken the forces of Judaism and of the Jewish religion by indifference to the synagog." With this in mind, he immediately proposed several innovations, including some that had already been suggested by Rabbi Cohon: replacing the Sunday morning service with one on Friday evening, incorporating more Hebrew into services, and reviving the bar mitzvah ceremony.[15]

The new Friday night service represented the first step in Temple Israel's transition from a classical to a modern Reform synagogue. It also reflected larger cultural changes; when the Fair Labor Standards Act became law in 1938, most industries instituted a forty-hour workweek with a two-day weekend. As a result, Jews no longer had to "choose between the American pattern of work and the Jewish day of rest." They could, as Liebman observed, now "proudly embrace both." In the late 1930s, as Rabbi Levi's health declined, fewer members had attended the Sunday service. Hoping to "bring about a revival of interest in the Synagogue," the board was willing to give the new rabbi a "free hand."[16]

Liebman hoped to appeal to younger members and Eastern European Jews who had grown up in Orthodox homes and might prefer Friday services for spiritual as well as practical reasons. "A dignified Friday evening service with a ritual beautifully traditional in form and richly Jewish in content," he declared, would offer "greater opportunity for awakening a deeper Jewish consciousness in the souls of our people." Its centerpiece was a Torah service that included a Torah reading in Hebrew with a brief commentary "in light of the rabbinic or midrashic literature and its application

Joshua Loth Liebman

Joshua Loth Liebman (1907–1948) was born in Hamilton, Ohio, and raised in Cincinnati. Descended from a long line of rabbis, Liebman earned a B.A. from the University of Cincinnati in 1926 at the age of nineteen. He taught German and Greek philosophy at his alma mater during his rabbinic studies and received his rabbinic degree from Hebrew Union College in 1930. A year in Jerusalem as a visiting fellow at Hebrew University confirmed his commitment to Zionism. "I came to Palestine a young man," he recalled, "I left Palestine a Jew . . . a member of a cosmic race." Rabbi Liebman returned to HUC in 1931 and completed a doctorate in Hebrew literature three years later. For the next four years he served as the rabbi at Temple Israel in Lafayette, Indiana and at K.A.M. Congregation in Chicago, Illinois. He married Fan Loth Liebman (his first cousin) in 1928. In 1947, the couple adopted fourteen-year-old Leila Bornstein, a Polish survivor of Auschwitz.

Hired by Temple Israel in 1939, Rabbi Liebman helped the congregation move toward modern Reform Judaism by introducing Friday night services, incorporating more Hebrew prayers, and reinstating bar mitzvah. A scholar and intellectual, he published *Peace of Mind* (1946), a spiritual guide to healing and forgiveness that became an international bestseller. At the height of his fame, Liebman died suddenly of a heart attack at the age of forty-one.

Rabbi Joshua Loth Liebman
(Courtesy of Temple Israel Archives)

to the modern world." Even so, the tone of the Friday night service more closely resembled the "church-like" Sunday service than a traditional Sabbath ritual.[17]

As members were not used to attending services on Fridays, Liebman enjoined trustees to set an example by attending every service with their families: "You are the leaders of this congregation and you cannot expect others to follow where you do not lead." Liebman's plan worked; in a matter of weeks, the board reported that 1,200 people had attended one Friday night service. By the following May, Liebman informed a colleague, the new service was a "phenomenal" success, and had become "the talk of New England." As one member recalled, "each time I attended, I left feeling not only spiritually the better person, but also intellectually the better person."[18]

As the Friday evening service became more popular, efforts were made to enhance the religious and social experience of attendees. In 1941, the music of organist and choir director Herbert Fromm, a distinguished German composer who would serve as music director until 1972, became an important feature. In 1942, the Sisterhood and Brotherhood instituted the "Oneg Shabbat" (a social event held in the vestry after services) as a way of promoting fellowship.[19]

Friday night services were only one prong of Rabbi Liebman's plan to increase membership, enlarge the congregation's influence, and enhance "Jewish consciousness." He saw education as key, but his goals were quite different from those of his predecessor. Rabbi Levi thought that religious education should focus on ethics; Liebman sought to emphasize the "majesty of Jewish history" and the Jewish contribution to civilization "as a creative antidote to the antisemitic poisons of our time." He wanted children to learn about the "present vitality of the Jewish people" rather than past persecutions, "to feel a sense of responsibility for their brethren everywhere," including Palestine, and "to feel the tremendous significance of Zionism and of its social ideals and of its literary and ethnic creativity." Studying Hebrew, demography, history, literature, and religion would, he hoped, "help students become integrated personalities, part of Kellal Yisroel" — "the Jewish people as a whole."[20]

The rabbi, the Education Committee, chaired by lawyer Frank L. Kozol, and the Parent-Teacher Association (PTA), led by future civic leader Ida Mae Kahn, worked together closely in this period to energize the education program. Kahn later recalled that the PTA became "the spearhead and the sounding board of all the new things that were coming to Temple Israel." It would also become a training ground for volunteer activists at the temple, most of whom were women.[21]

A consultant was hired to evaluate and determine ways to improve the religious school. His report echoed Rabbi Liebman's vision of an updated curriculum that would incorporate modern teaching methods and focus on current Jewish living, ethics, folklore, music, social service work, and interfaith understanding. It also proposed administrative reforms, including a clearer line of decision-making authority, greater pedagogical guidance for teachers, and a more active club program.[22]

The temple recruited an educational director to institute the curricular changes, supervise and hire new teachers, organize club and youth activities, arrange holiday services, and edit the temple bulletin. When he left a year later, the temple hired a new assistant rabbi, Leo Bergman (1940–1942), who specialized in Jewish education. Under Bergman's direction, the Ariel Club was founded in 1939 for junior high school students, with the goal of "saving our young people for Judaism and keeping them away from unhealthy extremes," including "some communist meeting down town." In its first year, 150 teenagers joined.[23] By November 1939, parents could comment that the children seemed to enjoy the new curriculum and student discipline had improved.[24]

The next year, Hebrew classes became compulsory for all grades—"a clear statement that . . . knowing Hebrew was not a thing of the past, a relic of Eastern European Jewish culture, but a wave of the Jewish future in America." Two full-time teachers were hired to instruct three one-hour sessions every week; the curriculum included the mechanics of writing and reading Hebrew, selections from traditional Hebrew prayers, excerpts from the Bible, modern stories and folk songs from Palestine, and conversation. Hebrew study rekindled interest in bar mitzvah. In 1941, in response to a growing demand, the religious school reinstated the ceremony. When Robert M. Fechtor became the first bar mitzvah, Rabbi Liebman noted that the new ceremony strengthened a young Jewish boy's "allegiance to his faith and his people," and encouraged "a mature attitude toward religious duties."[25]

Rabbi Liebman saw marketing as another means of increasing the temple's visibility and attracting new members. With his encouragement, the congregation hired a Boston publicist to feed articles about major Temple Israel activities and previews of Liebman's sermons to the Boston newspapers. Although the temple could not long afford to keep an outside publicist,

*Young People's Congregation
calendar of events for 1940–1941.
(Courtesy of Temple Israel Archives)*

the membership committee was inspired to create a marketing handbook and brochure that became a model for other congregations. Such tactics, along with reduced rates offered to new members, helped to compensate for the mass defection to Temple Sinai in the wake of Rabbi Cohon's resignation. Within a month of Liebman's arrival, sixty-two members had joined Temple Israel, and more than 350 families signed up during his first two years — "a record in American Reform Jewish congregations," as the new rabbi proudly noted. By December 1941, approximately 860 households belonged and 480 students were attending the religious school.[26]

Other Reform synagogues were adopting new administrative structures, and as the congregation increased in size, Temple Israel followed suit.

When the sexton, Louis Selig, who had been at the temple since 1918, retired in 1942, the board hired longtime congregant Louis L. Martinson, a thirty-year veteran of the *Boston Evening Transcript*, as the temple's first full-time administrator, or "executive director." Replacing both the sexton and clerk, he would serve until 1955.[27]

"TESTED AS NEVER BEFORE"

Like his predecessor, Rabbi Liebman was a "radio rabbi." While in Chicago, he had broadcast sermons on NBC's network radio program, "Message of Israel." In 1942, he would take over the ailing Rabbi Levi's popular regional broadcasts on Boston's WNAC; he later preached over the ABC and CBS national networks. Listeners appreciated Liebman's psychological approach and he became, as librarian Fanny Goldstein noted, "something of a new rabbinical rocket bomb." Reform leader Rabbi Stephen S. Wise of New York's Free Synagogue congratulated Liebman for taking Temple Israel's religious message beyond New England "in these critical days." As World War II escalated in Europe and tensions at home worsened, Liebman warned the congregation of the "menace of these tragic times" and the crisis ahead. "We American Jews are going to be tested as never before," he predicted. "Those men and women who occupy positions of responsibility in congregational life will have to become leaders in many new and unsuspected ways."[28]

Rabbi Liebman at the microphone. (Courtesy of Temple Israel Archives)

Rabbi Liebman's visibility enabled him to publicly confront antisemitism. As a member of Massachusetts Governor Leverett Saltonstall's Commission for Racial and Religious Understanding, he worked closely with civic and religious leaders and the police to study and combat religious prejudice and racism in Boston. The group designed a course on race and interfaith relations to help police officers better distinguish between "those who deliberately are waging an anti-Semitic crusade" and "innocent boys who only want to sock each other." Police Commissioner Thomas Sullivan would later credit Liebman with "wiping out practically all of Boston's anti-Semitism."[29]

Liebman also worked with Rabbi Levi, Temple Israel congregants, and others to aid European Jewry. During the 1930s, American Jews had become increasingly alarmed by the escalating antisemitism in Nazi Germany. By 1938, the widespread destruction of Jewish homes and businesses on *Kristallnacht*, reports that German Jewish refugees had been prevented from entering Great Britain, the United States, and other countries, and the invasion of Poland confirmed their fears. When the local newspaper, the *Jewish Advocate*, began to report firsthand accounts in October 1941 of deteriorating conditions for the Jews of Europe, Boston Jews responded by raising funds and awareness through a "Combined Jewish Appeal," led by Temple Israel member Louis Kirstein.[30]

Like most American Jews, Temple Israel members believed that a quick Allied victory would be the most effective way to save European Jewry. As the United States mobilized for war after the Japanese attack on Pearl Harbor in December 1941, Rabbi Liebman urged the congregation to lead the Jewish community in "the successful prosecution of the war effort." Offering the use of the temple buildings for war work, he also recommended the appointment of a special "Civic Cooperation" or "War Emergency" Committee to work with the governor and defense authorities to coordinate war activities.[31]

As in World War I, the Sisterhood and Brotherhood led the congregation's war efforts. The Sisterhood sold war bonds, collected food, clothing, and medical supplies for shipment overseas, sewed for the Red Cross, and raised funds for the March of Dimes. The Brotherhood contributed materials, money, and volunteers to the Jewish Welfare Board's Army and Navy Club on Commonwealth Avenue, and set up a Soldiers and Sailors Committee that sponsored events for military personnel stationed in Boston. The Brotherhood also provided personal encouragement to Temple Israel's

Brotherhood and Sisterhood World War II service activities. (Courtesy of Temple Israel Archives)

soldiers through *G.I. News*, a bulletin that contained information about temple happenings and reproduced letters from servicemen and servicewomen. As the first issue noted approvingly, these soldiers' actions demonstrated "patriotism and valor . . . and a proud consciousness of their religious heritage which speaks well for the Jewish future in America."[32]

In November 1942, when Rabbi Wise began to publicize documented Nazi atrocities, Americans at last grasped the terrifying implications of Hitler's "final solution." December 2 was designated a national "Day of Mourning and Prayer" for Nazi victims, and, shortly thereafter, Rabbi Liebman broadcast a timely sermon entitled "How Can I Believe in God Now?" "We cannot look to God to save us from man-made evil," he argued; in the end, man must take responsibility because "whatever each one of us does, affects the whole world."[33]

Several months later, on May 2, 1943, twenty thousand people filled Boston Garden and ten thousand more stood outside to protest both the Nazis' mass murders of Jews and Allied policies that limited Jewish resettlement. The largest gathering of Jews in Boston's history, the rally was attended by the governor, mayor, and religious leaders of all denominations. In a "characteristically stirring address," Rabbi Liebman argued that "a democratic world fighting for human liberty" must not permit the annihilation of European Jewry. In recognition of his efforts, Liebman was elected a representative to the American Jewish Conference, which convened a few months later to compile a list of Jewish demands for the Allied powers, including a "Jewish Commonwealth" in Palestine and the repeal of immigration restrictions.[34]

After D-Day in June 1944, the Allied troops began a rapid advance across Nazi-occupied territory. Later that year, as concentration camps were liberated, the world was stunned to learn that more than five and a half million Jews had been murdered in the Holocaust. Recognizing that the "tasks of peace will be as great as the emergencies of war," American Jews began to focus on postwar settlement and aid for survivors even before the Japanese surrendered in August 1945.[35]

"PEACE OF MIND" IN THE POSTWAR ERA

In the aftermath of World War II, Rabbi Liebman, believing that Americans needed to mourn, to grieve, and to mend, turned his attention to healing. "Mine has been a rabbinate of trouble, of depression, Hitler's rise, world crisis, global war, the attempted extermination of my people," Liebman noted. "My text has had to be: 'Comfort ye, comfort ye, my people.'"[36]

Liebman's training in philosophy and psychology, and his years in psychoanalysis, as well as his rabbinical experience, convinced him that psychiatry and spirituality could together heal the soul and foster human growth. This theory, first aired at Temple Israel, was eventually fully developed in

Peace of Mind, a spiritual guide to healing and forgiveness published in 1946. Liebman's book employed the language of psychiatry in the context of theology to resolve the difficult problem of finding inner peace in a turbulent world. "What we need," he concluded, "is a disturbed conscience and a serene mind, a conscience disturbed about the injustice, the cruelty and the evil in the world, but a mind that finds peace in balance and maturity." [37]

Peace of Mind quickly rose to the top of the *New York Times* best-seller list. More than one million copies were sold and the book was translated into ten languages. "One of the many signs that Jews stood on the threshold of acceptance into the religious mainstream," *Peace of Mind* made Liebman, as one historian noted, "the first 'iconic Jew' of postwar America." Liebman received thousands of letters every week; his radio audience soared into the millions and he was invited to preach throughout the Northeast. [38]

Liebman's fame also had a ripple effect on Temple Israel as membership increased. When he turned down an offer to lead New York's Temple Emanu-El in 1947, the grateful Temple Israel board granted Liebman life tenure, a raise, a life pension with survivor's benefits for his wife, and increased staff support so that he could focus more on the problems of world Jewry. Together, Liebman and the synagogue embarked on a five-year plan to make Temple Israel "the foremost Pulpit in the land." [39]

As the temple's flagship program, the religious school was key to the new plan's success. After the war, as postwar prosperity and the desire for a normal family life led to a marriage and baby boom, synagogues across America focused on education as a way to attract and engage young Jews. In

Samuel Nemzoff, religious school principal, 1942–1974. (Courtesy of Temple Israel Archives)

1942, when Assistant Rabbi Leo Bergman left, the board had hired Samuel Nemzoff, a teacher at Boston Latin School, associate of the Bureau of Jewish Education, and director of Camp Chebacco in Essex, Massachusetts, to be the principal. During Nemzoff's twenty-eight-year tenure, Temple Israel's religious school experienced extraordinary growth (from 412 students in 1942 to 1,156 in 1953), and became one of the strongest in the country. Nemzoff endorsed Liebman's initiatives and introduced several of his own. Concerned about teacher turnover, Nemzoff achieved stability by hiring qualified professional educators with solid Jewish training and advanced degrees in education; many stayed for decades, helping the school achieve an "outstanding reputation." By 1946, Temple Israel's curriculum and teaching methods had become a national model for religious school teacher training. Students at Hebrew Teachers College could earn course credit for a yearlong apprenticeship at the temple.[40]

Nemzoff later recalled that his strategy was to strike a balance between the child's non-Jewish environment and Jewish education, recognizing the competing activities in a busy child's life. Because religious school classes met for only a few hours each week, educators reinforced the child's connection to Judaism not only by providing traditional supplemental activities such as youth groups, but also through new summer programs, trips, and, especially, Jewish camps. As the primary grades consistently had a much larger enrollment than the high school, Nemzoff tried to combat the high dropout rate after bar mitzvah and confirmation by instituting several new high school courses and reviving other extracurricular activities. In 1947, he established the *Torchbearer*, a yearbook edited by the confirmation class, to promote school spirit.[41]

With postwar membership at an all-time high, the auxiliaries searched for new ways to fulfill the social, cultural, and educational needs of the adult population. In 1948, for example, the Brotherhood and Sisterhood together put on a musical variety show, "Of T.I. Sing," that was so successful that it joined the Sisterhood luncheon and the Brotherhood dinner as an annual fund-raising event. That year, the Sisterhood also launched a Garden Club that arranged floral decorations for religious services, decorated the Sukkah, and participated in local flower shows. The popular Supper Club, introduced by Rabbi Liebman, encouraged married couples to learn "basic concepts of religion, Reform Judaism and Jewish history" in a social setting.[42]

(Courtesy of Alan and Cecily Morse)

In the late 1940s and 1950s, the Brotherhood and Sisterhood staged a series of popular musical productions, including "Of T. I. Sing" and "Of the People." Above, John Morse, Berthold Stern, Phoebe Woolf, and Selma Yesley rehearsing in the 1950s.

TEMPLE ISRAEL BROTHERHOOD *presents*

OF THE PEOPLE

✷ an original revue ✷

TEMPLE ISRAEL

OF T.I. SING

PAGES FROM OUR FAMILY ALBUM

Presented by the SISTERHOOD AND BROTHERHOOD

(Courtesy of Temple Israel Archives)

IMPRESSIVE TRIBUTE PAID RABBI LIEBMAN

Thousands in Mourning at Services Held at Temple Israel --- Leaders of City, State and Nation Join in Ceremonies

THOUSANDS PAY FINAL TRIBUTE
Photo shows only a part of huge crowd that turned out yesterday to pay final tribute to Rabbi Joshua Loth Liebman during funeral services at Temple Israel, yesterday. The casket is shown being borne from the temple after the services.

Rabbi Liebman's sudden death and elaborate funeral were front-page news in Boston. (Boston Post, June 12, 1948)

Temple Israel flourished during this period due to its active auxiliaries and its famous rabbi, but the incessant demands on Rabbi Liebman's time had an adverse effect on his health. On June 9, 1948, only a few weeks after he celebrated the birth of the State of Israel, the forty-one-year-old rabbi died suddenly of a heart attack. For days, the newspapers were filled with tributes praising Liebman's "brilliant mind" and "sweet and lovable character." U.S. Congressman John W. McCormack, for example, called him "an outstanding American and a great spiritual leader." Boston's public schools were closed on the day of Liebman's funeral in his honor and thousands lined Commonwealth Avenue. In the crowded temple, Board President Joseph H. Cohen expressed the congregation's desolation: "A great light has been extinguished prematurely . . . a light that led Israel and all mankind."[43]

A RABBI FOR "THESE CHALLENGING TIMES"

The grieving congregation decreed a six-month period of mourning, during which no social or musical activities were held in the synagogue. Assistant Rabbi Irving A. Mandel (1948–1950) became the acting senior rabbi. A

1947 graduate of Hebrew Union College, Mandel had turned down several rabbinic positions to work with Liebman, but he did not arrive until shortly after the famous rabbi's demise. In December 1948, the congregation began to search for a new rabbi to replace its "modern prophet."[44]

In the aftermath of Rabbi Levi's long tenure and Rabbi Liebman's short but stellar one, the congregation — by now the fourth largest in the country — had high expectations for its new spiritual leader. "He must be a gifted scholar . . . a good organizer, a dynamic leader," Cohen declared, "who possesses the ability to work with people . . . to stimulate their best, creative efforts." In addition, he must "be a competent, talented representative of the Jewish people . . . in their relations with other great religious and public groups in our population."[45]

After a yearlong search from a pool of more than two hundred candidates, the board chose thirty-four-year-old Abraham J. Klausner, a former World War II army chaplain and the provost of Hebrew Union College–Jewish Institute of Religion. Rabbi Klausner had spent several years working with displaced persons in Germany after the war to ameliorate living conditions and reunite broken families through the aid of "Sharit ha-Platah" (Surviving Remnants), volumes containing lists of survivors.[46]

Rabbi Klausner was highly respected, but the decision about Liebman's replacement "was a controversial one, as any choice would have been." Klausner may have had reservations as well; he insisted on a two-year trial rather than a long-term contract. In his first address to Temple Israel's congregation, Klausner discussed the key role of religious institutions in "these challenging times," as well as the need for a secure state of Israel. Paying homage to his predecessor, he prayed "that the memory of the immortal Rabbi Liebman will be a guide at my right hand and a teacher before me."[47]

In his first few months at Temple Israel, Rabbi Klausner reestablished a more pastoral rabbinate, paying more than seventy-five visits to members. This role, so central to Rabbi Levi's approach, had noticeably declined under Rabbi Liebman. Klausner endorsed Liebman's educational programs, including a greater focus on Hebrew, and expanded the "Shabbos with the Rabbi" series for teenagers that had been created in 1948. With Principal Nemzoff, he helped to set up a two-year post-confirmation course. In 1950, in response to the growing interest in early childhood education, the school opened a kindergarten class. In 1951, with the support of the Sisterhood, Klausner and Nemzoff hired Aaron Gordon, one of the teachers, to direct youth activities, including dramatics and music, for two age groups:

Abraham J. Klausner

Born in Memphis, Tennessee, Abraham J. Klausner (1915–2007) moved to Denver, Colorado, as a child. He earned B.A. and M.A. degrees from the University of Denver in 1938. After his ordination from Hebrew Union College in 1941, he served at a synagogue in New Haven, Connecticut, until 1944, when he enlisted as an Army chaplain.

Rabbi Klausner arrived at Dachau, a concentration camp near Munich, Germany, in May 1945, shortly after it was liberated by the U.S. Army. After the war, he stayed for several years to work with and advocate for displaced persons, helping to reunite families and improve living conditions in the camps. In 1946, he officiated at the "Survivor's Seder," the first postwar seder in Germany, a poignant event attended by hundreds of survivors and Jewish-American soldiers. When he returned to the United States in 1948, he was hired by the United Jewish Appeal and then became provost of the newly merged Hebrew Union College–Jewish Institute of Religion.

In 1948, Rabbi Klausner was hired as the senior rabbi at Temple Israel. He focused on religious education and developing stronger pastoral relations with congregants. While in Boston, he married Judy Haskell. In 1954, he became the senior rabbi at Temple Emanu-el in Yonkers, New York. He and his second wife, Judy Steinberg, married in 1966 and had four children. In 1989, after thirty-five years of service, the Klausners retired to Santa Fe, New Mexico. Klausner published several books and a memoir. He was featured in the Oscar-winning Holocaust documentary, *The Long Way Home* (1997). Rabbi Klausner died of Parkinson's disease in June 2007.

Rabbi Abraham J. Klausner
(Courtesy of Temple Israel Archives)

teenagers between fifteen and eighteen and young adults between eighteen and twenty-five. Klausner also helped to revitalize the temple auxiliaries, organizing, for example, a lecture series on the highlights of Jewish history for the Supper Club. In 1952, Klausner presided over the temple's first televised Kol Nidre service, sponsored by the Brotherhood.[48]

Despite all this activity, some members had difficulty adjusting to the new rabbi, and, as membership began to level off, questions were raised about Klausner's oratorical skills and personal warmth. In 1950, Assistant Rabbi Irving Mandel left to become the founding rabbi at Temple Shalom in Newton, a synagogue designed to serve the Reform Jewish families who had been moving to western suburbs like Newton and Needham since the 1930s. Reform rabbis and lay leaders, including those at Temple Israel, had encouraged the establishment of suburban synagogues for years, but when a number of congregants left Temple Israel to follow Rabbi Mandel, some attributed the defections to dissatisfaction with Rabbi Klausner rather than the desire for convenience. By mid-1951, as congregants voiced complaints about the rabbi's "uninspiring" sermons, the board tried to boost attendance by inviting guest speakers to preach at services and holding more music services that highlighted the compositions of renowned director Herbert Fromm and the temple choir.[49]

In October 1951, the board held a special meeting to discuss "general dissatisfaction" and "unrest in the Congregation." In the end, Klausner's contract was extended for another two years with the understanding that, unless further action was taken, he would leave in June 1953. The board and the congregation confirmed this plan in January 1953. Klausner did not contest the board's decision, even though he was convinced that the congregation's expectations—"demanding of a Rabbi what is not of a religious nature"—had been problematic from the beginning and would not "be resolved with the exchange of Rabbis." Klausner defended his record at the annual meeting by pointing to a packed calendar of events and noting proudly that the synagogue "has gone from strength to strength . . . whether you look to membership, income or school enrollment." Nevertheless, Klausner readily agreed that he and Temple Israel were not compatible. "To those of you who have spoken critically of me and said 'Lo zeh ha-ish . . . this is not the man,' I say to you with all my heart, 'You are right.'"[50]

Klausner left to become the rabbi at Temple Emanu-el in Yonkers, New York, where he served for thirty-five years. While Rabbi Klausner might not have been a good fit for Temple Israel at that time, he also recognized that it

Rabbi Klausner greeting a young congregant. (Calendar of events for 1952–1953, courtesy of Temple Israel Archives)

would have been difficult for anyone to meet the expectations of a congregation that had so suddenly and tragically lost its brilliant, charismatic, and celebrated young leader. As Leon Jick, assistant rabbi from 1954 to 1957, later noted, "Temple Israel was not psychologically prepared to find a successor for Liebman. In their opinion, no one could compare with him and they didn't want anyone else . . . no matter how great they may have been."[51]

5. PROPHETIC JUDAISM AND THE
"SYMPHONY OF AMERICAN LIFE"

1953–1973

In the 1950s, American Jews felt increasingly self-confident. The generation that grew up during the Great Depression and lived through World War II focused on enjoying postwar prosperity—marrying, having babies, and moving to the suburbs. Overt antisemitism had declined in the wake of the Holocaust and the establishment of the State of Israel. But this period was also a time of deep anxiety as the Cold War triggered McCarthyite paranoia and fears of nuclear war. Convinced that the survival of the "free world" depended on the defeat of "godless Communism," Jews, along with their Christian neighbors, sought the comfort and security of established religious institutions that would provide community and transmit positive values to their children. During the "age of conformity," Jewish families joined synagogues in ever greater numbers.[1]

In 1953, in the midst of this complicated time, Temple Israel began a rabbinic search, hoping to find a dynamic leader who could "inspire confidence," make the temple more "Jewish in spirit and content," manage an increasingly large, complex organization, and help the congregation regain national renown. The congregation chose Roland B. Gittelsohn, the founding rabbi of Central Synagogue of Nassau County in Rockville Centre, New York. Rabbi Gittelsohn, who had also been a competitive candidate to replace Rabbi Liebman in 1948, had "all the prerequisites that the congregation wanted." He had made his reputation as a Marine Corps chaplain during World War II and was an experienced congregational rabbi, a nationally recognized leader in Jewish education, and a staunch advocate for social justice with "a reputation for having the courage to fight for the ideals in which he believed."[2]

Gittelsohn had strong ideas about his rabbinic role. Having taken an active role in policymaking at Central Synagogue, he expected to do the same at

Temple Israel. In addition, while acknowledging his primary responsibilities as "preacher, teacher and pastor" to the congregation, he insisted on his right to remain a "crusading rabbi" who would sermonize about pressing issues "in the context of the moral principles of Judaism." "I do not promise . . . to preach always what you want to hear," Gittelsohn declared. "I believe that there is a two-fold function of a preacher: to comfort the troubled and to trouble the comfortable."[3]

Like Rabbis Liebman and Klausner, Rabbi Gittelsohn was a product of his generation. The political, social, and religious values of all three were shaped by the Great Depression and World War II, but in different ways. Liebman and Klausner focused on individual and communal healing and comfort; Gittelsohn's deep awareness of the world's racial and political inequities inspired him to encourage members to become agents for social change. Working with the Union of American Hebrew Congregations (UAHC), he would push Temple Israel in the direction of social action through education and community initiatives.

When Rabbi Gittelsohn arrived in 1953, he instituted a number of changes designed to align Temple Israel with contemporary Reform trends. Some, like his decision to wear a "tallit" (prayer shawl) over his robe while on the bima, followed traditional ritual practices. Others, like encouraging Sisterhood members to light Sabbath candles at Friday night services, were designed to add to the "warmth and dignity" of the weekly celebration. Still others were intended to connect Temple Israel to the broader Jewish community. Gittelsohn established a "Rabbi's Discretionary Fund" that supported individuals and organizations, including the American Jewish Archives and the Central Conference of American Rabbis (CCAR). He also expanded Temple Israel's media outreach, adding a televised monthly service to the Brotherhood's monthly radio broadcasts.[4]

Even so, Temple Israel retained its formal atmosphere, and the regular Friday night service remained quiet and reflective. Attendees were expected to arrive on time and decorum was, as one member recalled, "austere." Parents of noisy children were "subject to public admonishment from the pulpit" and whispering teenagers might be expelled. Services were seen as social and spiritual events for adults, who might have the opportunity to mingle at the Oneg Shabbat with luminaries such as Jennie Loitman Barron (the first female Massachusetts Supreme Court Justice), Abram Sachar (the president of Brandeis University), Sidney, Norman, and Irving Rabb (the owners of Stop and Shop Supermarkets), and Kivie Kaplan (a well-known

Roland B. Gittelsohn

Roland B. Gittelsohn (1910–1995) was born in Cleveland, Ohio, to a Russian immigrant family. Gittelsohn attended Sunday school at the local Reform synagogue, but he became a bar mitzvah at the Orthodox shul where his grandfather served as rabbi. He graduated from Western Reserve University in 1931 and earned a rabbinic degree from Hebrew Union College in 1936. The same year, he became the founding rabbi of the Central Synagogue of Nassau County, in Rockville Centre, New York, staying for seventeen years. Gittelsohn had married Ruth Freyer in 1932; they had two children, David and Judith.

Although Gittelsohn was a pacifist, he enlisted as the first Jewish chaplain in the Marine Corps during World War II. His oft-quoted sermon at the cemetery at Iwo Jima — "Here no man prefers another because of his faith or despises him because of his color" — became a symbol of brotherhood. In 1947, he served on President Harry Truman's Committee on Civil Rights; in 1952, he won a Freedom Foundation award for his outspoken criticism of McCarthyism.

Rabbi Gittelsohn came to Temple Israel in 1953. An advocate for civil rights, the peace movement, and other causes, Gittelsohn was also a prolific author who published thirteen books. During his twenty-four-year rabbinate, the congregation grew to a record size and became deeply involved in social action initiatives. After his retirement, Gittelsohn cofounded the Association of Reform Zionists of America (ARZA) in 1978, serving as president until 1984. He married Hulda Phillips Tischler in 1978, and remained the rabbi emeritus of Temple Israel until his death in 1995.

Rabbi Roland B. Gittelsohn
(Courtesy of Temple Israel Archives)

philanthropist, civil rights activist, and owner of a successful leather company). Many enjoyed broadening their synagogue connections in exclusive social settings such as the Belmont Country Club.[5]

When Temple Israel celebrated its centennial in 1954, Rabbi Gittelsohn used the occasion to reflect on the synagogue's past and articulate his vision for its future—a tripartite focus on spiritual education, Jewish tradition, and social action. In the past, he argued, synagogues had been primarily social and communal centers; in the postwar era, they must focus on teaching. The lessons learned from the pulpit and classroom would guide members of all ages to become Jews not "by the accident of birth . . . but by deep conviction and faith." Like Rabbi Liebman, Gittelsohn believed in Jewish distinctiveness; he encouraged congregants to "establish a mutually reciprocal relationship" with non-Jews "on the basis of positive acceptance" rather than "apologetic denial." By applying the teachings of prophetic Judaism to "the symphony of American life," Jews could help to "eliminate our most grievous social ills."[6]

Most members were receptive to Gittelsohn's ideas. By the mid-1950s, the culture of Temple Israel was changing and, while some from the old "German" segment regretted what they saw as a "return" to Orthodoxy, others, who had come from traditional Eastern European backgrounds, felt more comfortable in services that included Hebrew prayers. They liked the new "ceremonials," the temple's educational and social programs, Gittelsohn's sermons, and the focus on the new State of Israel. As one congregant later recalled, the rabbi made members "feel that it was wonderful to be Jewish and to be able to take part and make whatever contribution you could to this wonderful movement."[7]

Soon after his arrival, Gittelsohn took aim at pew ownership, a classical Reform tradition still in effect at Temple Israel but increasingly rare elsewhere. Pew ownership required those without pews to stand in the rear or sit in the balcony, even when reserved seats were left empty by owners not in attendance. In 1956, on the recommendation of the Temple Committee, all seats were opened during the High Holy Days ten minutes after services began. Shortly thereafter, unreserved seating became the practice at Friday night services, with spaces in the rear reserved for latecomers, but it took two more years for members to approve a similar policy for the High Holy Days.[8]

Gittelsohn also introduced the concept of "family worship." Wanting to re-create "something of the family spirit which always prevailed on Shabbos

Temple Israel's centennial (which was also the Sisterhood's fiftieth birthday and the tercentennial of Jewish settlement in America) was commemorated with a yearlong celebration and fundraising campaign. Its theme—"Growth and Achievement"—was also the title of the synagogue history published for the occasion. The gala June finale, a "glittering" banquet at Boston's Hotel Statler, included a student pageant written by teacher Helen Fine and the ceremonial burning of the Meeting House mortgage. (Courtesy of Temple Israel Archives)

in Jewish homes," he instituted occasional Friday night family worship services, often connected with festivals, that were designed for youngsters aged nine and up. Families were encouraged to "sit together, sing together, and worship together," and children could receive special birthday blessings.[9]

BRINGING UP JEWISH BABY BOOMERS

In the 1950s and 1960s, the synagogue experienced dramatic membership growth. Temple Israel had about 1,400 families at the time of Gittelsohn's installation; by 1968, it was larger than ever before or since, with 2,140. As in the past, most members were parents with young children. While much of this growth could be attributed to the baby boom, new members were also attracted by Temple Israel's reputation, Rabbi Gittelsohn, and the religious school. Improved public transportation and automobile access in the late 1950s also increased the temple's appeal. The opening of the "Highland Branch" of the MBTA (later called the "D" or "Riverside" Green Line branch) in 1959 made public transportation increasingly convenient for congregants and students from the western suburbs. The 1956 acquisition of the Berners Square parking area, located behind the Meeting House, and the congregation's right to its exclusive use four years later, facilitated parking. Soon thereafter, members A. Alfred Franks, Charles M. Goldman, and others initiated negotiations (that would continue for decades) with MASCO (the Medical Academic and Scientific Community Organization, Inc.) for a parking garage on the Berners Square site.[10]

Religious school enrollment mushroomed from 350 in 1939 to almost 1,300 in 1955, leading to severe overcrowding, particularly in the younger grades. As a result, classes were staggered throughout the day on both Saturdays and Sundays in each of the temple's buildings. In 1955, the board decided that there was an urgent need for an addition to the religious school. Financed through required supplemental member payments to the Building and Improvement Fund, as well as donations and naming opportunities, the construction began in April 1957. The Rabbi Joshua Loth Liebman Wing was dedicated in December. Located along the west side of the existing religious school structure, the addition provided several new classrooms, a room for the Sisterhood (later named in honor of Rabbi Levi's widow, Ruth), a lounge, and an enlarged Waterman Library. With the space problem alleviated, the religious school continued to grow, and by 1960, there were almost 1,350 pupils in the religious school—a record high.[11]

Parents of school-aged baby boomers were attracted to the religious school's serious approach to Jewish education and its up-to-date curriculum. Rabbi Gittelsohn, a former chairman of the CCAR Commission on Jewish Education, was also a dedicated teacher who had authored several textbooks. He admired and built on the curricular innovations, including the focus on Hebrew language study and modern Israel, that had been introduced by Rabbi Liebman, Rabbi Klausner, and Principal Samuel Nemzoff.[12]

The temple's integrated, eleven-year religious school program began in kindergarten and ended with a two-year, voluntary post-confirmation class; parents were encouraged to enroll their children at an early age. In the primary years, children focused on Jewish holidays and biblical and post-biblical stories; third graders learned ethics, the Hebrew alphabet, and basic prayers, while fourth through ninth graders concentrated on Jewish ethics, history, biblical literature, and Israel. High school students studied comparative religions and prepared for confirmation by investigating theology and Jewish values. Gittelsohn and Nemzoff tried to involve parents by holding visiting days for all grades and encouraging adult participation in the

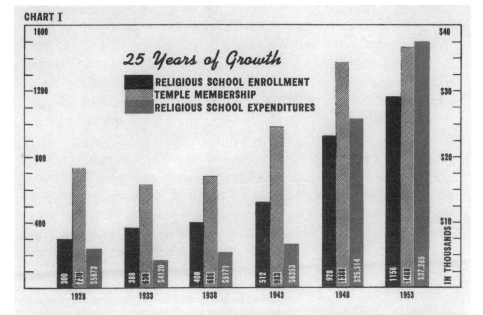

CHART I

25 Years of Growth

- ■ RELIGIOUS SCHOOL ENROLLMENT
- ▨ TEMPLE MEMBERSHIP
- ■ RELIGIOUS SCHOOL EXPENDITURES

Left axis: 1600, 1200, 800, 400

Right axis (IN THOUSANDS): $40, $30, $20, $10

Year	Enrollment	Membership	Expenditures
1928	300	730	$5873
1933	388	630	$4120
1938	400	636	$5171
1943	512	933	$6353
1948	928	1361	$25,514
1953	1156	1463	$37,285

In 25 years, membership in Temple Israel has doubled, but enrollments in the Religious School have nearly quadrupled. There just isn't the facility to properly handle the student body. And although costs have increased better than 6 times since 1928, Chart II proves conclusively that in relation to school costs in Boston, Temple Israel Religious School operations have been conducted with practical economy.

A Religious School class jammed into the Meeting House *kitchen*. Poor lighting . . . Poor ventilation . . . without room for an open book, let alone an open mind.

The cramped, dull Temple *library* is a poor setting indeed to study the glorious history of the Jewish People and indicates the real need for more classrooms.

Building campaign brochure for new religious school wing, 1955. (Courtesy of Temple Israel Archives)

confirmation class so that the entire family could gain a more "enriching and inspiring" understanding of Jewish religion and history."[13]

In the fourth grade, students could enroll in a five-year, two-day-per-week diploma program in Hebrew that included reading, writing, conversational Hebrew, and preparation for bar mitzvah. Bar mitzvah had been reintroduced at Temple Israel in 1941, and, by the mid-1950s, more than 150 children were involved in the Hebrew program. Convinced that "the religious education of future generations will be largely in the hands of your daughters, the future mothers in Israel," the education committee encouraged parents to enroll their daughters alongside their sons in Hebrew school. In 1956, when bat mitzvah was introduced, the number of girls who entered the Hebrew program nearly doubled, and, in October, Lois Isenman became the first bat mitzvah at Temple Israel. That year, with almost two hundred children in the program, fifty-one boys and four girls became b'nai mitzvah. Over time, the number of girls gradually increased.[14]

The religious school insisted on high standards of performance and behavior. With the full support of the Education Committee and the Parent-Teacher Association (PTA), Gittelsohn and Nemzoff instituted dress codes, attendance regulations, graded homework assignments, and other measures that were codified in a handbook for parents in 1956. While some parents viewed these standards as unreasonable, complaining that weekday classes

1956 Hebrew class, with three of the first female b'nai mitzvah. Row 1 (left to right): *Douglas Berrick, Leonard Meuliner, George Chefitz, Peter Rabinowitz,* **Lois Isenman,** *Herbert Jacobs, Stanley Satz;* Row 2: *Mr. Maurice Korinow, Steve Rabin, Arthur Cikins, Eugene Burgin, Martin Blank, William Bornstein, Mrs. Lillian Beauvais;* Row 3: *Jeffrey Myers,* **Eunice Gorman,** *Peter Jackson, Barry Zimmer,* **Pauline Gorman.** *(Courtesy of Temple Israel Archives)*

Teacher Helen Fine (pictured here in Israel) wrote several popular children's books, including G'Dee *(1953) and* At Camp Kee Tov *(1970). (Courtesy of Sandie Bernstein)*

conflicted with secular activities, most welcomed them. The board was also supportive, observing that education had always been a primary mission of the synagogue, and that "with the advent of Rabbi Gittelsohn, the entire School and especially the Confirmation Class has been revitalized."[15]

Teachers agreed, and one recalled the Gittelsohn/Nemzoff era as the "halcyon days" of the religious school. A "sympathetic" administrator who taught history at Boston Latin School for many years, Nemzoff became Temple Israel's first full-time religious school director when he retired from teaching in 1961. He later noted that while he and Gittelsohn had "different personalities" and teaching methods, "there was an understanding between us and a compatibility in terms of our own outlook on Jewish education." A founding member of the National Association of Temple Educators (1954), Nemzoff hired highly educated, skilled teachers, many of whom had been his colleagues at Boston Latin, and allowed them a "free hand" in developing courses and trying new methods. The principal and the teachers were responsible for the day-to-day instruction, management, and curriculum, but Gittelsohn's scholarly reputation, commitment to Jewish education, and ability to excite the staff also had a tremendous impact. The school attracted a talented and loyal teaching staff, including Helen Fine, author of several Jewish books for young children; Selma Finstein, former Roslindale High

1960 Confirmation class. (Courtesy of Temple Israel Archives)

School teacher and *Torchbearer* advisor; Rose Flax; and Judge Reuben Lurie, who taught several generations of students.[16]

Inspired by their teachers, a high percentage of students stayed in the program for confirmation and post-confirmation classes. The confirmation class used several of Gittelsohn's textbooks, including *Modern Jewish Problems* (1943) and *Little Lower Than Angels* (1951), while the increasingly popular two-year post-confirmation study class, taught by Judge Lurie, featured special lectures by the rabbi and invited guests. Lurie, by all accounts a gifted teacher, focused on different themes each year — comparative religion, courtship and marriage, Jews in the modern world — that would spur students to become active in the congregation and beyond. In 1956, Gittelsohn established a discussion group for college students that focused on contemporary issues and problems.[17]

Nemzoff also promoted Israeli culture and Israeli-American connections, hoping that "Israel-centered" programs would help to ensure the "preservation of the Jewish people." In May 1958, for example, the religious school celebrated the tenth Israeli Independence Day with a special assembly that included a play, a film, and songs. In September 1960, the post-confirmation class "adopted" a child in Israel with tzedakah funds, and the following year, students established a relationship with the Sholem Aleichem School in Lydda, Israel. The school and the Sisterhood also initiated classes on Israeli culture, including folk dancing and singing, and sponsored study opportunities in Israel.[18]

Nemzoff, the teachers, and the PTA designed a range of extracurricular activities designed to involve children in the life of the temple. As one teacher later recalled, "we had a wonderful PTA" and a "powerfully inter-

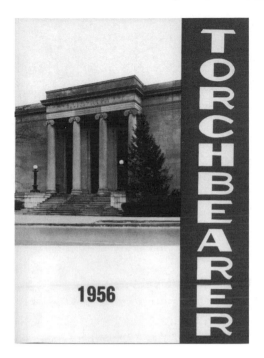

Torchbearer, *religious school yearbook,*
1956. (Courtesy of Temple Israel Archives)

ested group of parents" who planned Sabbath luncheons, Chanukah and Purim parties, dancing classes, model Seders, carnivals, and films. Other activities were designed to demonstrate that "a Jewish school could be like anything else." The *Torchbearer*, a yearbook produced by the confirmation class between 1947 and 1970 with the help of faculty advisers Selma Finstein (1947–1961) and Lillian Beauvais (1962–1970), won the prestigious Columbia Scholastic Press Association award in 1953 and 1954. The Temple Juniors, led until 1961 by longtime director Aaron Gordon (who, with his wife Blanche, directed Camp Tevya in Brookline, New Hampshire, for years), offered older students social activities, including dances, sponsored trips, and, beginning in 1953, a basketball team that won several Jewish Community Center League Championships. In 1960, the school established a youth group for students in the seventh through ninth grades as a prelude to the high school group.[19]

A POINT OF CONNECTION TO THE LARGER WORLD

The religious school's objectives—discovering Jewishness through learning, social activities, and a focus on Israel—reflected Rabbi Gittelsohn's goals for the entire congregation. Gittelsohn tirelessly promoted a "spiri-

Congregational trip to Israel, 1970. (Courtesy of Temple Israel Archives)

tual and cultural love" for Israel. His sermons, for example, frequently discussed Israel's history, culture, and standing in the world. In 1957, when
future prime minister Golda Meir (then foreign minister) asked Americans
to support Israel by purchasing bonds, Temple Israel, like other American
congregations, founded an Israel Bonds Committee. In April 1958, Roland
and Ruth Gittelsohn and Board President John Morse (1956–1958) and
his wife Aline participated in a month-long, official UAHC pilgrimage to
Israel where they met government officials, the chief rabbi, and various cultural and intellectual leaders. Gittelsohn was deeply moved. "Israel helps
to perpetuate a sense of Jewish peoplehood, so important to Jews, particularly after the Holocaust," he observed. "After an intensive visit to Israel, no
American Jew need wonder again who he is or where he belongs." Gittelsohn would return to Israel several times to travel, study, and teach, and he
led congregational trips in 1970 and 1975.[20]

After Israel's Six-Day War in June 1967, American Jews raised millions of
dollars in aid, convinced that another Holocaust could only be prevented
by ensuring the survival of the Jewish homeland. The Temple Israel board
voted to contribute $25,000 to the Israel Emergency Fund, and members
individually purchased more than $75,000 in Israel bonds. In 1970, the tem-
ple's Israel Committee organized the first of many Israel Independence Day
celebrations with "Israel Week," featuring a special service, book exhibit,
birthday party, and a pageant written by Helen Fine.[21]

Adult learning was another way of fostering Jewishness in the congregation. After Israel became a nation in 1948, more Jews had begun to see knowl-

edge of the Hebrew language as a "bridge . . . between the Jews of Israel and ourselves." When Gittelsohn introduced more Hebrew into the liturgy, the Sisterhood instituted a women's course on prayer-book Hebrew taught by Selma Finstein's husband, Joseph. Hoping to encourage congregants to participate more fully in services, Gittelsohn and his assistant, Rabbi Leon Jick (1954–1957), who later became a noted scholar of American Jewish history, also offered "intensive" study courses for men and women on such topics as "The Bible as Living Literature" and "Jewish Life Today." By 1959, the adult education program served several hundred people every year. In 1961, Temple Israel adopted the Sephardic pronunciation of Hebrew favored in Israel and increasingly used in other American Reform congregations.[22]

The growing awareness of and pride in Jewish cultural identity also helped increase involvement in the temple auxiliaries. The Young Married Couples Club was organized in 1955 with twenty to forty couples meeting monthly for a "Jewishly oriented" cultural program. Like the Supper Club, which celebrated its tenth anniversary in 1955, the Couples Club was a way to interest and involve younger members in temple activities.[23]

Flyer for Israel Independence Day celebration, 1971. (Courtesy of Temple Israel Archives)

The Sisterhood and Brotherhood, led by committed members such as Phoebe Woolf and Robert E. (Bob) Levi, the son of Rabbi Harry Levi, remained the heart of the temple's auxiliary program. For homemakers, the Sisterhood continued to provide a social outlet; as one member recalled, "I found what I was looking for there in the belonging, in the warmth and friendliness." Forty-nine departments offered a wide range of activities; Sisterhood members could join the decorative arts committee, choral group, or Garden Club, for example, or plan the annual Sabbath service and various social events. Other committees sewed layettes for babies in local hospitals, provided clothing for poorer confirmands, hired transcribers of Braille books, sent gifts to hospitalized veterans, and sold "Uniongrams" (Jewish notecards) for the National Federation of Temple Sisterhoods. The organizational skills that women learned through Sisterhood prepared them for work in the larger community and many went on to hold leadership positions in Jewish organizations and other Boston agencies.[24]

The legal opinion that paved the way for the institution of bat mitzvah in 1956 also led to women's greater participation in ritual life at Temple Israel. As the temple's legal advisor, Frank L. Kozol, argued, "We would be false to

Program for the Garden Club's annual Spring Flower Show, 1959. (Courtesy of Temple Israel Archives)

FUND HONORS HIRSCH GUTMAN

Makes Possible Ideals
He Gave His Life For

As a fitting tribute to its first member to give his life in the service of his country in the present conflict, Temple Israel Brotherhood announces establishment of the **Lt. HIR-SCHEL L. GUTMAN FUND** for the furtherance of those American ideals which First Lt. Gutman, holder of the Distinguished Flying Cross and other high awards, died for.

Originally the private undertaking of the family and friends, the Brotherhood Board accepted sponsorship when it became apparent that many Brotherhood members were interested in official commemoration of Lt. Gutman's sacrifice and in giving support to the worthwhile project which the Fund makes possible.

Lt. Hirschel L. Gutman

Under the plan worked out, the Fund this year will make possible free scholarships in Inter-Cultural Education at the Harvard Workshop, or at some similar institution, for six Greater Boston public school teachers and it is hoped these teachers will sow the seeds for better understanding among all creeds and races when they return to their own classrooms.

Announcement of the Brotherhood's sponsorship of the Gutman Foundation, in G. I. News, February 1945. (Courtesy of Temple Israel Archives)

our concept of full equality if we excluded females from any of our religious practices." The Sisterhood had led an annual Torah service for decades, and over the next several years, the Temple Committee authorized women to recite Torah blessings and lead services.[25]

The Brotherhood also offered men a variety of ways to connect to Temple Israel. As one future president, Bob Levi, noted in 1957, "Our religious services benefit the souls of our members, our educational program develops their minds and our Brotherhood activities touch their hearts." Initiatives included a glee club, an annual arts festival, regular father-son nights, and lectures on such topics as nuclear science, civil rights, and Israel. The organization also sponsored a range of service projects, including the Simons-Gutman Foundation, a Veterans Committee, a Prison Rehabilitation Committee, and interfaith work through the Jewish Chautauqua Society. In 1964, it was named Brotherhood of the Year by the North American Federation of Temple Brotherhoods.[26]

The Gutman Foundation (established in 1945 and renamed the Simons-Gutman Foundation after the death of founder Paul Simons in 1956), was at the forefront of the effort to put the principles of social justice into practice. Designed to promote democratic ideals and "better understanding among all people," the foundation provided scholarships for underprivileged and minority students and educators, launched a civil education project to

develop "enlightened" textbook material, and helped build the Human Relations Center at Boston University. In 1955, the Brotherhood marked ten years
of achievement in "the fight against bigotry and the quest for the improvement of human relations" by honoring Thurgood Marshall, the prominent
civil rights attorney who had just argued and won the historic *Brown v. the
Board of Education of Topeka* Supreme Court desegregation decision.[27]

CRUSADING FOR SOCIAL ACTION

The Simons-Gutman Foundation was a harbinger of American Jewry's
increasing focus on social action in an era not known for progressive ideas.
Rabbi Gittelsohn and temple members Bob Levi and Kivie Kaplan, future
president (1966–1975) of the National Association for the Advancement of
Colored People (NAACP), had served on a UAHC social action commission in the mid-1950s. All were deeply involved in creating a blueprint for
"Judaism in Action," a project that developed and published case studies
about religion in the public schools, civil rights, civil liberties, world peace,
mental health, and community relations that congregations who wished to
meld education and action could use as models. Gittelsohn generated interest in the project at Temple Israel through sermons that discussed contemporary problems and advocated actions that would lead to social change. In
1957, he led a two-year adult education course on "Justice and Judaism" that
incorporated the national curriculum he had helped to design.[28]

By 1959, when Temple Israel established a Social Action Committee, two
hundred other congregations had already founded similar groups. Arguing
that the temple "must go beyond prayer and rituals and religious schools,"
the new committee, with representation from the Brotherhood's Simons-
Gutman Foundation and Rehabilitation Committee, the Sisterhood's Public
Affairs Committee, and the Youth Committee, strove to educate and engage
members in finding solutions to societal problems. In this era of "violent
social upheavals," one member observed, the group hoped to "translate into
action and understanding the precepts which Judaism has always taught
concerning oppressed minorities." The committee and its leaders, including
founding chairman Dr. Joseph W. Copel and future chairs Sidney and Adele
Robbins, distributed a survey to Temple Israel's member families to determine issues of greatest interest. Excited by the enthusiastic response, the
committee obtained official board status and set up subcommittees focusing on discrimination, church-state separation, nuclear testing, and capital
punishment.[29]

Social action energized many temple constituencies. "I was more interested in the social action than anything at Temple Israel," one member recalled, "so Gittelsohn was my kind of guy." In 1961, the annual college homecoming service focused on "The Threat of Nuclear War — Its Impact on the Campus." In 1962, Temple Israel participated in a "Turn Toward Peace Sabbath" that included a "Walk for Peace" and rally at Boston Common.[30]

In the aftermath of President John F. Kennedy's assassination in November 1963, civil rights rose to the top of Reform Judaism's social action agenda, and the congregation vowed "renewed dedication" to the fallen president's ideals. In 1964, in conjunction with the Program for Racial Justice adopted by the UAHC and CCAR, the Temple Israel board affirmed that Jews, with their own history of ghettoization, had a special obligation to fight racism. In this spirit, Kivie and Emily Kaplan established the Social Action Fund for projects not covered by the congregational budget. The Social Action Committee initiated projects like the Boston-Ruleville Interfaith Committee, which helped to build a social center for a rural Mississippi community, and the Massachusetts Interfaith Social Action Committee, which assisted in local social welfare programs. Other Temple Israel groups followed suit. The Couples Club participated in the Congress of Racial Equality's study of Boston's housing conditions and urban renewal proposals. The Temple Juniors, along with several church groups, organized a food drive for Mississippi sharecroppers.[31]

Some rabbis and members personally took part in civil rights actions. On March 24, 1965, for example, a Boston delegation of Jewish clergy and laypeople, which included Temple Israel's associate rabbi, Harvey J. Fields (1963–1968), marched from Selma to Montgomery, Alabama. One participant, Temple Israel high school student Louis Grossman, called the march "one of the greatest experiences of my young life." He was particularly moved by the solidarity between the impoverished black Southerners and the marchers, the anger of the local white population, and the stirring speeches of the Reverend Dr. Martin Luther King, Jr., and other leaders. One month later, Dr. King preached at a Passover service at Temple Israel's Riverway Meeting House. Overflow crowds filled the foyer and the social hall below, where speakers had been set up. As religious school student Helaine Klein reported, King was "truly inspirational," speaking for forty-five minutes, without notes, about "the striving of men for freedom from hunger, ignorance, and oppression."[32]

By the mid-1960s, the ongoing civil rights struggle, the emerging coun-

Temple Israel Bulletin

ROLAND B. GITTELSOHN, RABBI; HARVEY J. FIELDS, ASSISTANT RABBI

VOLUME LV
NUMBER 30
APRIL 20, 1965

FROM THE RABBIS' DESK

Dear Friends:

The days immediately following the receipt of this Bulletin will be busy and productive ones in the life of our congregation.

First of all, at our Yizkor Service for the concluding night of Passover, we shall be greatly honored by the presence in our pulpit of The Rev. Dr. Martin Luther King. In view of the fact that there will undoubtedly be many hundreds of non-members who will be anxious to hear Dr. King, may we urge that our members plan to arrive in ample time to obtain seats. The Service will be held in the Rabbi Harry Levi Auditorium of the Meeting House at 8:30 P.M. Thursday evening, 22 April. Especially those members of the congregation who have lost loved ones during the past year are urged to be present for Yizkor at this Service.

On Friday morning, 23 April, we shall hold our Family Worship Service for the concluding morning of the Passover Holiday. Rabbi Fields will speak at this Service.

Our regular Friday evening Worship Service for Shabbat will take place at 8:30 P.M., the same evening, Friday, 23 April. Rabbi Fields and I will participate in a pulpit conversation on SHOULD WE JEWS MISSIONIZE? The question of whether Jews should follow the common Christian precedent of actively seeking converts has been under discussion for some time. Since Rabbi Fields and I happen to differ in our views on this matter, our pulpit conversation should shed light for members of the congregation.

A special treat is in store for us at the Friday evening Service. Mr. Myron Schoen, Director of the Commission on Synagogue Administration of the Union of American Hebrew Congregations, will be present to present a Diploma as Fellow in Temple Administration to our Executive Director, Mr. Bernard I. Pincus. The F.T.A. degree is given only to those Temple Administrators who successfully pass a rigorous examination in Jewish history and ideology as well as in administration and who write a creative paper.

We have long known of Mr. Pincus's immeasurable services to our congregation and will rejoice with him on Friday evening as he receives this well-merited national recognition on our pulpit.

We look forward to the opportunity of seeing many of our members over this busy and inspiring weekend.

Faithfully yours,

Roland B. Gittelsohn

ADDENDUM

We regret that we omitted the fact that the original review of Mr. Fromm's concert by Mr. Allan Sly reported in last week's Bulletin was originally published in the Jewish Advocate.

(Courtesy of Temple Israel
Archives)

Concluding Passover Services
at the meeting house

Thursday Evening, April 22, at 8:30 P.M.

Memorial (Yizkor) Service

REV. DR. MARTIN LUTHER KING
will speak

◇—◇

Friday Morning, April 23, at 10:30 A.M.

Passover Family Service

Rabbi Fields will speak

RABBI ROLAND B. GITTELSOHN, D.D., Sc.D.

TEMPLE ISRAEL

BOSTON, MASSACHUSETTS 02215

April
13th
1965

Dear Friend:

Within the last few days you have received an invitation to attend a reception in honor of the Rev. Dr. Martin Luther King on Thursday 22 April 1965 at 3:00 p.m. in the Oval Room of the Sheraton Plaza Hotel. This invitation indicated that the purpose of the meeting was to afford you the pleasure of meeting Dr. King personally and, if you so desire after hearing him, of providing financial help for the work he is doing in the struggle for civil rights.

I am writing to underscore this invitation and to tell you that I look forward personally to the pleasure of seeing you on that occasion. This meeting has been organized by an interfaith group of religious leaders in Boston who are convinced that Martin Luther King is one of the most inspired and inspiring prophetic men in our world. His work has been extremely demanding of financial resources and must be supported by all men of religious good will.

We at Temple Israel have a special responsibility in this because Dr. King has consented to be our guest preacher at the concluding Passover evening Service on Thursday 22 April at 8:30 p.m. This will be his only appearance for a Jewish group in Boston. I have promised him that especially in view of the courtesy and honor he is showing us, there would be a goodly representation of our members at the 3:00 p.m. meeting that day. Please try to come if you possibly can.

Cordially yours,

Roland B. Gittelsohn

Rabbi Roland B. Gittelsohn

terculture movement, and especially the escalating war in Vietnam, began to influence the way Americans viewed their government. The outspoken Rabbi Gittelsohn was one of the first clergymen to question America's involvement in Southeast Asia. When he supported the March on Washington for Peace in 1965, the American Legion, which had just declared Gittelsohn a recipient of its Good Government Award for his World War II service and past leadership of the Jewish War Veterans, rescinded the honor. This very public and controversial decision brought Gittelsohn much attention. Criticized by supporters of American foreign policy, he was lauded by congregants, fellow clergy, and colleagues nationwide who felt he had a right to "speak publicly as his conscience dictates," even when they did not agree with him.[33]

Most members supported Rabbi Gittelsohn's social justice work, but his position on the war led some to question the propriety of a rabbi addressing political topics from the pulpit. A few months earlier, Gittelsohn had preached a Rosh Hashanah sermon advocating civil disobedience (entitled "When Is It Right to Break the Law?") that some members found inappropriate. Gittelsohn agreed that he would not "represent" the congregation unless specifically authorized to do so, but he insisted that he would continue "to speak out vigorously on every moral issue" affecting "the fate of humanity." Years later, he remarked that the congregation "deserved an enormous amount of credit" for being able "to say we disagree with much that our Rabbi says, but we respect his right to say it."[34]

Over the years, Rabbi Gittelsohn also continued to lead other social action efforts. In December 1968, with the support of the Massachusetts Board of Rabbis, he became a proponent of Cesar Chavez's national grape boycott in support of migrant farmworkers. In 1976, Social Action Committee member Ronya Schwaab and others convinced him to advocate for Soviet refusniks who had been denied visas to the United States and Israel, laying the foundation for a major Temple Israel initiative in the mid-1980s.[35]

"A MAJESTIC IMAGE AND
AN IMPRESSIVE APPEARANCE"

By the late 1950s, despite the construction of the new religious school wing, space for the myriad activities of the congregation had again become a serious concern. Because increased traffic and difficult parking near Boston University discouraged use of the Commonwealth Avenue building, most activities took place at the Riverway campus, and the sanctuary was opened only for the High Holy Days, consecration and confirmation, and an occasional wedding or funeral. In 1959, the board appointed a Long Range Study Committee to examine the problem, with a focus on cost, parking, and accessibility.[36]

For several years, the committee debated various solutions: building additional facilities next to the Commonwealth Avenue structure, constructing a new sanctuary next to the Riverway Meeting House, and moving the temple to an entirely new site on the Newton-Brookline border. By 1963, with more than half of the congregation's 1,600 members living in Brookline and Newton (predominantly in Cleveland Circle and Chestnut Hill), such a move would follow the historical precedent set by Temple Israel and other congregations of relocating to accommodate the changing residential patterns of members. In 1967, however, the congregation approved the most cost-efficient option — uniting all of the temple's facilities on the Riverway site, where members could count on convenient access by car and public transportation.[37]

This decision was a milestone for Temple Israel; it solidified the synagogue's commitment to remain an urban synagogue that would serve Boston as well as the surrounding suburbs. Having made this choice, the board hoped to complete the "temple centre" first envisioned in the 1920s — a complex with a "majestic image" and "impressive appearance." The board

Sanctuary addition under construction, 1972. (Courtesy of Temple Israel Archives)

The Riverway facade of the sanctuary addition was completed by Louise Nevelson's massive wall sculpture, "Sky Covenant," installed in 1973. Commissioned by a committee chaired by Irving Rabb, the sculpture consists of twenty-five "apparently unconnected" geometric boxes made of corten steel intended to portray "a Jewish view of the universe." (Courtesy of Temple Israel Archives)

initiated a capital campaign, and, as in the past, the auxiliaries played a key role in raising money for the new sanctuary. In 1968, the temple sold the Commonwealth Avenue building to Boston University, which renamed it the Alfred L. Morse Auditorium. Because the new sanctuary would not be completed for several years, the university allowed the congregation to lease the auditorium for religious services.[38]

After the sale, the newly appointed building committee hired The Architects Collaborative (TAC) of Cambridge to do a feasibility study and draw plans. A team led by TAC Vice President H. Morse Payne designed an addition that included a soaring interior sanctuary, an airy skylit atrium lobby connecting the older and newer buildings, and a chapel. Ground was broken in 1972 and the structure was finished in October 1973. Two months later, the congregation dedicated "Sky Covenant," a sculpture commissioned from noted artist Louise Nevelson, to enhance the Riverway entrance. In 1974, Goody, Clancy and Associates designed a social hall to seat five hundred that completed the project.[39]

The new building was designed to symbolize the lofty ideals of social justice, spiritual education, and Jewish tradition that characterized Rabbi Gittelsohn's vision of Judaism. At the same time, the finished complex was intended to enhance the congregation's sense of community by consolidating all temple programming in one place. By the time it was dedicated in 1973, however, that sense of community was already being tested, as membership declined and younger Jews began to agitate for reforms that would make Judaism—and Temple Israel—less formal and more inclusive.

1973–1988

Temple Israel's new sanctuary epitomized both the achievements of the Gittelsohn era and the desire for change that would characterize the 1970s. At the formal dedication in October 1973, Rabbi Gittelsohn focused on the "theological truths" embodied in the new worship space, calling attention to the ark, "with sloping sides to symbolize Mt. Sinai"; the menorah, "a gentle, graceful, flowing tree"; and the hanging Ner Tamid (eternal light), whose "subtle motion suggests that the Torah is not static but alive." All, he observed, were intended to "symbolically rekindle" the "living energy with which Judaism infuses our lives." But the sanctuary's design, with its imposing bima, also represented a formal, more hierarchical synagogue style that was being questioned by many Reform Jews who sought greater inclusiveness, deeper spirituality, a more participatory, family-like worship setting, and a stronger sense of community. In the 1970s, Temple Israel and other American congregations would experience tension, turbulence, and a shifting balance of power. Experimenting with all aspects of Jewish life from ritual to social action, Jews would transform their synagogues and, in the process, the course of American Reform Judaism.[1]

Temple Israel's 1973 dedication festivities expressed this new dialectic between participation and performance. The now complete "campus," built in part to attract younger members and retain older ones, would provide increased space for "programs of education, study and sociability" and promote community by bringing "the generations and individuals within the congregation closer together." The original plans for the dedication had centered on formal, adult-oriented celebrations, including the premiere of a cantata commissioned from Emeritus Music Director Dr. Herbert Fromm for the occasion. But some members insisted on adding a family-focused program, a Yom Hamishpacha (Family Housewarming Day), that offered

Bima of Temple Israel sanctuary, 1973. (Courtesy of Temple Israel Archives)

entertainments, exhibits, and activities for families "at every corner of the building." When the well-attended event proved a success, its organizers felt empowered to advocate for more such programs.[2]

The dedication exposed a congregational identity crisis whose first signs had been steep and visible declines in membership and religious school enrollments due to changing demographics. Between 1968 and 1973, the number of household units dropped almost twenty percent, from 2,140 to 1,770. Religious school enrollment decreased from a peak of 1,402 in 1966 to fewer than 750 in 1973. As Temple Israel baby boomers completed religious school, many of their parents, especially those who had joined primarily for the educational program and had never personally participated in the temple's adult activities, resigned. At the same time, young adults and families influenced by the "movements" of the 1960s tended to view large synagogues as overly bureaucratic representations of the "establishment."

Notice for Yom Hamishpacha (Family Housewarming Day), in Temple Israel Bulletin, *October 16, 1973. (Courtesy of Temple Israel Archives)*

DEDICATION CELEBRATION

On Saturday evening, October 27, at 8:0u p.m. we will celebrate the dedication of our new Synagogue. All are cordially invited to attend these memorable Community Festivities.

The premier performance of Dr. Herbert F. Fromm's "Festival Cantata," especially commissioned for this occasion, will be presented.

The dedication of the Rabb-Cahners Social Hall and a reception will follow.

Everyone's invited to

YOM HAMISHPACHA
Family Housewarming Day

October 28, 1973
12 noon to 5 pm

Please note the times of the following special events scheduled for this exciting afternoon:

1:00 pm: THE MANDALA FOLK DANCE ENSEMBLE

2:00 pm: ELEANOR BOYLAN'S PUPPET THEATER

2:00 pm: THE FALL OF AMERICAN JEWRY

3:00 pm: MEZUZAH DEDICATION

3:15 pm: WOMEN OF VALOR

4:15 pm: JACK AND THE BEANSTALK

Plus: Lunch ($1 apiece), Refreshments, Supervised Children's Activities, Teen Activities, Israeli Dancing and Fun for Everyone.

Come early and stay late. Bring the entire family for a festive and joyous afternoon.

TEMPLE ISRAEL (Reform) COLLEGE FORUM presents a
SUNDAY EVENING SERIES on

LIBERAL JUDAISM
CONFRONTS THE 70's

February 8   Rabbi Albert Axelrad
                    Hillel Counsellor, Brandeis University
        FIGHTING SYNAGOGUE SENILITY

March 8   Rabbi Larry Halpern
                    Temple Israel
        RELIGION WITHOUT GOD

April 5   Joel Grishaver
                    Sophomore, Boston University 1969 graduate Institute
                    Jewish Youth Leaders from the Diaspora, Jerusalem
        SINGING THE NEW LEFT BLUES
                    or ISRAEL AND THE LIBERAL AMERICAN JEW

*Temple Israel offered independent study
programs, elective minicourses, lectures, and
social events for post-confirmation and college
students in the late 1960s and early 1970s.
(Courtesy of Temple Israel Archives)*

EASY
TO   FREE SUPPER!
GET   For reservations, phone
TO: RABBI FRANK WALDORF
        LO 6-3960
        BY THE THURSDAY BEFORE
        EACH MEETING
        5:00 p.m.

Looking for a closer, more personal connection to Judaism, many who saw Temple Israel as impersonal and formal chose to cultivate their Jewish identity by joining smaller synagogues, attending Hillel services, or establishing their own informal worship groups. The net effect was an aging Temple Israel congregation much reduced in size.[3]

Temple Israel's demographic trajectory reflected national trends. In the aftermath of the civil rights movement, the Vietnam War, and the Watergate scandal, Americans turned inward; the Jewish communal agenda shifted toward revitalizing Jewish spirituality and focusing on "personal and spiritual growth." As historian Jonathan Sarna observed, Jews increasingly "defined themselves through those elements of Jewish tradition that they *chose* to embrace. They felt free to explore many options . . . and they picked their way 'cafeteria style' among the diverse laws and customs that governed Jewish life."[4]

"OUR STRONGEST BUT ALSO OUR WEAKEST POINT"

In the 1970s, despite an endowment fund established in 1959, the loss in membership revenue and the debt burden of the new construction created a fiscal crisis. Between 1971 and 1979, Temple Israel consistently ran an annual deficit in the tens of thousands of dollars. Over the years, the board implemented a number of new financial strategies, including freezing the budget, eliminating a third rabbinic position added in the 1960s, restructuring the debt, directing the temple's portfolio manager to focus on income rather than growth, instituting a voluntary dues increase program, and finally, after much debate, raising dues and streamlining the dues schedule.[5]

In addition, Temple Israel's education program was no longer its strongest magnet. In response to changing educational theories of the 1960s, families began to demand a less formal atmosphere and a curriculum that included more creative arts and electives. A two-year evaluation initiated in 1970 led Principal Nemzoff and the Education Committee to implement changes that made experiential learning "central to the educative process." Incentives like field trips, weekend retreats, and informal "Ask the Rabbi" classroom visits encouraged some junior high school and high school students to remain in the program; even so, enrollment continued to decline. In 1974, Nemzoff retired after thirty-two years at Temple Israel; a year later, when his replacement resigned, school coordinator Lillian Beauvais became the principal.[6]

Lillian Beauvais, Temple Israel Religious School Principal, 1972–1981. (Courtesy of Temple Israel Archives)

In 1974, hoping to stem resignations and increase membership, the board appointed a committee to study and evaluate members' needs. Chaired by Dr. Herbert Schilder (board president, 1982–1985) and Dr. David S. Rosenthal, and representing all segments of the congregation, the committee contacted a random sample of members and interviewed those who responded, including a number who considered themselves "uninvolved." Many expressed deep dissatisfaction. They saw the temple as "impersonal," feeling that their concerns had been ignored; others were offended that the synagogue reached out to members primarily through weekly bulletins and mimeographed mailings that contained repeated requests for money. As the committee noted, "There must be attempts by one means or another to give the feeling to our members that they are needed and that their participation is desired."[7]

Many of the respondents' suggestions focused on building community among different constituencies through specialized programming and services. College students, young couples, and unmarried adults wanted more social and cultural programs. The elderly requested a senior center and services such as transportation to and from the temple. Parents with school-aged children asked for more frequent family services, a meeting place for high school and college students, and family "havurot" (fellowship/study groups).[8]

The 1974 survey marked a turning point for Temple Israel. As members demanded more targeted services and more individual attention, the committee recognized—probably for the first time in the congregation's long history—that "our size and prestige" are "not only our strongest, but also, our weakest point." In addition, when various constituencies had made it clear that they wanted to play a more central role in setting the institutional agenda, lay leaders and clergy recognized that they must involve more groups in temple governance. The committee concluded that the problem was neither facilities nor "manpower"; rather, the temple lacked "the organization to make it work."[9]

Implementation of the findings would also require rabbinical changes. While nearly half of the interviewees had joined the temple because of Gittelsohn's reputation, the senior rabbi was, as the committee observed, so "rightfully" busy "with the leadership of the whole reform movement and with a prominent role in social action" that he had little time to serve the congregation's everyday needs. Rabbi Gittelsohn had by this time been at Temple Israel for two decades, and many of the members who wanted a

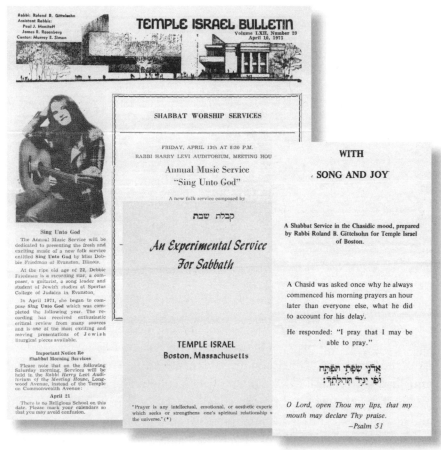

Cultural changes of the 1970s were reflected in several experimental worship services prepared by the clergy and invited guests, including the budding liturgist Debbie Friedman. In 1973, Friedman, now "one of the "Reform movement's most influential and charismatic liturgical composers," introduced "Sing Unto God," her new Sabbath liturgy, at the temple's annual music service. (Courtesy of Temple Israel Archives)

more informal, collaborative, and open synagogue considered him "old-fashioned." While the congregation revered their rabbi's erudition and social conscience, many also considered him authoritarian and uncompromising. Over the years, a number of families had had confrontations with Gittelsohn over school attendance, confirmation, weddings, and other matters. Some who had felt alienated had left the congregation; others harbored feelings of anguish and resentment that lingered for decades.[10]

Over time, Rabbi Gittelsohn's style of governance had also antagonized some members of the board. Despite the fact that CCAR (Central

Assistant Rabbi Paul Citrin and members of the PTA, 1977. (Courtesy of Temple Israel Archives)

Conference of American Rabbis) guidelines affirmed that the "administration of the practical affairs of the congregation is primarily the responsibility of the lay leaders," Gittelsohn insisted on attending every board meeting
and "had a great deal to say about . . . what should be done about every
phase of the temple." Before his arrival, the board had been fairly small
and autonomous; during his tenure, however, it gradually expanded, with
many of the new members his handpicked allies. When efforts were made
to nominate others, including a 1964 campaign to elect Bob Levi, son of
the former rabbi, as board president, Gittelsohn reacted strongly. Furthermore, functions traditionally performed by lay leaders were gradually being
handed over to professional staff who worked under the direction of the
rabbi and Bernard Pincus, the executive director from 1956 to 1979. During
this period, at Temple Israel as elsewhere, it was clear that the age-old balance between lay leaders and rabbis was shifting toward rabbinic control,
and many members worried that this would be "an unsatisfactory development in the long run."[11]

The challenge of implementing some of the congregants' suggestions fell
primarily to Assistant Rabbi Paul J. Citrin (1974–1978). In the early 1970s,
many young Jews had been attracted to "havurot" due to their "egalitari-
anism, informality, cohesive community, active participatory prayer, group
discussion, and unconventional forms of governance." Boston had been a

leader in the havurah movement and *The Jewish Catalog: A Do-It-Yourself Kit* (1973) further popularized the idea. In 1975, with Rabbi Citrin's guidance, Temple Israel began to establish havurot for various groups to help them "feel rooted in a large synagogue community," offer a "specific context" for their Jewish affiliation, and provide "a shelter from some of the numbing, impersonal aspects of the mass society which dominates our lives." By 1977, six havurot had been established; as one member observed, they helped "pull us—lukewarm congregants—into Temple life." The same year, Citrin coordinated various singles groups, served as liaison for the temple's well-established Couples Club, and ran a b'nai mitzvah program

(Courtesy of Temple Israel Archives)

The Ruth and Jack Gottlieb Memorial Garden, completed in 1976, was a project of the Garden Club, led by Alice Sherman. It was designed as a "biblical garden," where plants mentioned in the Bible were grown. (Courtesy of Temple Israel Archives)

for adults. He and the Social Action Committee reached out to the congregation's elderly by arranging transportation to Friday night services. The board also initiated various changes, including making the family worship service a monthly event for all congregants. "Family Services are not Children's Services," Citrin reminded members. "While the liturgy at a Family Service is shorter than usual, the prayers speak to people of all ages . . . its message knows no generational barrier." Together these new programs engendered a greater sense of community.[12]

The new efforts also paved the way for women's entry into leadership roles. Women had always been active in auxiliaries such as the Sisterhood, the

Religious School Committee, and the PTA. In earlier generations, although many were college-educated, most married women, particularly those with young children, did not engage in paid work. Many had become active in volunteer work in the 1930s, 1940s, and 1950s because it gave them "a chance to get out of the house and do something worthwhile." They enjoyed the camaraderie of working with "like-minded women," whether participating in social action or preparing for an Oneg Shabbat. These women, who spent so much time at the temple, intimately understood the workings of the congregation. Even so, while some represented their groups on the board, they were not invited to become officers of the temple.[13]

By the 1960s and 1970s, however, many Sisterhood members became determined to change its "lace, linens and silver coffee pots" image. Like their counterparts elsewhere, women like Betsy Abrams, Roberta (Bobbie) Burstein, Sylvia Cooper, Alice Sherman, and others resolved that "Sisterhood is not going to be known as 'the women of the kitchen' anymore." They initiated a variety of programs including an annual interfaith luncheon, women's leadership training, and, together with the Brotherhood, participation in social action activities such as improving child welfare, helping victims of domestic violence, and aiding Soviet refusniks. In recognition of its new focus, the Federation of Temple Sisterhoods would be renamed Women of Reform Judaism (WRJ) in 1993.[14]

Younger women — baby boomers and slightly older activists influenced by the feminist movement — also agitated to move the congregation in new directions. Most continued to work at least part-time after having children, and they applied their skills to the synagogue with the confidence that came from their professional experience. With formidable energy, women like Ruth Aisner, Anita Bender, Frances (Fran) Putnoi, Adele Robbins, and Genevieve Wyner moved from the Sisterhood, PTA, and Education Committee to other arenas, including administration and finance. As one congregant recalled, when "women found purpose, things just seemed to happen." In 1977, women's status in the temple was finally codified when a bylaw modification gave married women a vote for the first time by granting full voting privileges to each individual member rather than one per household.[15]

In the mid-1970s, congregational change was hastened by a sensitive situation concerning Rabbi Gittelsohn that led to his retirement. In 1975, Ruth Gittelsohn, who had suffered from progressive medical problems for many years, was diagnosed and hospitalized with "degenerative dementia." Later that year, during a congregational trip to Israel, Gittelsohn fell in love with

Under the leadership of Frances (Fran) Werman, twenty-five Sisterhood members worked for six years between 1974 and 1980 to create a large needlepoint tapestry, "Cycle of the Year." Designed by artist Nathaniel Jacobson (at left), the brightly colored tapestry, illustrating "the religious accounting of time and the commemoration of creation, the seasons, and the Jewish holidays," was installed in the Riverway stairwell. (Courtesy of Temple Israel Archives)

a widowed congregant, Hulda ("Bubbles") Phillips Tischler. Many in the congregation sympathized with his dilemma, but others were dismayed that their married rabbi—who had always held his congregants to a high "moral" and behavioral standard—would have a "girlfriend," even though his wife was "reduced in most respects to infancy."[16]

In September 1976, the sixty-six-year-old Rabbi Gittelsohn announced his intention to leave the following August, after twenty-three years at Temple Israel and forty years as a congregational rabbi. He had been granted life tenure in 1967, with the option of retiring anytime after his sixty-fifth birthday. The board agreed to retain Gittelsohn as rabbi emeritus, with an office at the temple. He would occasionally preach, perform life-cycle events when requested, and maintain his Sunday morning television appearances. Gittelsohn would also go on to co-found the Association of Reform Zionists of America (ARZA). In 1978, when his divorce became final, he married Hulda Tischler. He continued to support Ruth Gittelsohn in the nursing home until her death in 1980.[17]

"AN INSTITUTIONAL HUMANIZER"

With Rabbi Gittelsohn's departure, the board began to search for an experienced leader who would "reinforce the stability and viability of the congregation" while attracting a more diverse membership base. In response to the upheavals of the last several years, the board appointed a fifty-seven–member rabbinic search committee. Despite some fears that this committee could become a "Tower of Babel," its members soon agreed that, above all, the new rabbi must be "knowledgeable about Judaism" and "show concern for individuals." After a yearlong search, the committee came to consensus around forty-year-old Rabbi Bernard Mehlman of Temple Micah in Washington, D.C.[18]

With the hiring of Bernard Mehlman, Temple Israel, like many other synagogues in this era, made the decision to replace their "fiery" preacher with a more pastoral "teaching" rabbi. Rabbi Mehlman had never led a congregation of Temple Israel's size, but the search committee was impressed with his deep Jewish learning, his experience as an educator, and his approachability. Committee members also found Mehlman's thirty-four-year-old Boston-born wife, Emily (Shain), "completely charming" and "a great asset to him." They admired Mehlman's success in attracting members, noting that his Washington, D.C., congregation of young professionals had grown from sixty to four hundred families during his ten-year tenure. After a visit to Washington confirmed the committee's impression of Mehlman as "a fine human being, with humility, gentleness and an ability to establish a rapport with young people and with his congregation," lay leaders agreed that Rabbi Mehlman had the potential to galvanize Temple Israel and implement the ideas proposed in the 1974 survey report.[19]

For his part, Rabbi Mehlman clearly saw his election as a mandate for change. Recognizing Temple Israel as "a typical aging congregation in an urban setting with a suburban constituency," he was eager to take on the challenge of moving it forward. Over the years, Mehlman consistently

Bernard H. Mehlman

Bernard H. Mehlman (1937–) grew up in Brooklyn, New York. Mehlman graduated from New York University in 1957 and earned his masters and rabbinic degrees at HUC–JIR in 1963. He began his rabbinate as an Army chaplain in Texas and Germany. He married Emily Shain in 1964; they had two sons, Jonathan and David.

In 1965, Mehlman became the assistant rabbi at Temple Shaaray Tefila in New York. Two years later, he was hired by Temple Micah in Washington, D.C., a young congregation that expanded rapidly during his ten-year tenure. While in Washington, Rabbi Mehlman served as the Jewish coordinator for Interfaith Metropolitan Theological Education, Inc., an "experimental, interfaith, interracial, urban centered seminary for men and women" of all faiths. In 1973, he earned a doctorate in Hebrew Letters from HUC–JIR.

In 1978, Rabbi Mehlman became the senior rabbi at Temple Israel, serving for twenty-one years. Mehlman adopted a more inclusive team approach, broadened educational opportunities for all congregants, and worked to address multiple constituent needs. After retiring in 1999, he became professor of Homiletics and Midrash at HUC–New York. Mehlman served on the publishing team for *Mishkan T'filah — A Reform Siddur* (2007). He has chaired multiple committees and task forces of the CCAR and UAHC (now Union of Reform Judaism [URJ]) that address his commitment to lifelong Jewish education and the centrality of the synagogue in Jewish life.

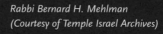

Rabbi Bernard H. Mehlman
(Courtesy of Temple Israel Archives)

maintained that he had been hired for two reasons: because he was an "institutional humanizer" who believed in building community, and because he had promised to bring Temple Israel into the "mainstream of modern Reform Judaism." A scholar and "teacher par excellence," he would work throughout his rabbinate to create a community where adults and children could "explore a Jewish lifestyle together."[20]

To achieve these goals, Rabbi Mehlman, the board, and his "kitchen cabinet" of like-minded lay leaders quickly moved forward on a variety of initiatives designed to build community and deepen congregants' connections to Jewish life and learning. While the board endorsed these "new directions," it also tried to focus the rabbi's attention on resolving the temple's continuing financial problems by increasing membership and attracting younger families who would shore up the shrinking religious school (in which fewer than one in five families had children enrolled). Mehlman believed that "if we had the right program, if we set the right tone, and we did it in the right way that membership issues would take care of themselves." Board members, on the other hand, recognizing that annual dues were the temple's primary source of revenue, felt that a more active approach was necessary. Eighty-three thousand dollars had been borrowed from the synagogue's endowment over the previous two years to cover essential expenses. While these deficits could partly be attributed to a struggling national economy, they needed to be addressed. As Irving Rabb argued, "We have a 'good bill of goods' to sell and we have to sell it. . . . We need 2000 members again."[21]

In 1978, the board established a public relations committee, chaired by Genevieve Wyner, to "extend a broader welcome to a wider segment of our community" through press releases, newspaper ads, and open houses. More than one hundred members joined in the first few months alone, raising the number of household units to 1,635 and adding seventy-four new religious school students. In 1979, the board approved a measure to offer new converts and newly married children of members a free year of membership, hoping that "exposure to the quality and beauty of our Temple" would encourage them "to continue their affiliation with us and with Jewish communal life." The membership committee also initiated a "Neighborhood Network" of volunteers who would improve the congregation's "feeling of belonging" by inviting new members to services and temple events. Such efforts proved successful; by October 1980, the temple had 1,735 membership units — its largest number since 1975.[22]

Family Kallah, 1981. In 1980, Temple Israel held its first family kallah at the UAHC's Eisner Camp in Great Barrington, Massachusetts. As one attendee noted, "The Kallah increased the number of friendly and familiar faces at the Temple." (Courtesy of Temple Israel Archives)

The renewed emphasis on community building also inspired lay leaders to find new ways of involving members in the work of the synagogue. In 1978, an ad hoc board committee established the Techiya seminar, a program designed to "nurture future leadership in the Congregation among men and women active in the [larger] Jewish community." Co-chaired by Margie Paley, Fran Putnoi, and Rhode Sapers, the initiative became a "catalyst for new conversations" that would "broaden the base of participation" in the temple's decision-making process.[23]

In addition to attracting new blood, the Techiya seminar positioned active female members for congregational leadership. In 1969, Phoebe Woolf had been the first woman elected as a vice president of the Board of Trustees. Thereafter, women more frequently become officers and, in the 1970s and 1980s, nine women would serve as vice presidents. In 1988, Fran Putnoi would become Temple Israel's first female president (1988–1991).[24]

Justin L. Wyner, the first board president elected after Mehlman's arrival, focused on improving communication among temple administrators, the board, and the congregation during his term (1979–1982). He held weekly office hours at the temple and encouraged the rotation of committee chairs so that more people could assume leadership positions. He instituted "Shabbatons" (retreats) for board members and their spouses so that the group could set "goals, priorities and perspectives as a congregational community." In 1981, he helped the temple install its first computerized membership database, a system that made it possible to address mailings to every individual in a household by his or her own name.[25]

The temple's finances also improved during this era, despite heavy inflation and high energy costs. Executive Director Bernard Pincus had retired in 1979 after twenty-four years of service. The new director, Norman Fogel (1979–1983), was able to balance the budget for the next three years due to the revenue generated by new members, a successful fund-raising campaign undertaken during Milton Linden's tenure as board president (1976–1979),

Torah bearers for Temple Israel's 130th Anniversary Service (1984). Front Row: Fran Putnoi, Betsy Abrams, Genevieve Wyner. Back Row: John Morse, Sr., Dr. Herbert Schilder, Joseph Winthrop. (Courtesy of Temple Israel Archives)

Executive Directors Bernard Pincus (1955–1979) and Norman Fogel (1979–1983). (Courtesy of Temple Israel Archives)

and a 1979 agreement to rent the Berners Square parking lot to the Medical Academic and Scientific Community Organization, Inc. (MASCO). The temple was able to complete substantial building repairs, security improvements, and energy-saving renovations, and in 1982, the Board of Managers paid off the building loan debt. This relative solvency made the various new programs Mehlman imagined feasible.[26]

BUILDING COMMUNITY THROUGH
CONGREGATIONAL LEARNING

Like his predecessors, Rabbi Mehlman saw the religious school, the adult education programs, and the pulpit as paths to Jewish learning. But he also saw study as a means of building community across generations and constituencies. Mehlman was determined to make the full range of Jewish texts—from Torah to Talmud to modern philosophy—accessible to and meaningful for Jews of all ages and backgrounds. He believed that every synagogue-related activity could become a teaching experience and encouraged congregants to gain the proficiency needed to grapple with the texts themselves.[27]

Well before his official arrival (in February, during the Blizzard of '78), Rabbi Mehlman was already convinced that it would be impossible for him to meet the expressed desire of his new congregation for more programs without a larger, more professional staff "team" to supplement his lay "companions, assistants, helpers . . . and co-workers." By the time Mehlman assumed his formal duties, Rabbi Citrin, who had taken on increasing

Rabbi Bernard and Emily Mehlman, Rabbi Emeritus Roland Gittelsohn, Board President Milton Linden, UAHC President Rabbi Alexander Schindler, and Associate Rabbi Ronne Friedman at Temple Israel's 125th anniversary service, 1979. (Courtesy of Temple Israel Archives)

responsibilities after Rabbi Gittelsohn's retirement, had accepted a position in Albuquerque, New Mexico. Mehlman proposed replacing him with an experienced rather than a newly ordained assistant rabbi; the candidate he had in mind was his former intern, Rabbi Ronne Friedman, whom he had mentored since 1971. The board took Mehlman's recommendation and hired Friedman, the assistant rabbi at North Shore Congregation Israel in Glencoe, Illinois, as the associate rabbi.[28]

When Rabbi Friedman arrived in August 1978, he and Rabbi Mehlman immediately turned their attention to instituting the changes to the religious school that the senior rabbi had been planning since his election. In fact, Mehlman had called a meeting of the Religious School Committee the very day after he was hired to propose improvements to the Hebrew language curriculum. The two rabbis introduced a three-unit post-confirmation class and a new curriculum for the eighth grade focusing on the Hebrew Bible. They wrote a teacher's manual to help raise and standardize the level of Hebrew instruction.[29]

In 1979, Mehlman and Friedman proposed that the high school meet on Monday nights so that the rabbis and cantor could teach younger students

Congregational learning across the life cycle. (Courtesy of Temple Israel Archives)

on Sunday mornings and older ones at a time most high school students would prefer. The three-hour evening session would include dinner, social time, and two classes. Although some parents worried that Monday night school would interfere with homework, the program was very successful. That year's confirmation class, with more than thirty students, was one of the largest in recent years. Eventually, the Monday night program became so popular that the eighth grade was added.[30]

Mehlman and Friedman also sought to strengthen the youth program through "Clergy Weekend" retreats and grade-specific youth groups. Again, they suggested expanding the staff to achieve this goal, and the temple hired a full-time youth director, Ellen Siegel, in 1980. The director was responsible for the youth program—Reform Youth Federation of Temple Israel (RYFTI)—curriculum development, and teaching. The temple youth group program soon became a national model, and RYFTI won the "Kavod Award" certificate of honor in 1980 from the National Federation of Temple Youth for its program focusing on social action, prayer, study, and Israel. Access to these and other religious school programs was extended by hiring an advisor for students with special needs.[31]

When Principal Lillian Beauvais retired in June 1981, Rabbi David Katz became the "Temple Educator." Rabbi Katz founded an adult program in 1983 called "The Academy"; it allowed parents to explore new areas of interest while their children were in class, to take intergenerational classes with their high-school-aged children, to join in suburban study groups, and to attend a Sunday night film series. In 1983, Katz successfully applied for a small grant from Combined Jewish Philanthropies for a Jewish Family Theater; its first play, "Post Bar Mitzvah Blues," was produced that December.[32]

When Rabbi Katz left in 1983, the Education Committee recommended that Rabbi Friedman, who had then been at Temple Israel for five years, be named temple educator. The new position added responsibility for the religious school, adult education programs, the library, and youth activities to Friedman's rabbinical duties. It also allowed him to focus on creating an integrated program "rooted in the idea of an organic temple community, a family, wherein the relationship of each member to every other member is important." Under Friedman's leadership, the religious school grew from 371 students in 1982–1983 to 508 in 1993–1994. Most of the growth was in kindergarten through seventh grade; as always, it continued to be a challenge to retain students after bar and bat mitzvah, with high school attendance remaining fairly consistent at slightly more than one hundred.[33]

nazis, Jews and goodness

The Rudolph Harold Wyner Memorial Lecture
In Search of Jewish Authenticity:
The Discovery of Jewish Folklore

The Rose Feinberg Memorial Lecture
Professor Philip P. Hallie, Wesleyan University.

TEMPLE ISRAEL
presents the first
SCHOLAR-in-RESIDENCE
PROGRAM
THE WEEKEND OF
NOVEMBER 16, 17, 18, 1979

Dr. Barbara Kirshenblatt-Gimblett	Friday evening
Chair and Professor of Performance Studies	April 18, 1986
New York University	Temple Israel
Tisch School of the Arts	8:15 p.m.

*Established by a grant from a
charitable trust founded by
Rudolph and Sara Wyner.*

featuring
DR. JAKOB J. PETUCHOWSKI
Professor of Jewish Theology and Liturgy
Hebrew Union College   Cincinnati, Ohio

The importance of Jewish knowledge is essential to the continuity of the Jewish people. We need a fuller understanding of the basic ideas, concepts, and teachings of Judaism. Our aim is to expand the horizons of our educational program and to share outstanding Jewish scholarship with the Academic, Christian Religious, and Synagogue communities of the Greater Boston area.

(Courtesy of Temple Israel Archives)

Rabbi Mehlman believed that adults should have as many educational opportunities as children. Shortly after his installation in 1978, he had inaugurated two Torah study classes that still continue today—one on Thursday mornings and another on Saturdays (before Shabbat services). He implemented a Sunday morning speaker series and special study groups for single parents, converts, adult b'nai mitzvah, and seniors. By the end of the year, Mehlman could claim that "every hour of the day there is something educational taking place at Temple Israel."[34]

These programs attracted new members and inspired additional ideas, including several adult education initiatives and endowed programs. In

March 1979, pathologist Aaron Lurie, attorney Joy Rachlin, and city planner Larry Koff established a Tuesday "Downtown Study Group" facilitated by Rabbi Mehlman that met during the workday in a Boston law office. The next year, the Sisterhood started a Tuesday morning study group focusing on Jewish womanhood. In December 1979, Bobbie and Maxwell (Mac) Burstein funded an annual Scholar-in-Residence program. The Rose Feinberg Memorial Lecture, an Israel-centered program, was added in 1982, and the Rudolph Harold Wyner Memorial Lecture (later renamed the Rudolph H. and Sara G. Wyner Lecture) in 1985. Eventually three other families endowed annual programs as well: the Herbert M. Karol Music Service in 1990, the Joy Ungerleider Jewish Book Month Program in 1995, and the Carl Steinbaum Program in 1999.[35]

TOGETHER IN SPIRITUAL CELEBRATION

"The creation of a Jewish family life style begins in the home, and extends to the synagogue," Rabbis Mehlman and Friedman observed in 1978. "It is clear that families who make the effort to attend Family Worship Services together are rewarded with a more enriching Jewish life — the prayers come true for grandparents, parents and children alike." Hoping to create an appealing experience for the entire "congregational family," the clergy modified the monthly family services by adding guitar accompaniment, replacing sermons with "stories," offering birthday blessings, and including prayer readings by various religious school classes in the service.[36]

In keeping with the new foci on congregational learning and community building, holiday services also became family-focused. In 1978, Mehlman, who was particularly fond of Purim, contrived to bring the generations together to celebrate the holiday. He recalled enlisting the "incredible, alert, smart doers" of the Sisterhood Sewing Group, who were mostly in their eighties, to create costumes for the religious school students to wear to a children's service that included a carnival, parade, and contest. Eager to see their handiwork, the Sewing Group members attended the event and the generations bonded. In 1979, the congregational seder was reintroduced after a five-year hiatus (during which Passover workshops were offered). Held on the second night of Passover, the seder affirmed the "spirit" of the "Temple Family." Whereas earlier congregational seders had been designed to teach holiday rituals to members, the new focus was "to bring us together in a spiritual celebration."[37]

Other holiday observances built on the same themes and established traditions that still continue. In September 1978, the clergy instituted a program for Selichot (the traditional midnight service that marks the beginning of the High Holy Days) that included a film, discussion, and refreshments, and culminated in a unique candlelight service designed to evoke a "mood of mystery." In 1984, the confirmation class began leading the service. On Yom Kippur, study sessions were added between the morning and afternoon services for members who wished to incorporate an educational component into their worship experience.[38]

The tone of regular Friday evening services also began to change when the clergy, in line with national trends, became determined to make them less a "performance" and more "a warm and religiously meaningful experience." Mehlman encouraged participation and employed interactive sermons that engaged congregants in a "dialogue" with the rabbi. Although some members found Mehlman's Socratic approach to preaching less dramatic than classical pulpit oratory, most came to appreciate his deep knowledge, "hopeful tone," and ability to "pull every bit of meaning out of the text."[39]

Mehlman's focus on text study and Hebrew also helped worshippers adjust to liturgical changes already under way before his arrival. The new UAHC prayer book, *Gates of Prayer* (*Sha'are Tefillah*), adopted at Temple Israel soon after its 1975 publication, reinstated many traditional Hebrew congregational prayers long absent from the Reform prayer book. When

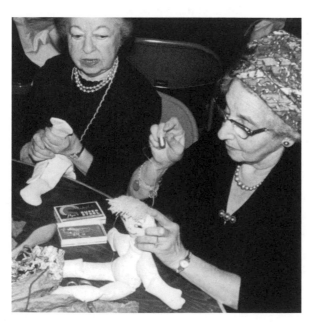

The Sisterhood Sewing Group (founded in 1912) met weekly to make dolls and stitch layettes for newborns at the Beth Israel Hospital. (Courtesy of Temple Israel Archives)

In the Mehlman era, Purim became a raucous family affair. The service was often based on a theme. Above, "The Wizard of Oz," 1982. (Courtesy of Temple Israel Archives)

the CCAR published a new High Holy Day prayer book, *Gates of Repentance* (*Sha'are Teshuvah*) in 1978, Temple Israel replaced the *Union Prayer Book* in use since the late nineteenth century.[40]

The music experience at Temple Israel also began to incorporate more traditional elements. Following a pattern set in the 1950s by other Reform synagogues, the temple had hired its first ordained cantor, Murray E. Simon, when Herbert Fromm, the longtime music director, retired in 1972. Cantor Simon was a well-known soloist who would serve as president of the American Conference of Cantors from 1979 to 1981. At Temple Israel, he revitalized the youth choir and, in 1981, established a volunteer adult choir called the Temple Israel Singers. By 1982, however, Cantor Simon was becoming dissatisfied with his position. While he was enthusiastic about Rabbi Mehlman's desire to supplement the organ with other instruments and use congregational singing to set a particular mood for each service, he increasingly resented the senior rabbi's determination to influence decisions about which music should be performed at services and other aspects of the music program. Hoping to make Temple Israel a test case for cantorial autonomy in American synagogues, he campaigned to report directly to the board. When his attempt to change the bylaws failed, Simon chose to let his contract expire and leave.[41]

The Sound of Music

Like other aspects of worship, the sounds of the service reflect cultural values and religious meaning. Those charged with musical direction at Temple Israel have shaped the synagogue's spiritual path, and some have had a profound impact on the development of sacred music worldwide. In the early years, the members of Congregation Adath Israel "davened" individually, chanting their prayers according to long-established regional traditions. With the institution of "reforms" in the 1860s and 1870s, the increasingly acculturated, upwardly mobile congregants created a more "American" atmosphere by hiring a professional choir with organ accompaniment. As music became an essential part of Reform worship, synagogues began to employ "music directors," and liturgical composers found a new market for musical arrangements of Jewish prayers and "hymns."

When Henry L. Gideon was hired in 1907 as Temple Adath Israel's first professional music director, music was already a central element of both worship and education. Gideon, a Harvard-educated organist and composer who taught at the Boston Conservatory of Music, published a popular religious school hymnal (1909). During his long tenure (1907–1938), the Sunday service was characterized by church-like choral settings for "traditional" Jewish prayers and hymns, primarily in English.

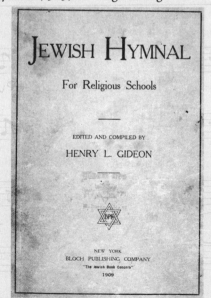

JEWISH HYMNAL

For Religious Schools

EDITED AND COMPILED BY

HENRY L. GIDEON

NEW YORK
BLOCH PUBLISHING COMPANY
"The Jewish Book Concern"
1909

(All images courtesy of Temple Israel Archives)

Herbert Fromm served as the music director and organist at Temple Israel from 1941 to 1972. Already a well-known composer and conductor when he fled Nazi Germany in the 1930s, Fromm became one of the "most prominent, most prolific, and most widely published composers of synagogue and other serious Jewish music" of his era. Fromm's music was "judiciously modern, yet imaginatively respectful of tradition." He composed numerous secular and liturgical works, many of which have become part of the standard synagogue repertoire, authored three books, and received several prestigious awards.

By the 1970s, many Reform synagogues were hiring cantors who had religious as well as musical training. Temple Israel's first cantor, Murray Simon (1972–1983), earned a master's degree from the Boston Conservatory of Music and a Ph.D. from HUC–JIR. While Simon retained his predecessors' emphasis on formal musical performance, as cantor he also took responsibility for the tone and atmosphere of the entire liturgy.

From 1979 to 1981, he served as president of the American Conference of Cantors.

In 1983, Roy B. Einhorn became Temple Israel's second cantor after graduating from HUC–JIR. Cantor Einhorn made music the central component of a more participatory, community-building worship experience. His two compact discs, *Lift Up Your Voice* (2005) and *Songs of Our Seasons of Joy* (2008), sponsored by members Eleri and Glen Dixon, demonstrate the range and diversity of the congregation's musical repertoire. In 2008, Einhorn received an honorary doctorate of music from HUC–JIR.

In 1983, the congregation hired Cantor Roy Einhorn, a recent graduate of HUC-JIR's School of Sacred Music in New York. Cantor Einhorn quickly became an integral component of the clergy "team," selecting the temple's liturgical music in conjunction with the rabbis, leading services, and directing the youth choir and Temple Israel Singers. He took an active role in the temple's education program, coordinating the b'nai mitzvah program and teaching classes. He also took on pastoral duties such as visiting congregants in the hospital and officiating at life-cycle events.[42]

The worship experience took on a new aspect when many members requested, and the temple committee approved, a shorter, Qabbalat Shabbat service at held at 5:45 P.M. that was tested in the summer of 1978. Held in the chapel, the service proved extremely popular, especially among families with young children, and soon became a seasonal fixture. By 1982, a number of members asked to extend the service to other times of the year. As one congregant explained, "The family services which happen once a month begin at my children's bedtime," while the Qabbalat Shabbat services "start at a reasonable hour, they last a reasonable amount of time, and the liturgy is accessible to young children."[43]

Other members, however, were determined to preserve the evening service. As one new congregant commented, she and her husband had joined the synagogue largely because of the cantor and professional choir. The 8:00 P.M. service "gives us a feeling of Shabbat rest. To get to a 5:45 service, my husband has to rush there from work and I take the 'T' in order to avoid having 2 cars at the temple. It is anything but a 'Shabbat Menucha' a restful Sabbath." Furthermore, she continued, the Qabbalat Shabbat was "not a very stimulating religious experience. The same 'camp-style' music is sung and there is no brief message from the rabbis to provoke some thought." After the service, "one goes home, makes dinner and it is business as usual — certainly no Shabbat — set aside and different from the rest of the week."[44]

For several years, the Temple Committee debated the pros and cons of each service — the "restful decorum," "mental stimulation," and sociability of an evening service with a sermon and Oneg Shabbat versus the informal, upbeat, child-friendly atmosphere of the Qabbalat service — and the possibility of offering both, against the backdrop of budget limitations, concerns about dividing the community between two services, and the clergy's clear preference for the early service. The committee tried to forge compromises that included holding congregational Shabbat dinners between Qabbalat and late services, moving the start time of the late service forward, and

Recipe for a Summer Evening
A Qabbalat Shabbat Service at 5:45 pm
One Dinner following at 6:30 pm
Mixed with plenty of Shabbat Fellowship
On August 5, 1983
You will have an opportunity to meet and welcome our new Assistant Rabbi Jeffrey Perry-Marx and Cantor Roy Einhorn and their wives.

for everyone's pleasure and convenience
Shabbat Menuchah   שבת מנוחה
A Restful Sabbath
If you attend a Qabbalat Shabbat Service at 5:45 or the later Evening Service at 8:15 pm, you will enjoy our Shabbat Dinner at 6:30.

January 11, 1985

Dinner by prior reservations only... none available at the door!
RSVP by Jan. 8th No exceptions! Send checks payable to Temple Israel
— Members at $8 each   To: Shabbat Dinner
— Children under 10 $6 each   Temple Israel
— Non-Members $10 each   Longwood Ave & Plymouth St.
— Total check enclosed $___   Boston, MA 02215

Name _____

Address _____

_____ Phone _____

(Courtesy of Temple Israel Archives)

extending the length of the Qabbalat service to thirty-five minutes to incorporate a reading or "sermonette."[45]

By 1984, the committee's attempts to please all constituencies were overruled by Rabbi Mehlman, who argued that the temple could "not raise people's expectations too high that they come to expect that we can run dual services throughout the year. We cannot tax the clergy that much." Mehlman's response, and his decision to gradually increase the number of Qabbalat Shabbat services, illustrated his belief that ultimately, it was the role of the clergy—not the temple committee—to interpret "the best of what Reform Judaism is all about," and implement the liturgy and services that would best achieve that goal.[46]

Various Qabbalat Shabbat liturgies were tested and eventually Assistant Rabbi William Berkowitz (1985–1990) codified the service to be published in booklet form. Many members who had initially objected came to love the spirit of the new service, where "a crying baby is part of the joy of the worship and part of the future." However, some who felt that their desire to celebrate Shabbat in a more "dignified" manner had been ignored would continue to harbor resentment against the rabbis, especially when additional Hebrew prayers and rituals were incorporated into the service. Some older members

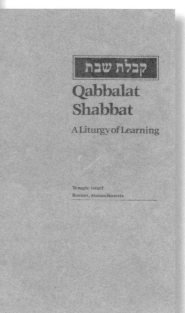

(Courtesy of Temple Israel Archives)

observed that the liturgy had become so "Orthodox" and "full of Hebrew . . .
that those of us who were brought up differently . . . can't follow it."[47]

"TIKKUN OLAM" (REPAIRING THE WORLD)

Rabbi Mehlman believed that the synagogue community was defined by
three concentric circles of caring: an innermost circle that included elements "critical to the immediate life of the congregation and its future"; a
middle circle of involvement in "various projects for human care and uplift"
in the larger Boston community; and, finally, a third circle of "responsibility
to the larger Jewish world." He saw education and family-friendly services
as essential, but also encouraged other ways of "humanizing this congregation's life," including providing aid to "people in nursing homes, who are ill,
infirm, and in need, who are lonely, who are in hospitals." Member Martha
Finn had long been concerned about such outreach and had led previous
"mitzvah" efforts with the Sisterhood and Brotherhood. Finn and Mehlman
strove to engage the entire congregation in "mitzvah committees" organized
by members in various towns to visit and aid hospitalized or housebound

members. In 1978, member Fannette Adelman established Aging Awareness (later renamed "Mature Adult Persons of Temple Israel" [MAPTI]) to serve the elderly. She and Rabbi Mehlman addressed the issue of aging through workshops, seminars, and other programs designed to help elderly parents and adult children communicate better and deal with practical, social, and emotional needs.[48]

These programs inspired a "Friendly Visitors" group, led by social workers Ruth Cowin and Vivian Freeman, to provide companionship for housebound elderly members. Endowed in 1982 by Michael Grossman as the "Marilyn Grossman Caring Committee" (in honor of his wife; it was later renamed the Marilyn and Mike Grossman Caring Community Fund), the committee eventually spawned other "caring communities" for widowed spouses, single parents, and convalescents. In 1982, Adele and Sidney Robbins, hoping to ensure the rabbi's ability to respond to urgent needs, established a discretionary fund to be used for medical, educational, and other assistance.[49]

Looking beyond the temple community, the Social Action Committee also became involved in various local, national, and international causes. Generally proposed by members with "a 'burning passion' about a particular issue," action groups focused on such issues as hunger and gun control in Boston, arms control and nuclear disarmament, apartheid in South Africa, and aid to Ethiopian and Iranian Jewry. Under the guidance of Dr. David Freeman and the Cooperative Metropolitan Ministries (an interfaith social action organization founded in 1966), members worked with organizations like the Greater Boston Food Bank and Shelter, Inc. to aid Boston's homeless. Rabbi Mehlman became particularly committed to Saturday's Bread/Sunday's Bread, an organization founded in 1983 whose mission was to feed the homeless on the weekends, when most other soup kitchens were closed. Congregants signed up to volunteer, and Mehlman went every Sunday for many years.[50]

The clergy and various members also continued the temple's long-term efforts to combat racism and foster interfaith and interracial relations in the city. In 1980, the Simons-Gutman Foundation and the UAHC cosponsored a Jewish-Black Dialogue/Workshop at Temple Israel and created a task force on Jewish-black relations. The temple appointed representatives to the Cooperative Metropolitan Ministries, the Archdiocese of Boston's Ecumenical Commission on Jewish-Christian Relations, and the Synagogue Council of Massachusetts (founded in 1981). In 1992, the temple's annual interfaith

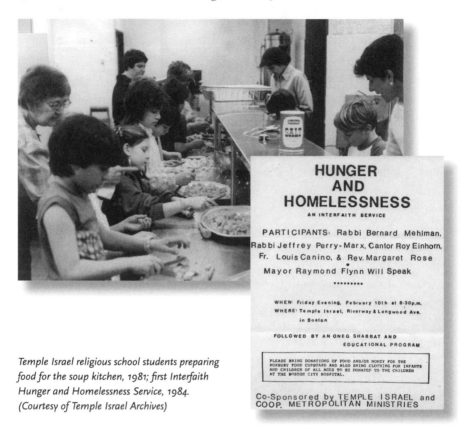

HUNGER
AND
HOMELESSNESS
AN INTERFAITH SERVICE

PARTICIPANTS: Rabbi Bernard Mehlman,
Rabbi Jeffrey Perry-Marx, Cantor Roy Einhorn,
Fr. Louis Canino, & Rev. Margaret Rose

Mayor Raymond Flynn Will Speak

• • • • • • • •

WHEN: Friday Evening, February 10th at 8:30p.m.
WHERE: Temple Israel, Riverway & Longwood Ave.
in Boston

FOLLOWED BY AN ONEG SHABBAT AND
EDUCATIONAL PROGRAM

PLEASE BRING DONATIONS OF FOOD AND/OR MONEY FOR THE
ROXBURY FOOD CUPBOARD AND ALSO BRING CLOTHING FOR INFANTS
AND CHILDREN OF ALL AGES TO BE DONATED TO THE CHILDREN
AT THE BOSTON CITY HOSPITAL.

Co-Sponsored by TEMPLE ISRAEL and
COOP. METROPOLITAN MINISTRIES

Temple Israel religious school students preparing food for the soup kitchen, 1981; first Interfaith Hunger and Homelessness Service, 1984. (Courtesy of Temple Israel Archives)

service on Hunger and Homelessness (established in 1984) became a joint service with the AME Zion Church on Columbus Avenue in Roxbury (Temple Israel's home from 1885 to 1907) in honor of the Reverend Dr. Martin Luther King, Jr.[51]

In the 1970s, at Temple Israel and other American congregations, concerns about the future of the State of Israel and the elusive search for peace in the Middle East became closely tied to Holocaust awareness. In the aftermath of the highly publicized trials of Adolf Eichmann (1961) and other Nazi war criminals, and the drama of the Six-Day War (1967), Jewish leaders and institutions were determined to raise the level of political and social responsibility among Jews and other Americans alike. They adopted the slogan "Never Again!" to reinforce the connection between the security of the Jewish people and the survival of a Jewish state.[52]

In 1975, Temple Israel had initiated a community Holocaust education program. The Social Action Committee participated in a training program in 1975 for secular school teachers that included a "kit" with resources and guidelines used by dozens of Jewish, Protestant, and Catholic educators at a Massachusetts Holocaust History Teachers' Conference at Bentley College. (Among this group was member Margot Stern Strom, who would found Facing History and Ourselves, an educational program about tolerance, in 1976.) In 1975, the temple also acquired and consecrated a Torah scroll rescued from Czechoslovakia during World War II.[53]

The Israel Committee began to sponsor a number of programs that encouraged liberal Jews to speak out regarding Israel and Arab-Israeli relations. In November 1977, Sidney and Adele Robbins sponsored a "Christian-Jewish dialogue on Israel" in their home. In April 1983, Rabbi Mehlman led a Brotherhood-sponsored congregational trip to Israel. At the same time, increasing numbers of religious school students began to participate in the Eisendrath Exchange Program, through which American Jewish teenagers traveled and studied for six months in Israel.[54] The Social Action Committee's efforts to engage Temple Israel members in global projects also included attempts to aid Jewish refugees from Iran and, later, Ethiopia. In 1978, outreach was extended to desperately poor Southeast Asian war refugees from Vietnam and Cambodia. The Taskforce on Indochinese Refugees, spearheaded by Ted and Dru Greenwood, helped to settle immigrants with sponsors, collecting furniture and clothing and assisting with housing and employment. The Tran family of five, and two other young men,

(Courtesy of Temple Israel Archives)

were hosted by temple members Edie and Guntram Mueller in their home for months.[55]

While all of these projects garnered congregational support, it was the movement to aid Soviet Jewry that truly captured the attention of the clergy and many members. In the decade following the 1967 Six-Day Arab-Israeli War, many Soviet Jews, dismayed by rampant antisemitism, had begun to apply for exit visas to Israel or America. Most were refused, or had their applications indefinitely delayed, and many were accused of disloyalty and labeled security risks. Often harassed, and sometimes even imprisoned, most refusniks also suffered financially because they had lost their jobs when they applied for visas.[56] At Temple Israel, Russian-born member Ronya Schwaab was the force behind the Soviet Jewry issue. In 1978, Schwaab organized an art exhibit, "From Moscow to Jerusalem," to raise awareness. With "dogged persistence," she initiated a Russian Jewry social-action task force to circulate petitions, write letters to Washington, and coordinate other temple activities. In 1981, a Russian Immigrant Scholarship Fund was established to pay the membership dues of Russian immigrant families who wished to join Temple Israel and enroll their children in the religious school; within a month, seven families became members. In 1981–1982, the clergy instituted a Shabbat service in English, Russian, Hebrew, and sign language and established a bar/bat mitzvah "twinning" program that paired Temple Israel's b'nai mitzvah with Soviet children.[57]

But the turning point occurred in 1986, when Rabbis Mehlman and Friedman went to the Soviet Union as representatives of the New England Region of Reform Rabbis to teach Russian Jews about Judaism. Soviet Jewry became a central focus of the clergy after this trip. The next winter, Rabbi Friedman and Cantor Einhorn returned to the Soviet Union with members Mark Yesley and Mike Grossman to make contact with refusnik families. Led by Mark and Marlene Yesley, the Social Action Committee coordinated a letter-writing campaign to the American and Soviet governments that culminated in 1987 when two families were allowed to immigrate to Boston. Mehlman, Friedman, and Einhorn took turns leading two more congregational trips to the Soviet Union, accompanied at various times by members Robert Shapiro, Donald and Fran Putnoi, John Lowenstein, and students Jessica Greenfield, Jeremy Morrison, Dana Kur, David Mehlman, and Andrew Snyder. The group became bolder each time, smuggling in medical supplies and prayer books, as well as objects of value that refusniks could sell, including blue jeans and cameras. By the late 1980s, Temple Israel

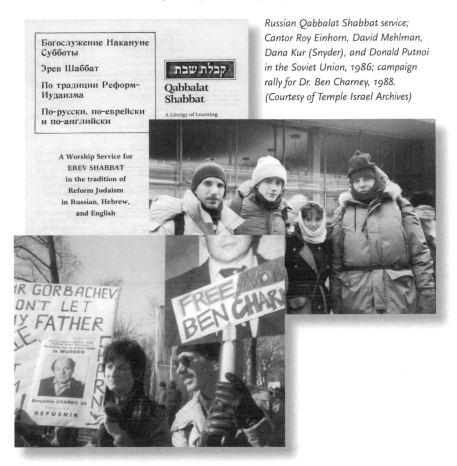

*Russian Qabbalat Shabbat service;
Cantor Roy Einhorn, David Mehlman,
Dana Kur (Snyder), and Donald Putnoi
in the Soviet Union, 1986; campaign
rally for Dr. Ben Charney, 1988.
(Courtesy of Temple Israel Archives)*

had become a leader in "the effort to fulfill the mitzvah of redemption of the captive for Jews in the Soviet Union."[58]

When Soviet Jews began to emigrate in greater numbers in the late 1980s in response to President Mikhail Gorbachev's increasingly liberal policies, Temple Israel established a committee to help recent arrivals learn English, find jobs, adjust to American life, and learn about Reform Judaism. In 1990, the clergy published a pamphlet, *Explaining Reform Judaism for New Americans*, and, as more immigrants became involved in the temple, the rabbis held religious wedding ceremonies for couples who had had civil marriages, established courses on the Jewish holidays, printed a Russian-language *Learner's Minyan* (1992), and offered a bar/bat mitzvah program for the children of new immigrants. Cantor Einhorn organized concerts and art shows to showcase the talents of the new Americans.[59]

By the late 1980s, myriad efforts to change worship, education, and social action had brought Temple Israel back into the mainstream of American Reform Judaism. Like other "cathedral congregations" faced with increasing numbers of Jews wanting a more intimate and spiritual worship experience, Temple Israel had begun to attract a younger generation, include more diverse groups in the governance process, and increase members' connections to the synagogue. As the century drew to a close, the congregation would continue to face the challenge of providing a "home for every constituency."

1988–2009

As the new millennium approached, Jewish Reform leaders began to reflect on the impact of the profound cultural changes in America since the 1950s. Synagogues, they realized, must become "big tents," "moral and spiritual centers responsive to the exciting demographic and religious realities of Jewish life." Temple Israel had already embraced this goal; in the 1980s, the synagogue committed itself to "opening its doors . . . to people of all ages, to varied kinds of families . . . who strive to create a Jewish home." In the 1990s and beyond, the board and clergy would work hard to create a welcoming atmosphere for underrepresented groups, including "Jews by choice," interfaith families, young unaffiliated singles, and gays and lesbians. As the congregation became "a community of communities," it also strove to serve as a spiritual home "where we can laugh and sing and dance, but sometimes cry as well: a place where we care and are cared for."[1]

The clergy's efforts to target various groups for special attention had begun early in Rabbi Mehlman's tenure. Programs such as MAPTI (Mature Adult Persons of Temple Israel, 1978) served seniors, a longtime constituent group, while the "Something Generation" (1987), which sponsored educational and social activities, represented the perennial efforts to connect post-college young adults with the temple. But Rabbis Mehlman and Friedman also reached out to new constituencies, including Jews by choice and interfaith couples. In the late 1970s, for example, they noted the involvement of Jews by choice such as Kathy Fogel (wife of executive director Norman Fogel), and Dru Greenwood, who spoke eloquently about her conversion experience at the first Techiya in 1978. Recognizing their needs, and those of interfaith couples, Mehlman, Friedman, and Greenwood set up an outreach program. Ultimately B'nai Abraham, the resulting educational/informational program for interfaith couples, would serve as a national model for other Jewish organizations under her leadership. In 1978, the Jewish

Family Connection began to sponsor a program, later financed by the Marilyn Grossman Fund, for those who wished to convert.[2]

These initiatives were prescient; in the 1980s, the percentage of synagogue members in interfaith marriages at Temple Israel and elsewhere would dramatically increase. By 1990, according to a National Jewish Population Survey, more than half of American Jews were married to non-Jews. These couples were producing increasing numbers of interfaith offspring, many of whom would not have been considered Jewish according to the traditional policy of matrilineal descent. In 1983, the Union of American Hebrew Congregations (UAHC) had addressed this issue by voting to consider any child born to either a Jewish mother *or* father Jewish.[3]

In 1986, Rabbi Friedman, Rabbi Mehlman, and the new librarian, Ann Abrams, undertook a similar effort to ensure that gay and lesbian Jews felt welcome at Temple Israel. That year, Marc Maxwell and David Passer became the first gay couple to apply for and obtain a family membership. In 1992, Temple Israel would establish a gay and lesbian "havurah," and Rabbi Friedman would perform the congregation's first same-sex commitment ceremony. Four years later, Aleinu, a support group for families and friends of gay, lesbian, and bisexual Jews funded in part by the Combined Jewish Philanthropies (CJP), would follow. Eventually, the clergy and the congregation would become active advocates for gay rights in the larger community.[4]

Another concern in these years was rebalancing the demographic composition of the congregation. For most of Temple Israel's history, the preponderance of members had been families with school-aged children. By the 1990s, however, the balance had shifted; in 1992, more than half the members were over the age of sixty, despite the steady growth and reputation of the religious school and the increasingly lively worship experience.[5]

This issue was addressed by a new initiative designed to attract and serve the needs of families with preschool-aged children, a population that had traditionally been slow to affiliate with synagogues. In 1988, Board President Fran Putnoi appointed an ad hoc committee to study the feasibility of a temple nursery school. Chaired by member Edith Sperber, the committee's goals were to attract younger members, take advantage of underutilized synagogue space, and bring in faculty who might also teach in the religious school. While the nursery school concept was not new (it had been raised in the 1930s, the 1950s, and the 1970s), earlier proposals had always been rejected due to competing priorities and considerable cost. This time, however, the board approved the project — *if* it could be accomplished "with-

Ann Abrams, Temple Israel's first full-time librarian, has made the Dr. Arnold L. Segal Library Center an active and welcoming place (bottom, Ellen and Harold Wald Children's Library; right, annual book fair, 1989). (Courtesy of Temple Israel Archives)

out drawing on the temple's operating budget and only if 'seed money' was obtained to fully cover the cost of renovations and startup expenses."[6]

When an initial gift from Dr. John and Bette Cohen was followed by a substantial donation from Murray Jacobson, a grant from the Richard Smith Foundation, and many other gifts, renovations to the education wing's basement began. Helen Cohen, Temple Israel's primary grades coordinator and the director of Congregation Kehillath Israel's highly regarded preschool in Brookline, was hired as the director, and the Frances Jacobson Early Childhood Center (FJECC) opened its doors in the fall of 1994 with sixty-eight children. In addition to proving valuable to the temple's educational programming, the FJECC's award-winning curriculum brought many young families into Temple Israel.[7]

WOMEN AND SPIRITUALITY

The new emphases on inclusiveness, community, and spirituality mirrored larger trends in the Reform movement and elsewhere. The women's movement, for example, had inspired feminist demands for the ordination of

Frances Jacobson Early
Childhood Center in the
1990s. Top: *Rabbi Ruth
Alpers teaching; Students
celebrating Shabbat;*
bottom: *Director Helen
Cohen greeting student,
1994; Rabbi Bernard
Mehlman chanting from
the Megillah, 1996.*
(Courtesy of Temple
Israel Archives)

Susan Abramson became Temple Israel's first rabbinic intern in 1978. One of the first fifty American women ordained (HUC–JIR, 1981), Abramson, now the longest-serving female rabbi in Massachusetts, became the rabbi of Temple Beth Shalom Emeth in Burlington in 1984. (Courtesy of Rabbi Susan Abramson)

women that were realized in 1973 when Sally Priesand became the first female rabbi ordained at HUC–JIR. Feminism also spawned a growing body of scholarly work that specifically addressed the relationship between women and Judaism. As more women entered the clergy, the changing gender balance began to reshape ritual practice and the style of rabbinical leadership.[8]

Rabbis Mehlman and Friedman had always supported women's efforts to participate more fully in all facets of synagogue leadership. Soon after his arrival in 1978, Mehlman had invited Susan Abramson, who had grown up in the congregation, to serve as the temple's first rabbinic intern; as such, she became the first woman to serve in a rabbinic capacity at Temple Israel. In the 1980s, as more women took on leadership positions, and services became more informal, the synagogue adopted increasingly non-hierarchical, gender-neutral liturgical language. In 1988, Fran Putnoi became the temple's first female board president. Thus, in 1990, when Associate Rabbi William Berkowitz accepted a pulpit in Portland, Maine, Mehlman thought it timely to consider the "advisability of the selection of a young woman" to replace him. The clergy chose Rabbi Elaine Zecher, a 1988 graduate of HUC–JIR who was working as a program director at Stoughton's Striar Jewish Community Center. "A young woman of high standards," Zecher was also a "seasoned candidate."[9]

The arrival of Temple Israel's first woman rabbi had a profound impact on the congregation. When Rabbi Zecher was installed by her sister, Rabbi

Deborah Zecher, many women, in particular, were deeply moved by the symbolism of the event. Zecher's presence catalyzed congregants to reconsider gender issues in the context of spirituality and community. As she later recalled, "There was a different kind of need in terms of learning, scholarship, and connection that women wanted through their spiritual leader." Some female members, eager to study Judaism from a gendered perspective, asked the new rabbi to help form a women's study group (still in existence). In the fall of 1991, the seeds planted by this and two additional study groups blossomed when feminist historian Ellen Umansky became the first female Burstein scholar. The following spring, the women's study groups organized the first Women's Kallah, a Shabbat worship and learning experience designed for and led by women, which became an annual event.[10]

In turn, the Women's Kallah inspired temple-wide liturgical experimentation with the goal of helping members "feel that they're connecting spiritually, to something beyond themselves, to the community as a whole." Often introduced by Rabbi Zecher, but encouraged by the clergy as a whole, such innovations were sometimes incorporated into Qabbalat Shabbat and holiday services. After one successful Women's Kallah experiment, for example, Zecher suggested bringing the Torah out of the Sukkah on Simchat Torah and unrolling it around the sanctuary, a ritual that has since become a popular tradition.[11]

Soon after her arrival, Rabbi Zecher established a Learner's Minyan to help congregants understand the structure of the Shabbat service. She also extended the Shabbat is for Kids program (established by children's dance company director and temple member Jeanne Traxler in 1986) and instituted another Sabbath program called Teenie Tiny Tots. In 1992, with the help of David Freeman and others, she instituted a monthly "Tefillat Refuat Hanefesh" (Service for the Healing of the Soul). Five years later, Rabbi Zecher, future board president Carol Michael (2007–2009), and others established "Heneinu," a community-building project designed to encourage members to "be present for one another in times of joy and sadness." Trained Heneinu volunteers led lay shiva services, visited the sick, and distributed candy for wedding blessings at services.[12]

ENVISIONING THE TEMPLE'S FUTURE

By the mid-1980s, the proliferation of targeted programs at Temple Israel had led to a corresponding expansion in staff and budget. Between 1985 and 1986 alone, the "increased services for the Congregation" raised expenses by

Rabbi Elaine S. Zecher and Spiritual Engagement

Raised in Monroeville, Pennsylvania, Elaine S. Zecher (1961–) graduated from Brandeis University in 1983 and was ordained at HUC–JIR in
1988. For the next two years, she was the program director at the Striar
Jewish Community Center in Stoughton, Massachusetts. In 1989, she
married Dr. David Eisenberg; they had three children: Jacob, Benjamin,
and Naomi.

Rabbi Zecher was hired as Temple Israel's first female rabbi in 1990.
Zecher has been deeply committed to creating spirituality through
individual engagement and community. After establishing an ongoing healing service at Temple Israel and then incorporating a healing
prayer into the regular service, she became the principal investigator for
a CCAR healing project. Her creative approach to liturgy as a means of
helping every participant create sacred space has earned her a national
reputation.

Rabbi Zecher was a significant contributor to Synagogue 2000 and
remains active in Synagogue 3000, national projects to revitalize congregational life. She was instrumental in the
preparation and publication of the Reform
movement's innovative prayer book, *Mishkan
T'filah — A Reform Siddur* (2007), serving as
an editor on both the editorial committee and
the production task force. Zecher is also the
chair of the CCAR's Worship and Practices
Committee.

(Photos by Ellen
Shub; courtesy
of Temple Israel
Archives)

(Courtesy of Temple Israel Archives)

ten percent. It was difficult to maintain a balanced budget, and the temple once again began to experience regular deficits. Because the majority of the trustees agreed with long-standing treasurer Sumner Rodman that "we must pay the price" to maintain "our pre-eminent position in Reform Jewry," the board launched a $4.5 million capital campaign in 1986 to build an endowment that would "guarantee the progressive and responsive direction in which we have been moving." Led by Fran and Donald (Don) Putnoi, the "Campaign for Temple Israel" was designed to set the institution on a firm, long-term financial foundation and to fund long-deferred maintenance.[13]

When leaks requiring major repairs were discovered in the clerestory behind the sanctuary choir loft in 1988, Rabbi Mehlman encouraged the board to allot capital campaign funds for a full-fledged sanctuary renovation. Like Rabbi Gittelsohn, Rabbi Mehlman saw the sanctuary as "the container in which the drama and content of our liturgy is realized," and he hoped to create a more intimate worship setting. He believed that removing the choir loft, installing a larger lectern at the front of the bima to be shared by the rabbi and cantor, and placing the choir next to the bima, facing the congregation, would improve participation and encourage dialogue. When some members who had a "strong preference for a 'hidden' choir" expressed concerns about exposing the singers, the renovations committee proposed adding a divider that would partially hide them. Completed in 1990, the new configuration, designed by architect and temple member Claude Menders, fulfilled Rabbi Mehlman's desire for a sanctuary that reflected "the new directions which our worship has taken." The capital campaign funded this renovation and much-deferred maintenance, with the remainder placed in the endowment.[14]

The congregation's balance sheet would be more significantly improved in 1989, when decades of negotiations with MASCO (Medical Academic and Scientific Community Organization, Inc.) for a long-term lease of the

Renovated sanctuary, 1991. (Photo by Wayne Soverns, Jr., Architectural Photography; courtesy of Temple Israel Archives)

Berners Square parking lot were successfully concluded. The land lease would ensure Temple Israel a regular, dependable, and sizable income stream for ninety-nine years. In 1991, MASCO opened a 300,000-square-foot mixed-use building on the site with a day care center, 60,000 square feet of office and retail space, and parking for 750 cars.[15]

By the beginning of the 1990s, Temple Israel's numerous targeted programs and activities, the sanctuary renovation, and increased financial confidence had engendered a feeling of positive energy that many attributed to Rabbi Mehlman and his clergy team. In 1986, the congregation had expressed

Berners Square parking lot; MASCO parking garage. (Courtesy of Temple Israel Archives and MDS/Miller Dyer Spears Inc.)

Temple Israel clergy, 1991:
Cantor Roy Einhorn, Rabbi
Elaine Zecher, Rabbi Ronne
Friedman, Rabbi Bernard
Mehlman. (Photo by Gary
Goodman; courtesy of
Temple Israel Archives)

its appreciation for the senior rabbi by granting him life tenure, with the option of early retirement (after age fifty-six) to pursue an academic career. In addition to his ongoing rabbinic role, Temple Educator Rabbi Friedman had brought national recognition to the congregation's educational programs (later highlighted in Joseph Reimer's *Succeeding at Jewish Education* [1997]). Cantor Einhorn was much admired for his engaging and accessible cantorial style, as well as his skillful management of the b'nai mitzvah preparation program. Rabbi Zecher rounded out the "dream team" with her creative approach to spirituality and innovative programming.[16]

But the future of this particular clergy team soon became an issue. In the fall of 1990, Rabbi Friedman, whose contract would expire in June 1991, decided that "it was time for him to return to a full-time pulpit as a senior rabbi." He had stayed at Temple Israel for twelve years because he and Rabbi Mehlman enjoyed working together; however, at the age of forty-four, Friedman felt that he had come to a "crossroads in his rabbinate." With "continued enthusiasm for the type of rabbinate he and Rabbi Mehlman have jointly created," Friedman, with his mentor's full support, proposed that he become "co-rabbi" and succeed Mehlman when he retired.[17]

In November 1990, President Putnoi formed an ad hoc committee, chaired by Richard Berkman (board president, 1997–1999), to consider this unprecedented arrangement. After much debate, the committee proposed that Friedman's new contract include a provision that the trustees vote by April 1993 "whether or not to recommend to the Congregation that it make a commitment to you . . . with the right to succeed Rabbi Mehlman . . . as Senior Rabbi." The board approved the contract in July 1991.[18]

In February 1992, when Friedman initiated the process of enacting the contract provision, the board held "parlor meetings" to discuss the "succession" issue. These conversations quickly revealed a number of conflicting views. Many trustees saw the idea of a "co-rabbinate" as an innovative and exciting way to affirm the temple's direction and showcase its leadership in the Reform movement. Others, including many who admired the rabbis, found the proposal problematic because they believed the process of rabbinic succession itself was at stake. According to tradition and the temple bylaws, rabbis were to be hired through an open search; no rabbi "had a right to select his own successor." In addition, the rabbinic search process, one of the board's most significant responsibilities, had historically proved an important opportunity for the congregation to assess priorities and rethink its future. Some believed that the proposed "co-rabbinate" would require a change in the bylaws; others felt that the arrangement was too open-ended (this objection would be removed in April when Mehlman stated his intention to retire in 1997).[19]

With the proposal under consideration, the debate inevitably came to feel like a personal referendum on the rabbis rather than a discussion of policy, and it became clear that there were disparate views about the rabbis' style of leadership and the process of governance. Many of these divisions harkened back to the late 1970s, when some members' dismay at Rabbi Gittelsohn's departure was exacerbated by the alacrity with which Rabbi Mehlman implemented institutional change. Others emerged in the 1980s, when the Gittelsohn-era classical Reform style of worship that many members enjoyed was phased out. In light of these concerns, some board members saw the proposal for the co-rabbinate as confirmation that the current rabbis did not respect the historic balance of power between board and clergy. Proponents, on the other hand, felt that a co-rabbinate arrangement would maintain and strengthen the positive direction of the congregation.[20]

In April 1992, the board voted forty to thirty-three to recommend Friedman's proposal to the congregation for a vote at a special June meeting. Congregants, however, turned out to be as conflicted as the board. Some resented the suggestion than they "rubber-stamp" the board's recommendation, and many were confused and upset by a series of rancorous mass mailings sent out by advocates for both sides, including past presidents and influential lay leaders. Supporters of the proposal argued that the choice hinged on the question of continuity of leadership: "Do you or do you not want to continue the kind of Rabbinic leadership we have had for the last

Since 1991, the Marilyn Grossman Café has offered an inviting atmosphere for Sunday morning conversation, meetings, and relaxation. Proceeds support the Kurson Transportation Fund. (Courtesy of Temple Israel Archives)

NEWELL & ELEANOR KURSON TRANSPORTATION FUND

Do You Need a Ride to Temple?

We Can Help!

fifteen years?" Opponents also lobbied for continuity—the continuity of precedent, contending that process should be more important than individuals in matters of policy. Both groups truly believed they were acting in the best interest of the synagogue.[21]

At the special meeting on June 16, after several hours of debate, the final vote was cast. When the ballots were counted, 736 had voted in favor of the proposal and 848 against. With the outcome determined, Board President Robert Hoffman (1991–1994), Rabbi Friedman, Rabbi Mehlman, and many others spoke eloquently about reuniting and healing the congregation. "This is not the first, and it will not be the last time the congregation wrestles with a difficult issue and makes a difficult choice," a former board president, Gerald Holtz (1985–1988), observed. "We must go forward in a spirit of acceptance" and "a spirit of cooperation." Accepting the defeat with extraordinary grace, Rabbi Friedman held himself, "rather than others, accountable." He would remain at Temple Israel for another two years before becoming senior rabbi at Temple Beth Zion in Buffalo, New York.[22]

"TOGETHER FOR THE COMMON GOOD"

In the days after the annual meeting, as one congregant recalled, "Life went on as usual, but with much less enthusiasm and great sadness." President

*Students at the 1991
Maccabiah, an annual
religious school event in
which teams competed
for medals in games and
activities. (Courtesy of
Temple Israel Archives)*

Hoffman urged members to "reach out in a spirit of partnership to those who differed" and come "together for the common good." By the fall, he and the board had agreed to establish a "Unity Commission" and a Long-Range Planning Committee to work toward these goals.[23]

The Unity Commission, co-chaired by Harry Hauser and Richard Berkman, addressed concerns relating to governance, decision-making, and communication. The eighteen volunteers "of proven ability and diverse opinions" conducted a study that confirmed members' perennial concerns about poor communication between the rabbi and the board and among board members, as well as between the board and the congregation. The commission's final report urged trustees to become more involved in the daily life of the temple so they could better appreciate the range of members' needs. It also recommended that the clergy work more closely with lay leaders and staff "for advice and consultation" and make a greater effort to communicate "new directions" to the congregation as a whole through Friday evening sermons and announcements, a column in the monthly bulletin, and special mailings.[24]

The issue of open channels of communication between the clergy and board, already a sensitive point, was reignited in the fall of 1992 when Rabbi Friedman performed a public blessing for a same-sex couple at an evening Shabbat service in advance of the temple's first gay commitment ceremony. The rabbis saw setting such precedents as a clergy prerogative, but some trustees felt that the clergy's decision to act without either consulting or informing the board repeated a problematic governance pattern. If lay leaders were to serve as representatives of and ambassadors to the congregation, some trustees believed, they needed foreknowledge of potentially controversial issues. President Hoffman established an ad hoc committee, chaired by Richard Goldman and Laurel Friedman (chair of the Temple Committee), to respond to the feelings expressed and to study issues concerning gay and lesbian Jews in the synagogue. The committee's report emphasized the need for educational programming and respect for opinions on all sides.[25]

The Unity Commission also recommended changes to the temple's governance structure that were designed to streamline the board's work, including a clear succession plan for the presidency through the new position of first vice president. As president-elect, the first vice president would work with the president during his or her (now) two-year term. An Executive Committee would handle day-to-day matters so that the larger board of trustees could focus on important policy issues. These proposals, and another new bylaw amendment permitting absentee ballots, were adopted at the annual meeting in 1993.[26]

The 1993 slate of officers was carefully selected. Genevieve Wyner, who had more than thirty years of experience on temple committees, including the PTA (Parent-Teacher Association), the Public Relations Committee, the Friends Campaign, and the Unity Commission, was nominated for president; James (Jim) Segel was proposed for first vice president. Both were admirers of the clergy and their innovations, but Wyner had also felt strongly about the need to maintain congregational control over the rabbinic selection process. Promising "a very open administration," she urged congregants to "celebrate diversity and see it as a strength."[27]

The preliminary report of the Long-Range Planning Committee was unveiled that November. Chaired by Paula Brody and Merrill Hassenfeld, the committee had conducted extensive member surveys; among other findings, it confirmed that people joined Temple Israel looking for community and spirituality. The committee pinpointed a number of goals: understanding more clearly the temple's constituency groups and providing more opportunities for interactions among them; improving communications with members and responding to their concerns, needs, and desires; and offering worship and nonworship programs that would serve the entire congregation.[28]

The committee also noted a decrease in membership that created a pressing need for greater economies, as well as new approaches to marketing
and fund-raising. "It is up to the Board," the report observed, "to enforce
the necessary discipline." In 1995, the trustees responded by hiring a new
executive director, Daniel Soyer. Three years later, with the help of a new
part-time development director, the temple would embark on a campaign
that raised one million dollars for renovating the library, the administrative
wing, and lobby; moving the Wyner Museum; and installing a service eleva-
tor near the Longwood Avenue entrance. In 2000, the temple would receive
the largest gift in its history from Melvin Nessel.[29]

The Long-Range Planning Committee's findings reflected concerns that
had been reiterated for decades. Despite the fact that the synagogue touted
its success at creating community, many older and younger congregants continued to feel that their needs were not fully addressed. Meeting such needs
in an inclusive way was a central goal of all American Reform synagogues
in the 1990s as they tried to balance tradition and innovation. The perennial focus on services, for example, reflected the deeply symbolic nature of
the worship experience and the meanings attached to ritual. Most temples
experimented with a variety of worship opportunities. Like Temple Israel,
a majority of Reform synagogues had increased the proportion of Hebrew
prayers in the liturgy and added new rituals that responded to the increasing demand for "tangible symbols rooted in Jewish memory." Some larger
congregations chose to offer multiple Shabbat services of different types, led
by clergy members in rotation. But the Temple Israel clergy rejected that
model in favor of offering a single service each Shabbat—predominantly
the Qabbalat Shabbat, but sometimes the more formal later service—so
that the clergy and the entire congregation could gather as a community.[30]

In May 1993, a joint meeting of the Unity Commission and the board to
air this issue made it clear that members continued to hold strong views
about the timing, duration, location, format, tone, music, and content
(including sermons) of the Friday night service. Taken individually, these
concerns "might seem trivial," but as a group, they "define for many the
spirituality of the service." The issue was turned over to the Temple Committee, which recommended a three-month experiment for late 1994; both
Qabbalat Shabbat (at 5:45) and traditional services (at 8:00) would be held,
with an Oneg Shabbat in between. In the end, however, the board voted
the following September to make the Qabbalat Shabbat service a weekly
event, after which it became, in effect, the primary service. By 1996, the

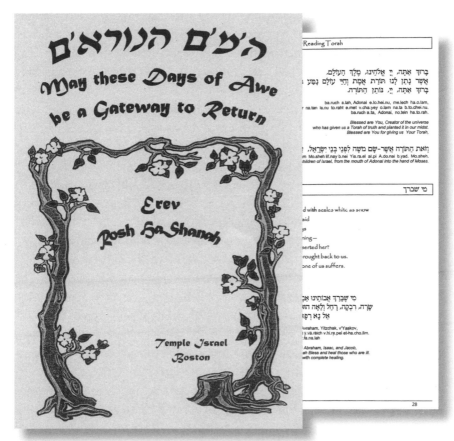

Erev Rosh Hashanah Purple (formerly "D") Service, 2006, cover and page 28, with English prayers and translations by member Edie Aronowitz Mueller. (Courtesy of Temple Israel Archives)

monthly 7:45 family service had also been folded into the Qabbalat service. "Late" services, many of which included special lectures or other programs, were held approximately twice per month in the fall and spring. Each year, however, fewer were scheduled, and by September 1997, the late service had been discontinued.[31]

In its place, a variety of other services that addressed the needs of specific groups were introduced, mostly at Rabbi Zecher's instigation. By the mid-1990s, the annual Women's Kallah (1992), the monthly healing service, and Shabbat is for Kids had been joined by Shul Within a Shul, a ten-week Shabbat workshop for twelve families with children. The Winter Kallah, a day-long event including worship and education for all congregants, initiated in 1995 by the Men's Study Group, was endowed by Paula Brody and Merrill

Hassenfeld in 1996. In 1998, Rabbi Zecher and the rabbinic intern, Jeremy Morrison, with much creative input from members Susan Levin and Edie Mueller, developed an "experiential and experimental" High Holy Day service called the "D Service" ("D" for "different"). Now referred to as the "Purple Service," the liturgy continues to evolve.[32]

The 1993 self-studies encouraged other initiatives designed to help those who "felt abandoned due to the emphasis on young families, children, singles, [and] Russian families" feel more connected to the temple. Vivienne Kalman established Adult Outlook (1992), which offered weekday study groups, arranged for lectures by Rabbis Gittelsohn and Zecher, and operated a monthly "drop-in" lounge for older members. These activities, along with ongoing Brotherhood and Sisterhood programs, did much to alleviate the "sense of alienation and frustration" in this cohort. In 1996, the Grossman Caring Community and the Newell Kurson Transportation Services created "Home for Life" programs for seniors who were housebound. The FJECC connected the temple's oldest with its youngest members through Generational Link, a volunteer program that brought seniors into the classroom to serve as occasional aides.[33]

Two major Wyner Museum exhibitions also reinforced a sense of community while strengthening the bonds between different age groups. In 1994, Helene Bailen and others installed "Mazel Tov! 140 Years of Weddings at Temple Israel," an exhibition that incorporated cherished memories and artifacts from many generations of members and paid tribute to a central event in their lives. In 1995, Fran Putnoi, Susan Porter, Barbara Levy, and others, in conjunction with the Jewish Women's Archives, embarked on an oral history project in which thirty-two women over the age of eighty were interviewed by a committed group of younger women. The life stories of the older women inspired "Women Whose Lives Span the Century," a project that resulted in two complementary exhibitions. "Reflections," at the Wyner Museum in 1998–1999, focused on the "universal and unique themes" that ran through the interviews, using the women's "own words, photographs, documents and personal artifacts in a richly-textured evocation of their experiences." "Contemporary Artistic Interpretations," at the Levanthal-Sidman Jewish Community Center's Starr Gallery in Newton in 1998 (later installed in Temple Israel's Smith Lobby), featured artwork by female artists that was inspired by the women's oral histories.[34]

The Continuing Education Committee, long led by Steve Subrin, helped to integrate disparate groups through study and learning. In 1994, the com-

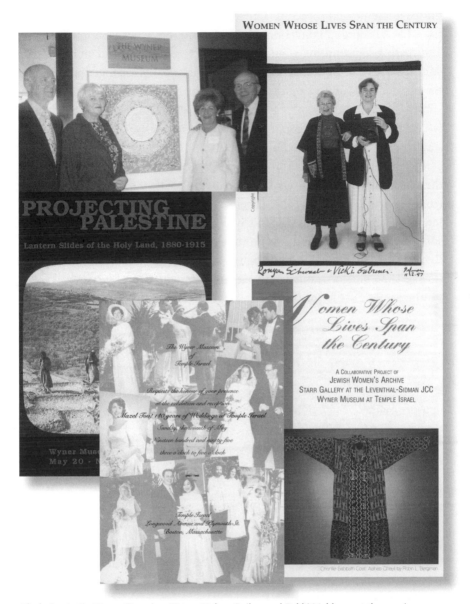

Clockwise: Justin Wyner, Genevieve Wyner, Helene Bailen, and Rabbi Mehlman at the opening of "Mazel Tov! 140 Years of Weddings at Temple Israel," 1994; "Women Whose Lives Span the Century," 1998–1999; invitation to "Mazel Tov!"; "Projecting Palestine," 2001. In 1986, a naming gift from Justin and Genevieve Wyner funded a permanent museum at Temple Israel to display the Sisterhood's collection of Judaica and rotating temporary exhibitions. The Museum and Cultural Affairs Committees, led over the years by Fran Putnoi, Barbara Levy, Harriet Greenfield, Carole Diamond, and Pam Goodman, have overseen a variety of historical and cultural exhibitions in the Wyner Museum. (Courtesy of Temple Israel Archives)

mittee implemented the Long-Range Planning Committee's recommendation that continuing education programs adopt a cohesive annual theme. The yearly programming would alternate between a focus on an historical/ cultural topic and a book of the Torah. The first year, the congregation commemorated the temple's 140th anniversary by studying the history of Judaism from the founding of Temple Israel (1854) through the Dreyfus Affair (1898); the next year, the congregation studied Genesis. Successful from the start, the program remained intact for almost a decade.[35]

In September 1993, with numerous adult education initiatives under way, the temple was able to hire a family educator with the help of a donation from members John and Bette Cohen and a grant from the Commission on Jewish Continuity (a joint CJP and Synagogue Council effort). The first person selected, Aviva Scheur, was promoted to interim temple educator when Rabbi Friedman moved to Buffalo in 1994. In 1997, the family educator position became budget-funded, and Meir Sherer, who would serve until 2005, was hired. One of Sherer's duties was to implement Kesher, a voluntary pro-

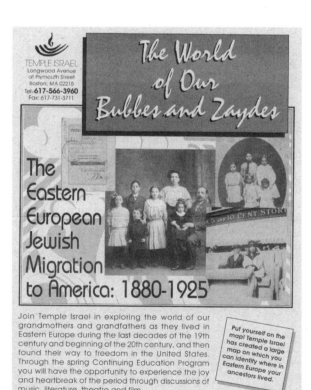

Announcement for 1996– 1997 continuing education program. (Courtesy of Temple Israel Archives)

Family educator Meir Sherer
and a young congregant,
Purim 2004. (Photo by
Allan E. Dines; courtesy of
Temple Israel Archives)

gram sponsored by the Jewish Family Connection, for religious school families with children in grades two through seven. Parents were encouraged to study topics related to their children's curriculum on Sunday mornings. Periodically the adults and children would come together to learn in family groups.[36]

These and other programs, as well as holiday and life-cycle events, were well attended by the temple's growing interfaith population. Many non-Jewish partners increasingly played vital roles on temple committees. In 1992, the Outreach Committee, chaired by Susan Levin, had established an interfaith havurah that offered lectures, services, and counseling. Two years later, she and Paula Brody set up a task force to examine the role of non-Jews in temple governance with the goal of aligning the bylaws with synagogue practice. It studied other Reform temples, reviewed UAHC policies, and held open forums for members. After much debate, the majority recommended that, as the congregational vote was the "bottom line of membership," all members, including non-Jewish partners, should have voting privileges. But they agreed that board membership and committee chairmanships should be reserved for Jewish members. This balance, approved at the 1997 annual meeting, would encourage "participation in temple activities of the entire family" while keeping governance in the hands of "members of the Jewish faith."[37]

THE "ALTNEU" RABBI

In June 1998, Rabbi Mehlman announced his intention to retire in August 1999. Determined to ensure a thorough, open search process for the new senior rabbi, President Richard Berkman appointed former board president

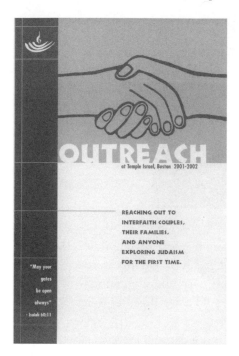

Program detailing interfaith outreach opportunities at Temple Israel, 2001–2002. (Courtesy of Temple Israel Archives)

Jim Segel (1995–1997), who had done a remarkable job of consensus building during his tenure, to chair the search committee. After holding a series of open forums to discuss future directions for Temple Israel and expectations for the senior rabbi, the committee codified the congregation's core values as "worship, lifelong education, social justice, diversity, community, dedication to continuity, and excellence." The search committee would look for a leader to personify these values, attract young families—particularly the unaffiliated and intermarried—and collaborate effectively with other clergy, lay leaders, and staff.[38]

Despite the CCAR's observation that "serving as senior rabbi of a large, urban temple is not the 'be all and end all' that it used to be," and the fact that several other large urban congregations were also engaged in searches, a number of applicants, including Rabbi Ronne Friedman, decided to apply for the position. When the applications had been reviewed and the finalists interviewed, it was clear that Friedman, a seasoned senior rabbi who had "proved himself in Buffalo and emerged as a major voice in Reform Judaism," was "unquestionably the strongest" candidate.[39]

At a special congregational meeting in March 1999, Rabbi Friedman was elected as senior rabbi of Temple Israel. Friedman acknowledged his unique

Simchat Torah, 1999. (Photo by Gary Goodman; courtesy of Temple Israel Archives)

situation in his acceptance speech. "I am the Altneu Rabbi," he noted, "and this is my Altneuschul" (a reference to Prague's "Alt Neu" [Old-new] synagogue). "I am the same and different five years later and so is Temple Israel," he observed. "This synagogue, if it is to be an Altneu Schul, a place which cherishes the past and nourishes the future, must enable each individual member of every Jewish family to discover here the holy spark that he or she possesses." Friedman hoped to "create an environment in which the individual Jew and the community of which he/she is a part will explore Jewish civilization as a treasure trove of values, traditions and behaviors through which meaning and purpose, comfort and connectedness, joy and hope may be discovered." Delighted to be "once again home," he hoped to be "available and accessible as a teacher, a mentor/model, counselor and 'professional friend,'" and to create "a genuine partnership between the rabbi and lay leadership."[40]

Upon his arrival in September 1999, Rabbi Friedman asked lay leaders, clergy, and administrative staff to focus on ways to increase inclusiveness and build community. Board President Elizabeth (Liz) Levin (1999–2001) had already established a strategic planning committee to study "the internal and external environments" of the synagogue and to ensure that clergy and board initiatives aligned with members' needs. In addition, a transition

Quabbalat Shabbat service,
2001. (Photo by Gary
Goodman; courtesy of
Temple Israel Archives)

committee had arranged a series of parlor meetings where the new rabbi could greet and converse with congregants.[41]

By December, Friedman was ready to present several new proposals designed to move "our Congregation to a new place." Some originated with members; others reflected the realities of an institution struggling to meet its financial obligations. All were seen as ideas to be discussed and considered rather than as faits accomplis. "We must embrace change," Friedman observed, "and use it to create new opportunities." The projects included reintroducing occasional classical Reform evening services with a sermon, opening a midweek satellite Hebrew school in a western suburb, and expanding upon an earlier concept for a program for post-college young adults.[42]

Rabbi Friedman was determined to address the needs of the entire congregation. When the Strategic Planning Committee's survey clearly indicated, for example, that many members still pined for the late Friday evening service, "an adult service replete with a classical sermon" was reinstated on a monthly basis. Meanwhile, the weekly 5:45 Qabbalat Shabbat service, with its guitar and tambourine accompaniment, became so popular that it eventually outgrew the atrium and had to be moved into the sanctuary.[43]

Rabbi Friedman also modified the clergy's approach to interfaith weddings. Despite Rabbi Mehlman's recognition of the need to create a liturgy that would "acknowledge the special relationship non-Jewish partners accept as they enter life in the Jewish community," he could not in conscience preside over an interfaith marriage ceremony. Rabbi Friedman had arrived at a different conclusion in Buffalo, and when he returned he established more inclusive guidelines for interfaith couples who wished to be married by Temple Israel clergy. While these guidelines allowed each member of the clergy to follow his or her own conscience, they also reflected

Ronne Friedman

Raised in Washington, D.C., Ronne Friedman (1947–) earned a B.A. from Lafayette College in 1969. He matriculated at HUC–JIR and served as a rabbinic intern with Rabbi Bernard Mehlman in 1971–1972 at the Interfaith Metropolitan Theological Education, Inc., in Washington, D.C. Friedman married Irene Neumann, an industrial designer, in 1972. They had two sons, Jesse and Zachary. After studying at Jerusalem's Hebrew University in 1974–1975, Friedman earned a master's degree and was ordained at HUC–JIR in 1975. Upon graduation he became assistant rabbi at North Shore Congregation Israel in Glencoe, Illinois.

In 1978, Rabbi Friedman was hired by Rabbi Mehlman as associate rabbi of Temple Israel; in 1983 he also became the temple educator. In addition to his work on Jewish education, Rabbi Friedman was deeply engaged in the resettlement of Southeast Asian and Soviet Jewish immigrants, the establishment of interfaith dialogue, the pursuit of social justice, and the advancement of equity issues. In 1994, he left to become the senior rabbi at Temple Beth Zion in Buffalo, New York.

In 1999, Rabbi Friedman returned to Temple Israel as senior rabbi; he was granted life tenure in 2004. During his rabbinate, he has fostered the development of social action programs and outreach to young Jews, interfaith couples, and gays and lesbians. Friedman has served on many URJ and CCAR committees as well as other boards. He has been the chair of the Joint Rabbinical Placement Commission of the UAHC, CCAR, and HUC–JIR.

Rabbi Ronne Friedman
(Courtesy of Temple Israel Archives)

changing demographic realities and resolved an issue that had caused angst among members for many years.[44]

A proposal to open a satellite religious school campus was intended to address the fact that, by 1998, the majority of families were choosing to have their children tutored in Hebrew at home rather than sending them to Hebrew classes at the temple on Tuesdays and Thursdays. When a temple committee investigated the idea, however, it became clear that, while a suburban campus would decrease the commute for many families, it would not solve the fundamental problem: families at Temple Israel (and elsewhere) found a three-day-per-week Hebrew schedule onerous. In 2002, therefore, the temple eliminated Thursday classes, extended class time on Tuesdays and Sundays, and commenced the program in second rather than third grade. The change had the desired effect; in the first year, more than half the students being tutored enrolled in Hebrew classes, where they could learn while building relationships with other Jewish children.[45]

Rabbi Friedman's proposed outreach program for young, unaffiliated Jews took shape in 2001, when newly ordained Rabbi Jeremy Morrison, who had grown up at Temple Israel and served as youth director from 1993 to 1995, was hired to lead the initiative. Both had been interested in this issue for years; in fact, Morrison had co-led the "Something Generation" program while youth director. The two imagined an "urban satellite" project in the South End where Jews in their twenties and thirties could develop "a more active and positive Jewish identity." The board agreed to retain Morrison for one year to pilot the program. Ultimately funded by a generous donor, the Riverway Project has successfully deepened hundreds of young Jews' connection to Judaism through study, worship, and social activities. In addition to sponsoring events in the South End and Cambridge, the Riverway Project holds popular programs at the synagogue, including Torah and Tonics, Salsa Under the Sukkah, Riverway Tots, and Soul Food Friday (a well-attended monthly Friday evening worship service and social hour). Many participants have become active members of Temple Israel.[46]

Rabbi Friedman's approach to the Riverway Project exemplified his extraordinary capacity to encourage other people's ideas and work. A strong believer in the collective strength of a "clergy team," his leadership approach has been to serve as the "quarterback who leads by inspiring and enabling others to be the stars." Rabbi Friedman built on the strengths of his preexisting relationships with Rabbi Mehlman, Rabbi Zecher, and Cantor Einhorn to foster connections among the clergy "team" and mentor new clergy

Riverway members at Salsa Under the Sukkah; celebrating Shabbat with Rabbi Morrison. (Courtesy of Temple Israel Archives)

live band • free food

soul food

FRIDAYS

@temple israel
Riverway, Boston

a shabbat service like no other.
validated parking is available in the 375 longwood avenue garage located next to Temple Israel

may 2 • 7:30pm

617.566.3960 • www.riverwayproject.org

to become leaders at the synagogue, in the larger community, and in the Reform movement as a whole.[47]

"A TZEDEK SYNAGOGUE"

In the late 1990s, a determined group of lay leaders pressed the congregation to take a more public role in social action. While Temple Israel had long been involved in various local *tzedekah* projects, including Saturday's/Sunday's Bread, the Greater Boston Food Bank, and the Jewish Coalition for Literacy, the new initiatives would focus on political efforts. In 1998, member Frances (Fran) Godine and others encouraged the congregation to join the newly formed Greater Boston Interfaith Organization (GBIO), a coalition of faith-based organizations designed to build relationships that transcend race, class, geography, and religion and "develop local leadership and organized power to fight for social justice." The next year, Rabbi Jonah Pesner, who had served as an assistant rabbi in Westport, Connecticut, for two years (and had known Rabbi Zecher since he was a teenager at camp), became the new assistant rabbi (1999–2006). Pesner, who had a particular

Temple Israel member Fran Godine and Reverend Burns Stanfield of the Fourth Presbyterian Church, South Boston, at GBIO action, 2006; Rabbi Jonah Pesner and Cantor Roy Einhorn with Catherine D'Amato of the Greater Boston Food Bank, 2005. (Courtesy of GBIO and Temple Israel Archives)

interest in social justice issues, quickly became engaged in social action efforts at Temple Israel and GBIO.[48]

In 2002, with Rabbi Friedman's support, a dedicated Social Action Committee and Rabbi Pesner initiated "Ohel Tzedek" (Tent of Justice), a campaign to determine and act on the congregation's social justice priorities. Rooted in the belief that group action based on shared core values is inherently more powerful than even the most devoted efforts of a single person, Ohel Tzedek was designed to build relationships within the synagogue community and then turn the energy generated into social action. After many "one-on-one" conversations and house meetings that revealed the issues that mattered most to the congregation, action "hevrot" were established: to advocate for affordable housing, support the legal rights of gay and lesbian families, reach out to senior citizens, strengthen interfaith bonds, and help those in career transitions make professional connections. The hevrot would take action in and out of the temple in partnership with other religious organizations. As excitement grew, the initiative spread to other temple arenas. In the religious school, for example, students in grades five through seven, with the support of their families, began to form action teams relating to such issues as homelessness, literacy, and animal rights in preparation for b'nai mitzvah.[49]

Over time, Rabbi Pesner's advocacy for faith-based community building made him a leader in GBIO, where he helped to coordinate campaigns to create an affordable-housing trust, improve working conditions for janitors and nursing-home workers, and initiate statewide health care reform, among others. In 2006, he left Temple Israel to become the founding director of Just Congregations, a grant-funded project at the Union for Reform Judaism designed to disseminate the Ohel Tzedek model among congregations and community groups across North America.[50]

Another long-standing congregational social justice issue came to the fore in 2002 when the Massachusetts Supreme Judicial Court agreed to consider the constitutionality of gay marriage. In keeping with the synagogue's history of support for civil rights, Temple Israel members and the entire clergy team became deeply involved in the campaign to guarantee the right of gay couples to marry. As Rabbi Friedman noted, because "marriage is a

Ohel Tzedek mural by artist Deborah Putnoi. (Courtesy of Temple Israel Archives)

Andrew Sherman and Russell Lopez, one of the many same-sex couples married at Temple Israel in 2004. (Courtesy of Temple Israel Archives)

paradigm for the ideals of cooperation, trust, mutual responsibility, continuity and affection . . . it is no more in the interest of society to deny legal status to same-gender marriages than it would be to abolish heterosexual marriages." In March 2004, after the court ruled in favor of the right of same-sex couples to marry, Friedman officiated at the wedding of Temple Israel's first legally married same-sex couple; by May, the clergy had conducted eleven such marriage ceremonies.[51]

In the aftermath of the September 11, 2001 terrorist attacks, Temple Israel's longtime focus on interfaith dialogue took on new urgency. The clergy and members worked with other religious organizations to guarantee respect for all religious traditions during this difficult time. After Temple Israel, Trinity Church, and the Islamic Society of Boston held a joint memorial prayer service on the first anniversary of the attacks, members Carol Shedd, Edie Mueller, and others helped to establish the Boston Interfaith Dialogue, a "trialogue" to build relationships and learn about each other's traditions. Other initiatives, including multiple partnerships between the temple and the Bethel AME Church in Jamaica Plain, have also helped to further this goal.[52]

At the same time, Temple Israel, like other American synagogues, became more focused on Jewish security issues at home and in Israel. In the 1990s, the American Jewish community had been divided by political events such as the Israeli invasion of Lebanon, the Palestinian intifada, and the ongoing violence between Palestine and Israel. Clergy and congregants alike debated about appropriate ways to support Israel. Most continued to identify strongly with the Jewish state, but, while some saw Israel as a victim of terrorism and accepted the political need to protect its borders, others were convinced that a lasting peace could only be achieved through a two-state solution. During this time, the Temple Israel clergy developed a relationship with Or Hadash, a congregation in Haifa, Israel, Boston's sister city. Initiated in 1991, it has been reinforced over the years through exchanges and trips by staff, members, and students, as well as much-needed financial support from Temple Israel and others in Boston's Reform community. The temple has also been a longtime supporter of Seeds of Peace, an international program that brings Palestinian and Israeli children together at a summer camp in Maine. After 2001, although Temple Israel members continued to express a range of opinions about Israeli politics, fears about terrorism heightened American Jews' determination to support Israel's "quest for peace" in the Middle East.[53]

By 2004, when Temple Israel entered its 150th year, the energy generated by the FJECC, the Riverway Project, Ohel Tzedek, and other initiatives was palpable. For several years, a large committee led by a quartet of experienced temple leaders — Fran Putnoi, Carol Michael, Michele Fishel, and Eleri Dixon — had envisioned and planned a wide range of special events for the sesquicentennial anniversary to commemorate the congregation's

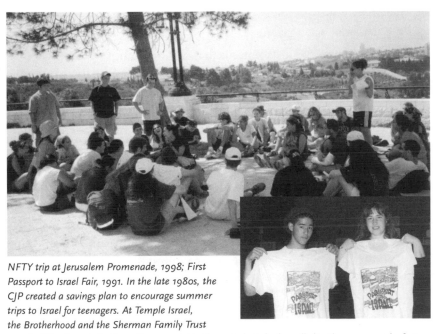

NFTY trip at Jerusalem Promenade, 1998; First Passport to Israel Fair, 1991. In the late 1980s, the CJP created a savings plan to encourage summer trips to Israel for teenagers. At Temple Israel, the Brotherhood and the Sherman Family Trust matched family contributions. By 1993, eighty-three students had enrolled in the program; the first Temple Israel group went to Israel by boat from Greece in 1995. (Courtesy of Temple Israel Archives)

past, celebrate its present, and look toward its future. In 2001, an archivist was hired to process and prepare the temple's archival collections for use in a Wyner Museum exhibition, lectures, and this volume. A capital campaign was initiated to update the building's systems, add classroom and storage space, and fund renovations; still under way, the campaign has raised the funds to transform the 1928 Levi Auditorium into a multipurpose worship and social space. The sesquicentennial celebration, like all such commemorations, highlighted patterns of continuity and change in Temple Israel's long history, strengthened the community, and underscored its long-held core values: "Torah" (learning), "Avodah" (worship), and "G'milut Chasadim" (deeds of loving kindness).[54]

TEMPLE ISRAEL IN 2009

In the years since the sesquicentennial, Temple Israel has continued to be guided by the principles of Torah, Avodah, and G'milut Chasadim. Members have found myriad ways to build relationships and engage in experiences that fulfill Rabbi Ronne Friedman's goal of "touch[ing] the core issues of peoples' lives . . . from the Jewish perspective." In 2009, the synagogue tries to serve as a multipurpose "beit" (house) where every member can find his or her own space. As a "Beit Tefillah" (a house of worship and prayer), Temple Israel creates Jewish worship experiences designed to address contemporary spiritual needs that embrace innovation even as they honor tradition. As a "Beit Midrash" (a house of study and Torah), Temple Israel offers lifelong Jewish learning programs for individuals and families that enrich their lives. As a "Beit Knesset" (a house of caring and action), Temple Israel works at being a welcoming, caring community and encourages the pursuit of justice in the world.[55]

Many of the initiatives of the past decade, including the Riverway Project and outreach to interfaith and gay and lesbian members, continue to advance these congregational goals and foci; Ohel Tzedek, in particular, has become central to the life of the congregation. As of this writing, members are working on several social justice initiatives—Youth and Safety, Aging with Dignity, creating an "internal caring community," and alleviating the suffering of Sudanese genocide victims—all of which are designed to help Temple Israel become a "Tzedek synagogue." Assistant Rabbi Stephanie Kolin, who arrived in 2006, works with these groups to help them forge links with GBIO and other external "action communities."[56]

Clockwise: Women's Kallah brochure, 2005; S'lichot, 2004 (photo by Ellen Shub); Sesquicentennial organizers with entertainer Hershey Felder, 2005; Wyner Museum historical exhibition and poster, 2004. (Courtesy of Temple Israel Archives)

In 2005, recognizing how difficult it had become for volunteer lay leaders to manage the increasingly complex administrative structure of the synagogue, the board of trustees, led by President Dean Richlin (2003–2005), approved, and the congregation ratified, major revisions to the bylaws designed to streamline and improve board operations. The new bylaws reduced the size of the board from more than sixty members to approximately fifteen, who meet monthly to engage in planning with staff and address and respond to issues. The bylaws also established a larger oversight group, the Leadership Council, which meets three times per year. Under the leadership of Presidents Brad Gerratt (2005–2007) and Carol Michael (2007–2009), the new plan has facilitated more efficient budget analysis and planning that has led to significant restructuring of staff positions.

In 2007, due to the generosity of numerous donors to the "Temple Israel Tomorrow" campaign, renovations began that will ultimately transform Temple Israel's physical space to meet the changing needs of the congregation, ensure the integrity of the historic structures, and make the facility more physically accessible. Many years of planning spearheaded by Marc Maxwell (the longtime Buildings and Grounds Committee chair), have culminated in a design by Leers Weinzapfel Associates. The first phase, to transform the Rabbi Harry Levi Auditorium into "a flat-floored, multi-

Temple Israel clergy, 2009: Rabbi Ronne Friedman, Rabbi Stephanie Kolin, Cantor Roy Einhorn, Rabbi Elaine Zecher, Rabbi Jeremy Morrison. (Photo by Ellen Shub, courtesy of Temple Israel Archives)

Renovated Levi Auditorium, 2009. (Courtesy of Marc Maxwell)

function space in which to pray, meet, dance, eat and celebrate," with new restrooms, coatrooms, and a catering kitchen, was completed in the fall of 2008. Further projects include restoring the historic Riverway entrance to the Levi Auditorium, making it and the sanctuary entrance fully accessible, and reconfiguring the chapel and other lower-level spaces. The work also includes safety, energy management, and fire protection improvements, along with other efforts to make the building more "green."[57]

In 2009, Temple Israel represents the growing diversity of Boston's Jewish community. The congregation comprises 1,633 member units with 2,666 adults and 1,271 children — including 600 singles, 417 interfaith families, and 70 gay and lesbian couples. The average adult age is between fifty and sixty, slightly lower than in the past two decades. In part, this change can be attributed to the fact that most of the eighty-four FJECC families and their ninety-eight preschool children are members. Four hundred and seven students attend the religious school. A new study program for members over sixty, the Temple Israel Lifelong Learning Initiative (TILLI), is in its initial year.[58]

There have also been remarkable continuities in Temple Israel's population over the years. Members reside in twenty-five cities and towns in

Dancing with the Torahs on Nessel Way between the temple and the parking garage, Simchat Torah, 2006. (Photo by Ellen Shub, courtesy of Temple Israel Archives)

metropolitan Boston, but, as has been the case for several decades, the majority (currently 81 percent) lives in Brookline, Boston, and Newton. Most members continue to work as professionals in law, medicine, business, and academia. An occupational profile reveals that 190 members are attorneys and 168 are medical professionals, while 88 are presidents or chief executive officers of their own companies.

As in the past, people continue to join synagogues to find "a spiritual home" where they can worship, study, engage in social action and fellowship, and celebrate life-cycle events. Because many of these professionals are women, however, the tone of synagogue life and leadership has changed. Today, members of both genders have the advantage of professional experience as well as the time constraints of full-time work. As the synagogue community becomes increasingly diverse, and members have less time to engage in volunteerism, meeting the varied needs of constituents has become more complex and more costly. But these challenges are not new, nor are they unique.

Over its 155-year history, Temple Israel has continually redefined itself to stay "on top of people's current mentality in order to remain relevant" in the changing context of the Reform movement and the shifting complexities of American life. As in other Reform synagogues, this goal has often required the congregation to "reformulate its theological orientation and rethink its practical implications." The process of "becoming American Jews" has been different for every generation and has had numerous meanings. American Judaism has changed, along with the shifting balance of lay and rabbinic governance and the ongoing tension between observance and assimilation. Even so, at Temple Israel, congregational values as a whole have remained constant: devotion to education and personal development, dedication to social justice, and a fundamental determination to make the synagogue a "second home" for everyone who enters its sacred space.[59]

APPENDIX

CLERGY, LAY LEADERS, AND PROFESSIONAL STAFF
OF TEMPLE ISRAEL, 1854–2009

SENIOR RABBIS

Joseph Sachs (Hazan)	1854–1856
Joseph Shoninger (Hazan)	1856–1874
Solomon Schindler	1874–1894
Charles Fleischer	1894–1911
Harry Levi	1911–1939
Joshua Loth Liebman	1939–1948
Abraham J. Klausner	1949–1953
Roland B. Gittelsohn	1953–1977
Bernard H. Mehlman	1977–1999
Ronne Friedman	1999–

ASSOCIATE & ASSISTANT RABBIS

Samuel Wolk	1923–1929
Lawrence W. Schwartz	1929–1930
Beryl D. Cohon	1930–1939
Leo A. Bergman	1940–1942
David B. Alpert	1943–1946
Albert A. Goldman	1946–1948
Irving A. Mandel	1948–1950
Earl A. Grollman	1950–1951
Maurice L. Zigmund	1951–1954
Leon A. Jick	1954–1957
Robert W. Shapiro	1957–1960
Charles A. Kroloff	1960–1963
Harvey J. Fields	1963–1968
Larry J. Halpern	1967–1970
Frank M. Waldorf	1968–1971
Paul J. Menitoff	1970–1973
James B. Rosenberg	1971–1974
Paul J. Citrin	1974–1978
Ronne Friedman	1978–1983
Jeffrey A. Perry-Marx	1983–1985

William L. Berkowitz	1985–1990
Elaine S. Zecher	1990–
Ruth Alpers	1994–1999
Jonah D. Pesner	1999–2006
Jeremy S. Morrison (Rabbinic Fellow)	2001–
Stephanie D. Kolin	2006–

MUSIC DIRECTORS & CANTORS

Henry L. Gideon (Music director)	1908–1938
Herbert Fromm (Music director)	1941–1972
Cantor Murray Simon	1972–1983
Cantor Roy B. Einhorn	1983–

BOARD PRESIDENTS

Moses Ehrlich	1854–1862
Bernard Heineman	1862–1863
Samuel Strauss	1863–1866
John H. Bendix	1866–1869
H[enry?] Weiss	1869–1870
Charles Morse	1870–1872
John Phillips	1872–1873
John H. Bendix	1873–1876
Charles Morse	1876–1883
Edward S. Goulston, Sr.	1883–1885
Lewis Hecht, Sr.	1885–1902
Jacob Morse	1902–1904
Daniel Frank	1904–1911
Louis Strauss	1911–1915
Jacob R. Morse	1915–1922
Felix Vorenberg	1922–1927

Carl J. Kaffenburgh	1927–1930	Louis Selig (Sexton)	1918–1942
Lee M. Friedman	1931–1942	Louis L. Martinson	1942–1955
Joseph H. Cohen	1942–1954	Bernard I. Pincus	1956–1979
James D. Glunts	1955–1956	Norman Fogel	1979–1983
John Morse, Sr.	1956–1958	Robert Hill	1983–1987
Hirsh Sharf	1958–1961	Deanne Stone	1987–1989
Frank P. Cohen	1961–1964	Leon Rothenberg	1989–1995
Lloyd D. Tarlin	1964–1967	Daniel Soyer	1995–2006
Solomon Stern	1967–1970	Leah Camhi (Interim)	2006–2007
Herman Snyder	1970–1973	William Varnell (Interim)	2007–2008
Morton I. Narva	1973–1976	Jane Doré Krantz	2008–
Milton Linden	1976–1979		
Justin L. Wyner	1979–1982	EDUCATION DIRECTORS	
Herbert Schilder	1982–1985	Samuel Nemzoff	1942–1974
Gerald J. Holtz	1985–1988	David Ginsberg	1974–1975
Frances Stieber Putnoi	1988–1991	Lillian Beauvais	1975–1981
Robert J. Hoffman	1991–1994	Rabbi David Katz	1981–1983
Genevieve Geller Wyner	1994–1995	Rabbi Ronne Friedman	1983–1994
James W. Segel	1995–1997	Aviva Scheur	1994–1996
Richard L. Berkman	1997–1999	Deborah Eisenbach-Budner	1996–2000
Elizabeth Kopp Levin	1999–2001	Aliza Beauvais	2000–2003
Barry Weisman	2001–2003	Lesley Litman	2003–2007
Dean Richlin	2003–2005	Uri Feinberg	2007–
Brad Gerratt	2005–2007		
Carol Brown Michael	2007–2009		
Leah Rosovsky McIntosh	2009–		

SEXTONS & EXECUTIVE DIRECTORS

Mr. Nelson (Shames)	1860–1865
Julius Gottlob (Shames)	
October–December 1865,	
August 1866–December 1870	
J. W. Strauss	1871–1875
(Messenger and Collector)	
Joseph Guggenheim	1875–1903
(Sexton)	
Abraham Guggenheim	1903–1918
(Sexton)	

NOTES TO THE TEXT

CHAPTER 1: THE SYNAGOGUE AND THE COMMUNITY (pp. 1–18)

1. Jonathan D. Sarna, "The Jews of Boston in Historical Perspective," in *The Jews of Boston*, 2nd edition, ed. Jonathan D. Sarna, Ellen Smith, and Scott-Martin Kosofsky (New Haven, Conn.: Yale University Press, 2005), 3–4; Ellen Smith, "Strangers and Sojourners: The Jews of Colonial Boston," in ibid., 21–42.

2. Stephen G. Mostov, "A Sociological Portrait of German Jewish Immigrants in Boston: 1845–1861," *American Jewish Studies Review* (1978): 127–130; Oscar Handlin, *Boston's Immigrants, 1790–1880*, 3rd ed. (Cambridge, Mass.: Harvard University Press, 1979), table VI, "Nativity of Boston, 1850," 243.

3. The origins of Boston's Jewish community are related in Solomon Schindler, *Israelites in Boston: A Tale Describing the Development of Judaism in Boston, Preceded by the Jewish Calendar for the Next Decade* (Boston: Berwick & Smith, [1889]), chap. 1. Although a fire destroyed the synagogue's original records written in German, other sources state that attendees of the initial meeting included William Goldsmith, Moses Ehrlich, Peter Spitz, Himan Spitz, Bernard Fox, Charles Hyneman, Jacob Norton, Isaac Wolf, and Abraham F. Bloch. See S[imon] Simmons, *The History of Temple Ohabei Shalom, Principal Events from Its Organization in 1843, to the Fiftieth Anniversary Celebration on February 26th, 1893* (Boston, 1893), 10–11; Jeannette S. and Abraham E. Nizel, *Congregation Ohabei Shalom: Pioneers of the Boston Jewish Community. An Historical Perspective of the First One Hundred and Forty Years, 1842–1982* (Boston, 1982), 6–8. For more on Ohabei Shalom, see Albert Ehrenfried, *A Chronicle of Boston Jewry* (Boston, 1963), 332–345; Schindler, *Israelites in Boston*, chap. 1; Sarna, "The Jews of Boston in Historical Perspective," 4–5; Smith, "'Israelites in Boston,' 1840–1880," in Sarna, Smith, and Kosofsky, *Jews of Boston*, 48–50; Mostov, "Sociological Portrait," 129, 150. Chevra Ahabath Achim (Society of Brotherly Love) Mutual Aid Society membership lists, in Albert Ehrenfried Papers, Jacob Rader Marcus Center of the American Jewish Archives, Cincinnati Campus, Hebrew Union College-Jewish Institute of Religion, Cincinnati, Ohio [hereafter AJA].

4. Smith, "Israelites in Boston," 52–56; William A. Braverman, "The Ascent of Boston's Jews, 1630–1918" (Ph.D. diss., Harvard University, 1990), 41.

5. U.S. Census (1850), Schedule 1 (Population); *Boston City Directory*, 1853.

6. Barbara Miller Solomon, *Ancestors and Immigrants: A Changing New England Tradition* (Boston: Northeastern University Press, 1989), 5; Ehrenfried, *Chronicle of Boston Jewry*, 337–338; Mostov, "Sociological Portrait," 129. Schindler, *Israelites in Boston*, chap. 1; Leon A. Jick, *The Americanization of the Synagogue* (Waltham, Mass.: Brandeis University Press, 1976), 21–27; Chevra Ahabath Achim Mutual Aid Society membership lists, in Ehrenfried Papers, AJA; *Boston City Directory*, 1853.

7. Jonathan Sarna, *American Judaism: A History* (New Haven: Yale University Press, 2004), 72–73; Leon Jick, *The Americanization of the Synagogue* (Boston: Brandeis University Press), 24–25.

8. Schindler, *Israelites in Boston*, chap. II; Stella Obst, *The Story of Adath Israel* (Boston, 1917), 6–7; Jick, *Americanization of the Synagogue*, 102–103.

9. *Boston Atlas*, 27 March 1854, 1. Ehrenfried, *Chronicle of Boston Jewry*, 347–348. The new congregation passed resolutions to this effect in April 1854 that were published in *Boston Evening Transcript*, 24 May 1854, 2.

10. *Boston Atlas*, 27 March 1854. Ehrenfried, *Chronicle of Boston Jewry*, 371. As no board meeting minutes before 1861 have survived, no further information is available about early members. Obst, *Story of Adath Israel*, 7. Susan Abramson, "History of Temple Adath Israel As Seen Through the Evolution of the Worship Experience" (senior honors thesis: Brandeis University, 1976), 66. Braverman, "Ascent of Boston's Jews," 154–155.

11. For Touro's will, see Ehrenfried, *Chronicle of Boston Jewry*, 269, 274; Morris Schappes, ed., *A Documentary History of the Jews in the United States, 1654–1875* (New York: Citadel Press, 1971), 337 n. 23. *Moses Ehrlich, President, v. Mendez Kursheedt and others*, 1856. State of Louisiana, Second District Court of New Orleans. Supreme Court of Louisiana Legal Archives (Mss 106), New Orleans, 1846–1861, Docket 4604. Louisiana and Special Collections Department, Earl K. Long Library, University of New Orleans, New Orleans, Louisiana [*Ehrlich v. Kursheedt*]. New Orleans lawyer Mendez Kurdsheedt, the defense attorney for the original congregation, was probably related to Touro executor Gershom Kursheedt.

12. Jonathan Sarna states that Bayers used the *Minhag Ashkenazi* rite, while Polanders preferred the *Minhag Polin* rite. Sarna, "The Jews of Boston in Historical Perspective," 5. For plaintiffs' description of services, see Deposition of Isaac Adda, 9 October 1855, in *Ehrlich v. Kursheedt*, 73. For Sachs, see Deposition of Bernard Wurmser, 21 November 1855, in *Ehrlich v. Kursheedt*, 253.

13. For Saroni's nativity, see U.S. Census (1880). As one German wrote, "The so called Polish Congregation consists of Polanders, Hollanders, English, Germans and other nations, and have also adopted the minhag" (*American Israelite*, 8 August 1856). Deposition of Alexander Saroni, 9 November 1855, *Ehrlich v. Kursheedt*, 126–127.

14. Document H, 19 May 1854, in Deposition of Alexander Saroni, 9 November 1855, *Ehrlich v. Kursheedt*, 245. Court records provide details of the bitter conflict, during which some of the plaintiffs characterized their opponents as "crafty" and "treacherous," while several defendants portrayed the seceders as "thieves" and "liars" (Plaintiff's Brief, 3; Defendant's Brief, *Ehrlich v. Kursheedt*, 5, 10). For the final decision, see "Opinion," *Ehrlich v. Kursheedt*, 4.

15. Temple Israel, Board of Trustees Minutes [hereafter Board Minutes], 14 September 1862, in Temple Israel Archives, Boston, Mass. [hereafter TI Archives]. An 1867 criticism of Joseph Shoninger's knowledge of the "Schita" makes it clear that the koshering of meat was important to both his "Honor and Livelihood." Board Minutes, 11 February

1867, 13 February 1867. (All quotations cited from the German-language board minutes are courtesy of Felix Edenfeld's excellent translation and transcription.) Karla M. Goldman, *Beyond the Synagogue Gallery: Finding a Place for Women in American Judaism* (Cambridge, Mass.: Harvard University Press, 2000), 40–59. Obst, *Story of Adath Israel*, 8. An 1882 *Boston Globe* article describing the city's synagogues notes that Adath Israel had 60 member families while Ohabei Shalom had 150 families. Boston's four other synagogues had much smaller memberships. "Jewish Churches," *Boston Globe* [hereafter *Globe*], 24 July 1882, 4.

16. Jick, *Americanization of the Synagogue*, 58; Burton Samuel Kliman, "The Jewish Brahmins of Boston: A Study of the German Jewish Immigrant Experience, 1860–1900" (senior honors thesis: Brandeis University, 1978), 172–173.

17. Jick, *Americanization of the Synagogue*, 58–59; Obst, *Story of Adath Israel*, 8; Schindler, "The History of the Congregation Temple Adath Israel of Boston, Mass.," 1906 typescript timeline of TI history, in Commonwealth Avenue Temple File, Buildings Collection, TI Archives; Bylaws of Temple Israel, 1879–1995, TI Archives; Ehrenfried, *Chronicle of Boston Jewry*, 374, 385–388.

18. Quote from Sarna, *American Judaism*, 80. For Jewish synagogue education, see Jick, *Americanization of the Synagogue*, 62–63 and Goldman, *Beyond the Synagogue Gallery*, 60–63. Joseph Sachs, quoted by Joseph Strauss, in "Letter to the Editor," *American Israelite*, 12 May 1856.

19. "Jewish Synagogues, 'Adath Israel,'" *Boston Herald* [hereafter *Herald*], 10 May 1863; Obst, *Story of Adath Israel*, 8; Sarna, *American Judaism*, 80–81; Joseph Reimer, "Passionate Visions in Contest: On the History of Jewish Education in Boston," in Sarna, Smith, and Kosofsky, *Jews of Boston*, 286. School Committee Report, Board Minutes, 1 June 1862.

20. Sarna, *American Judaism*, 9. Obst states that 37 new members joined between 1859 and 1860 (Obst, *Story of Adath Israel*, 9). Quote from Schindler, *Israelites in Boston*, chap. 1.

21. For minyans, see Board Minutes, 1861–1876; Obst, *Story of Adath Israel*, 8. For consultations, see Board Minutes, 7 November 1863. For other burial rulings, see Board Minutes, 7 May 1876, 18 June 1876. Sections of the original parcel were sold to Congregation Mishkan Israel in 1860 and the United Hebrew Benevolent Association in 1862 to raise money. Adjoining plots were purchased in 1881 and 1914.

22. Board Minutes, 4 September 1870; Ehrenfried, *Chronicle of Boston Jewry*, 361. Board Minutes, 17 September 1865. For the ladies' fair, see Board Minutes, 7 November 1875 and 2 January 1876; "The Jewish Fair," *Globe*, 3 December 1875, 5. See also Goldman, *Beyond the Synagogue Gallery*, 148. For fund drive, see Board Minutes, 4 February 1877.

23. Sarna, "Historical Perspective," 4; "Appendix A: The Jewish Population of Boston," in Sarna, Smith, and Kosofsky, *Jews of Boston*, 343. Mostov, "Sociological Portrait," 137–138, 150; Jick, *Americanization of the Synagogue*, 89. Kliman, "Jewish Brahmins," 172–173.

24. Congregation Mishkan Israel (now Mishkan Tefila), was formed in 1858 by twelve families from Posen who seceded from Ohabei Shalom. David A. Kaufman, "Temples

in the American Athens: A History of the Synagogues of Boston," in Sarna, Smith, and Kosofsky, *Jews of Boston*, 178. Quote from Isaac M. Fein, *Boston—Where it All Began. An Historical Perspective of the Boston Jewish Community* (Boston: Boston Jewish Bicentennial Committee, 1976), 30. Adath Israel continued to collect money for designated charitable causes (Board Minutes, 15 January 1866).

25. Barbara Miller Solomon, *Pioneers in Service: The History of the Associated Jewish Philanthropies of Boston* (Boston, 1956), 6–12; Susan Ebert, "Community and Philanthropy," in Sarna, Smith, and Kosofsky, *Jews of Boston*, 222.

26. Solomon, *Pioneers in Service*, 8, 11–12. See also Goldman, *Beyond the Synagogue Gallery*, 60–61, 145–149.

27. Quote from Abramson, "History of Temple Adath Israel," 90–91. Jonathan D. Sarna, "The Evolution of the American Synagogue," in *The Americanization of the Jews*, ed. Robert M. Seltzer and Norman J. Cohen (New York: New York University Press, 1995), 221–225; Sarna, *American Judaism*, 75–102; Jick, *Americanization of the Synagogue*, 174–179; Goldman, *Beyond the Synagogue Gallery*, 78–99.

28. Jick, *Americanization of the Synagogue*, 153. Board Minutes, 6 January 1878.

29. Board Minutes, 29 March 1863, 2 April 1865, 9 April 1865, 5 February 1870. Schindler, *Israelites in Boston*, chap. 2. See also Goldman, *Beyond the Synagogue Gallery*, 82–93.

30. Board Minutes, 26 August 1866. See also Goldman, *Beyond the Synagogue Gallery*, 82–93. Board Minutes, 26 August 1866. Committees began to submit reports in English in 1875 (Board Minutes, 19 September 1875), but the transition was not complete until 15 June 1879.

31. Board Minutes, 31 July 1870, 18 September 1870, 14 April 1872, 15 September 1872. When the board set up a committee to work with Shoninger to establish the long-awaited chorus in 1871, he acquiesced, but the chorus performed only intermittently. See Board Minutes, 7 February 1871, 9 April 1871, 20 November 1871. In September 1871, the board voted to improve congregational order by omitting the recitation of prayers for the sick. This reform also took years to take effect, in part because of the loss of income it involved. Board Minutes, 10 September 1871, 5 May 1871, 3 May 1874. For recommendations of reforms, see Board Minutes, 11 May 1873. For mixed seating, see Jick, *Americanization of the Synagogue*, 182–194; Sarna, *American Judaism*, 125–128; Goldman, *Beyond the Synagogue Gallery*, 82–83. Renovations to the synagogue took place in the summer of 1874. See Board Minutes, 22 March 1874, 3 May 1874, 7 June 1874, 16 August 1874, 30 August 1874, 6 September 1874.

32. Board Minutes, 8 June 1873, 7 September 1873, 12 October 1873, 22 March 1874, 3 May 1874.

CHAPTER 2. BECOMING A REFORM TEMPLE, 1874–1911 (pp. 19–53)

1. Board Minutes, 5 July 1874. Ehrenfried, *Chronicle of Boston Jewry*, 389; David Kaufman, "Temples in the American Athens: A History of the Synagogues of Boston," in Sarna, Smith, and Kosofsky, *Jews of Boston*, 177. The contract for the building renovations was

signed on 5 July 1874; Schindler was hired the same day and arrived on 28 July. The pews were completed in August, and the "choice" pews on both the lower floor and the gallery were auctioned in September. Board Minutes, 5 July 1874, 28 July 1874, 6 September 1874.

2. Solomon Schindler, "Laconicism—B," Sermon delivered at Congregation Adath Israel, 10 March 1877, in Solomon Schindler, "Sermons, Vol. 2, December 1867–Dec. 1877," esp. 29–32 (handwritten manuscript in Solomon Schindler Papers, Temple Israel Archives). Solomon Schindler, "Laconicism—C," Sermon delivered at Congregation Adath Israel, 14 April 1877, in Schindler, "Sermons, Vol. 2," 93–94. Board Minutes, 1873–1875, passim. Other synagogues embarked on similar paths of reform at the same time. For examples, see Alan Silverstein, *Alternatives to Assimilation, The Response of Reform Judaism to American Culture* (Waltham, Mass.: Brandeis University Press, 1994) and Peter Eisenstadt, *Affirming the Covenant: A History of Temple B'rith Kodesh, Rochester, New York, 1848–1998* (Rochester, N.Y.: Temple B'rith Kodesh, 1999).

3. Board Minutes, 16 August 1874, 30 August 1874; Ehrenfried, *Chronicle of Boston Jewry*, 388; Schindler, "History of the Congregation Temple Adath Israel." Sarna, *American Judaism*, 125; Goldman, *Beyond the Synagogue Gallery*, 93–99, 136. The German version of the Amidah translated the reference to the raising of the dead in the messianic age to "you keep faith with those who sleep in the dust" (See Abramson, "History of Temple Adath Israel," 110).

4. The Reform Committee had examined Wise's new prayer book in 1873 (see Board Minutes, 5 January 1873). For Huebsch's prayer book, see Board Minutes, 16 August 1874, 30 August 1874, 27 September 1874.

5. Board Minutes, 27 September 1874, 2 May 1875, 11 August 1875. B. O. Flower, *Progressive Men, Women, and Movements of the Past Twenty-Five Years* (Boston: New Arena, 1914), 173. See, for example, various sermons from 1877 in Schindler, "Sermons, Vol. 2." Quote from Board Minutes, 7 March 1875. Ehrenfried, *Chronicle of Boston Jewry*, 389. In 1876 there were eight confirmands; in 1877, twelve. Ohabei Shalom held its first confirmation in 1877 (see "Confirmation at the Synagogue Adath Israel," *Globe*, 30 May 1876, 5; "The Feast of Weeks," *Globe*, 19 May 1877, 8).

6. Most joined Ohabei Shalom or dropped any synagogue affiliation (see Schindler, *Israelites in Boston*, chaps. 2–3. He notes that members "yielded to the fashion of appearing in the temple with heads uncovered" by the 1880s). The UAHC first approached Congregation Adath Israel in 1874 (see Board Minutes, 23 August 1874, 30 August 1874). In an 1877 sermon, Schindler claimed that the members "were afraid of losing their independence and preferred rather to destroy Judaism all together rather than to give up a particle of their pretended rights" (Schindler, "Laconicisms—C," Sermon delivered at Congregation Adath Israel, 14 April 1877, in Schindler, "Sermons, Vol. 2," 95).

7. Some members were concerned about this transition (Board Minutes, 4 December 1875). A bylaw change in September 1875 included a provision recognizing civil marriage (Board Minutes, 12 September 1875). See, for example, Schindler, "Three Mottos," a sermon delivered at Adath Israel on 18 January 1877, in Schindler, "Sermons, Vol. 2," 41.

8. Figures from 1870 and 1880 membership lists, in TI Archives. Board Minutes, 7 November 1875, 3 September 1876. Schindler, *Israelites in Boston*, chap. 3.

9. For holidays, see "The Thanksgiving Observances," *Globe*, 1 December 1876, 2; Board Minutes, 30 September 1877. Dividing a part of the cemetery into family plots was first raised in 1866 (Board Minutes, 18 March 1866). The decision was finalized ten years later (Board Minutes, 18 June 1876).

10. "Laconicisms—C," Sermon delivered at Congregation Adath Israel, 14 April 1877, in Schindler, "Sermons, Vol. 2," 96–99; "Laconicims—B," Sermon delivered at Congregation Adath Israel, 10 March 1877, in ibid., 86–87. Board Minutes, 7 November 1875, 4 December 1875. For German, see Board Minutes, 24 December 1876, 25 March 1877. Obst, *Story of Adath Israel*, 13–14. "Annual Report, comprising the Attendance, the Deportment, and the Industry of every pupil of the Sabbath School, Temple Adath Israel, from Nov. 1, 1878 till June 1, 1879," in Religious School Files, TI Archives. Joseph Reimer, "Passionate Visions in Contest," 286.

11. Religious School Committee Report, Board Minutes, 16 January 1878; Board Minutes, 15 September 1878. Board Minutes, 11 September 1887, 16 September 1888.

12. Board Minutes, 8 August 1877; Religious School Committee Report, Board Minutes, 2 April 1878.

13. As was typical for matters regarding Schindler, the members were divided about offering him a longer contract (see Board Minutes, 5 May 1880). For committees, see Bylaws of Congregation Adath Israel, Board Minutes, 5 May 1879.

14. Sarna, *American Judaism*, 124. Smith, "Israelites in Boston," 55–56.

15. Smith, "Israelites in Boston," 52–61. See also chap. 3, "The Economic Ascent," in Braverman, "Ascent of Boston's Jews," 80–120.

16. Names from membership lists in TI Archives; occupations from U.S. Census (1880) and *Boston City Directory*, 1880. Occupations could be determined for 49 of 58 household heads listed; place of birth for 47. Only one head of household was born in the United States. The median age for male heads of household was 46; 36.5 for wives. They had a median of 4 children; the median age of the oldest was 18, the youngest 4.5. Calculated from U.S. Census (1880).

17. Sixty-four percent of members lived in Boston proper and 20 percent lived in Roxbury. Seventy percent had at least one servant, half of whom were born in Ireland; 15 percent were born in the United States to Irish parents; many of the rest were from Canada. Only 8 percent were from Germany or Prussia. Calculated from U.S. Census (1880).

18. Smith, "Israelites in Boston," 57. Ebert, "Community and Philanthropy," 222–223.

19. "Adath Israel," *Globe*, 4 February 1885; Board Minutes, 1880–1885; Abramson, "History of Temple Adath Israel," 77; *Growth and Achievement: Temple Israel 1854–1954*, Arthur Mann, ed. (Boston: Congregation Adath Israel, 1954), 31; Kaufman, "Temples in the American Athens," 183–184; Gerald Gamm, *Urban Exodus: Why the Jews Left Boston and the Catholics Stayed* (Cambridge, Mass.: Harvard University Press, 1999), 100–101, 135–136. The temple sublet the Pleasant Street structure to Congregation Shaaray Tefila

(now Mishkan Tefila). Ohabei Shalom also built a new synagogue in the new South End on Union Park Street in 1887. See Gerald Gamm, "In Search of Suburbs," in Sarna, Smith, and Kosofsky, *Jews of Boston*, 149–50.

20. The mayor was Hugh O'Brien, Boston's first Irish Catholic mayor; the ministers included Schindler's close friends, Minot Savage and Edward Everett Hale. Kaufman, "Temples in the American Athens," 184. "A Jewish Dedication," *Herald*, 4 February 1885. "Adath Israel," *Globe*, 4 February 1885.

21. Solomon Schindler to the Board and Members, Board Minutes, 6 April 1884; Report of the School Committee, Board Minutes, 26 April 1885. Membership List, 1885, TI Archives. *Boston City Directory*, 1885. Goldman, *Beyond the Synagogue Gallery*, 10–13.

22. Ebert, "Community and Philanthropy," 223–234; Braverman, "Emergence of a Unified Community," 65–66, 77.

23. Braverman, "Ascent of Boston's Jews," 121–122; Braverman, "Emergence of a Unified Community," 72; Sarna, "Jews of Boston in Historical Perspective," 7.

24. Solomon Schindler, "'A Word to the Wise,' Lecture delivered Sunday December 20th 1891 at the Temple Adath Israel," 13–16, in Solomon Schindler Papers, Box 1, AJA. Schindler, quoted in Solomon, *Pioneers in Service*, 15, and Ebert, "Community and Philanthropy," 223–224. Braverman, "Ascent of Boston's Jews," 121–122. "Noted Jewish Organization," [Boston] *Jewish Advocate* [hereafter *Advocate*], 11 August 1903. "Jewish People's Institute," *Advocate*, 3 August 1908.

25. Board Minutes, 7 June 1885, 21 June 1885; *Globe*, 14 January 1893; Isaac Mayer Wise, in *American Israelite*, 21 November 1879. Silverstein, *Alternatives to Assimilation*, 107. For library, see Obst, *Story of Adath Israel*, 17.

26. The teachers were Lottie Rosenfeld, Jennie Cohen, Grace Alexander, Rosie Benari, Jennie Hirshberg, and Fannie August (see Report of the School Committee, Board Minutes, 26 April 1885).

27. Arthur Mann, *Yankee Reformers in the Urban Age* (Cambridge, Mass.: Belknap Press of Harvard University Press, 1954), 56, 63–70. Abramson, "History of Temple Adath Israel," 97.

28. Schindler argued that traditional Christianity was forced to "cling to belief" rather than reason because "the belief that three are one and one three [is] a doctrine against which reason revolts." He admired Unitarianism because its rise was similar to that of Reform Judaism and because it had abandoned "the dogma of a trinity"; Jesus was regarded as merely "the ideal of a man" rather than the son of God. See Schindler, *Messianic Expectations and Modern Judaism* (Boston: S.E. Cassino, 1886), 34, 60–65, 272; Schindler, *Dissolving Views in the History of Judaism* (Boston: Lee and Shepard, 1888), 318–323.

29. "Declaration of Principles: The Pittsburgh Platform," 1885 Pittsburgh Conference, http://ccarnet.org/Articles/index.cfm?id=39&pge_prg_id=3032&pge_id=1656 (accessed 10 October 2008). Schindler, *Messianic Expectations*, 201–205. Schindler later came to support the Zionist movement (see Braverman, "Emergence of a Unified Community," 81–82; *Advocate*, 3 February 1916, 15 February 1917).

30. "Boston Mourns: Sudden Death of Rabbi Solomon Schindler," *Advocate*, 7 May 1915; Mann, *Growth and Achievement*, 49.

31. Smith, "Israelites in Boston," 56–57. See also Goldman, *Beyond the Synagogue Gallery*, 1–2. For services schedule, see Board Minutes, 9 September 1880.

32. Abramson, "History of Temple Adath Israel," 74. Schindler to the Board, 5 April 1884; Board Minutes, 26 April 1885. Report of the Committee Revising Bylaws, 24 April 1885, in Board Minutes, 26 April 1885; Board Minutes, 31 May 1885. See also Michael A. Meyer, *Response to Modernity, A History of the Reform Movement* (New York: Oxford University Press, 1988), 291.

33. In 1887, Schindler was offered a position at Philadelphia's Congregation Tefereth Israel. Adath Israel's willingness to increase his salary from $1,800 to $2,500 to ensure his stay may have encouraged him to push for Sunday services (see Board Minutes, 6 April 1887). "Sunday at Adath Israel," *Globe*, 8 October 1888; Schindler, *Israelites in Boston*, chap. 3; Board Minutes, 1 April 1888, 15 April 1888, 9 December 1888. For Jewish opinion regarding Sunday services, see Kerry M. Olitzky, "The Sunday-Sabbath Movement in American Reform Judaism: Strategy or Evolution?" in *American Jewish History*, vol. 2., *Central European Jews in America, 1840–1880: Migration and Advancement*, ed. Jeffrey S. Gurock (New York: Routledge, 1998), 77–84.

34. Mann, *Yankee Reformers*, 57–63. See, for example, "Unitarianism and Judaism," 16 December 1888, and "Nationalism as a Religion," 21 November 1890, in Schindler Papers, AJA. Mann, *Yankee Reformers*, 55, 57.

35. Board Minutes, 21 September 1890, 19 November 1891. Schindler, "A Word to the Wise," 20 December 1891, in Schindler Papers, AJA. M. Bourchier Sanford, "In Favor of the Jew," *North American Review* 152 (January–June 1891), 126.

36. Schindler had earlier opposed intermarriage (see *Israelites in Boston*, chap. 5; *Hebrew Observer*, 18 May 1883, 20 July 1883, 16 October 1885; Braverman, "Ascent of Boston's Jews," 167). "He Gave His Best," *Globe*, 25 October 1893. In *Israelites in Boston*, chap. 7, he noted that being an "efficient reader" and "good teacher" were "all that was formerly required of a Jewish minister." See also Sarna, *American Judaism*, 91–93; Braverman, "Ascent of Boston's Jews," 161.

37. The prayer book was written by Joseph Krauskopf of Philadelphia's Tifereth Israel. Board Minutes, 6 November 1892, 1 January 1893, 5 March 1893.

38. "Parting Words. Rabbi Schindler Takes a Backward Look," *Globe*, 8 January 1894. "Looking Forward. Rabbi Schindler Says His Farewell," *Globe*, 22 January 1894. Schindler's contract expired in June 1894 (see "Rabbi Fleischer Called," *Globe*, 20 March 1894). For press coverage of his retirement, see, for example, "Gave His Best," *Globe*, 25 October 1893. For his postrabbinic career, see "Boston Mourns," *Advocate*, 7 May 1915.

39. Meyer, *Response to Modernity*, 265–279. Board Minutes, 3 December 1893, 7 January 1894, 17 January 1894, 21 January 1894, 18 March 1894, 13 May 1894. After interviewing three candidates, the board had initially made an offer to Rabbi William S. Friedman, of

Denver, Colorado, but when Friedman declined, the trustees brought in two more candidates (Friedman would serve at Denver's Temple Emanuel until 1938).

40. "Rabbi Fleischer Called," *Globe*, 20 March 1894; Board Minutes, 28 May 1894, 2 September 1894, 14 September 1894. A few members resisted Fleischer's reforms, including one who declared that his wife and daughter "refuse positively to attend your reform services" (Board Minutes, 13 October 1894).

41. Board Minutes, 6 August 1895, 12 September 1897, 21 September 1902, 18 November 1906. "New Every Morning," *Globe*, 20 September 1895, 11 November 1895; Obst, *Story of Adath Israel*, 20.

42. The board was willing to engage in pulpit exchanges with other rabbis, "provided the expenses are not too large," but voted that special advance permission was required for these exchanges and for the rabbi to be absent from the temple (see "New Every Morning," *Globe*, 20 September 1895; Board Minutes, 1 December 1895). "Memorial Services," *Globe*, 25 May 1896; "In Wakefield Cemetery," *Globe*, 29 May 1899. For auxiliary society, see Obst, *Story of Adath Israel*, 19–20.

43. Free Religious Association, *Proceedings at the Twenty-Ninth Anniversary* (New Bedford, Mass.: Free Religious Association, 1896), 104. "Why He Gives Thanks," *Globe*, 26 November 1900, 7. "'My Country, Right or Wrong,'" *Globe*, 8 January 1900. Mann, *Growth and Achievement*, 82–83. *Globe*, 1 February 1897. "Republicans Control Board," *Globe*, 16 December 1896, 1.

44. Fleischer to the Board, 4 June 1898, in Rabbi Charles Fleischer Papers, TI Archives. Board Minutes, 7 December 1896.

45. "Lack of Patronage," *Globe*, 7 January 1901, 7. Board Minutes, 4 March 1900, 3 March 1901, 2 May 1903. "Sees Possible Danger: Rabbi Fleischer on Passage of Jewish Sabbath Bill," *Globe*, 20 April 1901, 4.

46. Obst, *Story of Adath Israel*, 21, 25. For Frank, see U.S. Census (1880, 1900). Women raised funds through balls and other events (see "Grand Entertainment," *Advocate*, 9 February 1906; "Council of Jewish Women," *Advocate*, 2 November 1906; Sisterhood Collection, TI Archives). See also Goldman, *Beyond the Synagogue Gallery*, 149–150.

47. For the sale of the Columbus Avenue building to the AME Zion Church, see Real Estate Agreement between Congregation Adath Israel and Henry Crine, 6 November 1902, in Columbus Avenue Files, Buildings Collection, TI Archives. The church took possession and rededicated the structure in June 1903. In turn, it sold its North Russell Street structure in the West End to an Orthodox synagogue (see Agreement; "Former Synagogue Now a Church," *Globe*, 7 June 1903, 13; Gamm, "In Search of Suburbs," 149–150). For the purchase of the Commonwealth Avenue property, see Special General Meeting, Board Minutes, 19 August 1903. The fund-raising campaign began immediately.

48. "Handsomest Synagogue in the United States is Dedicated," unidentified newspaper clipping, 2 September 1907, in Commonwealth Avenue Files, Buildings Collection, TI Archives; Gamm, *Urban Exodus*, 192–193.

49. For the temporary quarters, see "Daniel Frank President: Annual Meeting of the Congregation Adath Israel," *Globe*, 14 September 1903, 9; Obst, *Story of Adath Israel*, 20–21; Gamm, *Urban Exodus*, 105. For the 250th celebration, see *Advocate*, 1 December 1905.

50. Board Minutes, 20 May 1906, 18 November 1906.

51. For membership figures, see "President's Message to Congregation Adath Israel," Board Minutes, 1 March 1925. For dedication description, see Fleischer, "The Significance of the New Synagogue," *Herald*, 1 September 1907; *Boston Traveler*, 1 September 1907; "Handsomest Synagogue"; Obst, *Story of Adath Israel*, 24.

52. Fleischer to the Board, in Board Minutes, 18 December 1907; Board Minutes, 5 January 1908, 26 February 1908, 15 March 1908, 19 April 1908.

53. Fleischer had been offered a pulpit in Portland, Oregon, in 1906, but the Adath Israel board raised his salary to keep him in Boston (Board Minutes, 18 November 1906). Description of Fleischer in Mann, *Growth and Achievement*, 66. For Fleischer's public lectures and writings, see, for example, "Judaism the Universal Religion," *Globe*, 25 February 1895, 4; "Plea against Self-Sacrifice," *Globe*, 2 January 1899; "New Every Morning," *Globe*, 20 September 1895, 3. For quote, see Charles Fleischer, "Keynote Address at the Thirty-Third Anniversary of the Free Religious Association of America, 1900," in Free Religious Association, *Proceedings at the Thirty-Third Annual Meeting* (Boston: Free Religious Association, 1900), 131. Board Minutes, 20 October 1907. In 1900, Fleischer was told to "refrain from political lectures" and not to "absent himself from the city without the privilege of the president" (Board Minutes, 7 October 1900, 4 November 1900). See also Board Minutes, 5 May 1901, 16 April 1905.

54. For contract, see Fleischer to the Board, Board Minutes, 18 December 1907. Board Minutes, 5 January 1908, 26 January 1908, 26 February 1908, 15 March 1908, 19 April 1908. For Schindler's appointment as rabbi emeritus, see Board Minutes, 1 March 1908.

55. Fleischer to the Board, 8 May 1908, in Fleischer Papers. Board Minutes, 22 April 1908, 9 May 1908, 13 May 1908, Fleischer to Leo J. Lyons, 14 May 1908, Board Minutes, 24 May 1908. For Fleischer's changing ideology, see also Mann, *Growth and Achievement*, 79.

56. Board Minutes, 31 January 1909, 1 March, 1909; Announcement, 9 April 1909, 18 April 1909, 20 May 1909. For press coverage of the meeting and the community response, see *Advocate*, 23 April 1909. Rabbi Menaham Eichler of Ohabei Shalom, for example, commented that "Sunday Jews" would ultimately "be absorbed in the great ocean of the non-Jewish population."

57. Fleischer to the Board, Board Minutes, 30 January 1910; Board Minutes, 3 April 1910.

58. *Advocate*, 23 April 1909. Fleischer to the Board, 15 June 1910, in Fleischer Papers. "Fleischer Engagement is Not True," *Advocate*, 3 June 1910. "Adath Israel is Too Conservative — Fleischer Resigns," *Advocate*, 17 June 1910.

59. President's Message, General Meeting, Board Minutes, 29 January 1911; Board Minutes, 4 February 1911, 7 February 1911, 16 February 1911, 26 February 1911; "Elected to Succeed Fleischer," *Advocate*, 2 March 1911. Fleischer attempted to influence the board's choice

for his replacement by inviting various rabbis to interview. Fleischer's interference almost derailed the negotiations with Levi.

60. Max Heller, "A Recantation," *American Israelite*, 20 April 1911. "Confesses He Was Guilty of Five Errors," *Advocate*, 26 March 1911.

61. "Some Mistakes I Have Gladly Made," *Advocate*, 9 April 1911; "Favors Assimilation," *Advocate*, 14 April 1911. Mann, "Charles Fleischer's Religion of Democracy," 562. For Fleischer's last sermon, see *Advocate*, 2 June 1911. For his postrabbinic career, see "Dr. Fleischer Opens 'Sunday Commons,'" *Globe*, 8 January 1912; For a description of the Sunday Commons, see Felix Shay, "The Church of Citizenship," *Roycroft* 2, no. 2 (April 1918), 62–63. "Dr. Charles Fleischer Editor and Lecturer," *New York Times*, 3 July 1942.

62. The Immigration Restriction League was founded in Boston in 1894; by the 1900s, support for the movement had become so widespread that its leaders were able to successfully lobby Congress to establish a committee to examine restriction. The United States Immigration Commission (known as the Dillingham Commission) convened in 1907 and published its findings in 1911 (for the reports, see "Dillingham Commission, 1907–1910" http://ocp.hul.harvard.edu/immigration/themes-dillingham.html [accessed 10 November 2008]).

CHAPTER 3. THE ERA OF OPTIMISM, 1911–1928 (pp. 54–77)

1. "Rabbi and Congregation," *Advocate*, 31 March 1911, 8. Special General Meeting, Board Minutes, 26 February 1911; "Rabbi Harry Levi," *Advocate*, 1 September 1911, 8; "Elected to Succeed Fleischer," *Advocate*, 2 March 1911, 1. "Rabbi Levi Accepts Call," *Advocate*, 17 March 1911, 1. "Rabbi Harry Levi," *Advocate*, 1 September 1911, 8. After Schindler's highly publicized sermon, "Mistakes I Have Made," Levi wrote to him, "I am heartily in accord with the views you expressed in it . . . only a man of strong character could have made the confession it contains. It takes courage to acknowledge a mistake" ("Shares Schindler's Opinions," *Advocate*, 21 April 1911, 2).

2. Mann, *Growth and Achievement*, 84–89; *Advocate*, 8 December 1924.

3. "Asks for Friendship and Pleads for Loyalty to Judaism, In Inaugural," *Advocate*, 22 September 1911. Levi's address, "The Function of the Synagogue," was printed verbatim in the newspaper. Silverstein, *Alternatives to Assimilation*, 82–112; David Kaufman, *Shul With a Pool: The "Synagogue-Center" in American Jewish History* (Waltham, Mass.: Brandeis University Press, 1999).

4. The city's daily newspapers and the *Jewish Advocate* published excerpts of Levi's sermons every week with those of other religious leaders. "Atonement Services," *Advocate*, 6 October 1911. President Frank's Report, Board Minutes, 28 January 1912; Rabbi Levi's Report, Board Minutes, 7 April 1912, 5 May 1912. Temple Israel Membership Lists, in TI Archives. Susan Abramson, "The Social History of Temple Adath Israel, 1911–Present" (unpublished paper, 1973), 24, in TI Library. Information compiled on the 75 new members who joined between 1911 and 1914 (for whom nativity could be found), from U.S. Census (1900, 1910, 1920, 1930) and World War I Draft Registration Cards, 1917–1918.

5. For the decision to join the UAHC, see Board Minutes, 28 January 1912, 3 March 1912, 7 April 1912. The board did not specify the ritual they adopted. See Board Minutes, 1 June 1912, 13 October 1912, 13 November 1912, 1 December 1912; "Rabbi Levi's History, 1910–1939," "Scrapbook and Timeline of Temple Israel Events During Harry Levi's Rabbinate" [Levi Scrapbook], Rabbi Harry Levi Papers, TI Archives. For music, see Board Minutes, 14 January 1912, 13 October 1912, 2 March 1913, 11 January 1914; "Report of Special Congregational Meeting Concerning Religious Services and the Need for a New Building," n.d., circa 1917–1918, 2–3, in Special Collections, TI Archives.

6. U.S. Census (1900, 1910, 1920). "Rabbis Plead for United Efforts on Part of the Boston Community," *Advocate*, 26 January 1912. Board Minutes, 8 October 1911, 3 December 1911. For Hebrew, see Janet Printz Kaplan, interview by Rachel Alexander, 5 November 1997, transcript, Women Whose Lives Spanned the Century Oral History Project, TI Archives [WWLSC]. For school activities, see Board Minutes, 15 January 1913.

7. Levi Scrapbook, 30 November 1912; Board Minutes, 1 December 1912.

8. *TI Bulletin*, 16 April 1921, 20 March 1929.

9. For figures, see Board Minutes, 5 November 1911; *TI Bulletin*, June 1917. Levi Scrapbook, 1911–1921; Confirmation Programs, 1915–1928, TI Archives.

10. Board Minutes, 1 June 1912; Constitution and Bylaws of the Young People's Society of Temple Adath Israel [YPSOTAI] (undated), in Youth Committee Files, TI Archives. "College Fair of Temple Israel Full of Color," *Advocate*, 8 December 1911; Board Minutes, 2 March 1913; "Y.M.H.A. News," *Advocate*, 28 February 1913.

11. Board Minutes, 5 November 1911, 26 January 1913; Board Minutes, 14 January 1912, 11 January 1914. Harriet Segal Cohn, interview by Helene Bailen, 9 and 16 January 1997, transcript, WWLSC; Marion Guttentag, interview by Emily Mehlman, 4 June 1996, transcript, WWLSC.

12. Board Minutes, 2 March 1913. Address of Mrs. Daniel [Rose] Frank, Temple Israel Sisterhood, Tenth Anniversary Dinner, 30 November 1913, Sisterhood Collection, TI Archives. "Temple Israel Has a Week of Varied Activities," *Advocate*, 5 December 1913; Board Minutes, 11 January 1914; Obst, *Story of Adath Israel*, 25–26. "Women in Attendance," *Advocate*, 5 February 1915. For national Sisterhood, see Goldman, *Beyond the Synagogue Gallery*, 172, 185–192; Sarna, *American Judaism*, 142–143.

13. *Advocate*, 5 December 1913; Silverstein, 162–163. "Temple Israel Brotherhood," *Advocate*, 1 February 1917. Levi Scrapbook, 9 December 1917. For services, see Levi Scrapbook, 8 April 1914; "Temple Israel," *Advocate*, 4 June 1915; *Advocate*, 1 June 1916. In April 1914, for example, 1,500 people attended Sunday services at Temple Israel.

14. For the temple's prominence, see "Women in Attendance," *Advocate*, 5 February 1915; "Temple Israel," *Advocate*, 4 June 1915. For community service, see President's Message, Board Minutes, 28 January 1912. For Levi's speeches, see "Report to the Board of Trustees," January 1913, Levi Papers; Board Minutes, 8 October 1911, 3 March 1912; "Calls Play Unpatriotic," *Advocate*, 7 May 1915; "Symposium on Woman Suffrage," *Advocate*,

29 October 1915. For Levi's patriotism, see Braverman, "Emergence of a Unified Community," 78; "Temple Israel," *Advocate*, 9 November 1916.

15. "Temple Israel," *Advocate*, 4 June 1915; "Rabbi Levi Says Sunday Services Have Met a Real Need," *Advocate*, 20 May 1914; "Rabbis Plead for United Efforts on Part of the Boston Community," *Advocate*, 26 August 1912. "Appendix A," Sarna, Smith, and Kosofsky, *Jews of Boston*, 343. Braverman, "Emergence of a Unified Community," 77–82; Ebert, "Community and Philanthropy," 222–231; "Unity of Boston Jewry Demonstrated in Successful Results of Local Relief Campaign," *Advocate*, 21 February 1918.

16. Board Minutes, 13 October 1913. Levi Scrapbook, 8 November 1914. "Temple Israel," *Advocate*, 4 June 1915; "Temple Israel Sisterhood," *Advocate*, 10 September 1915. *TI Bulletin*, June 1917.

17. "Combined Boston Purim Celebration," *Advocate*, 27 January 1916; "3,000 Children Will Celebrate Purim," *Advocate*, 24 February 1916. For branch school expansion, see *TI Bulletin*, 1920–1939, passim.

18. "David A. Ellis Dies; Lawyer of Boston," *New York Times*, 28 July 1929; "David A. Ellis Passes Away at Age 56," *Advocate*, 1 August 1929. "Life of Mrs. Andrews a Three-Fold Success," *Advocate*, 22 January 1919; Sarah Deutsch, *Women and the City: Gender, Space, and Power in Boston, 1870–1940* (New York: Oxford University Press, 2000), 231–258; Ehrenfried, *Chronicle of Boston Jewry*, 639. Braverman, "Emergence of a Unified Community," 78–82.

19. "Interesting Zionist Discussion," *Advocate*, 19 January 1912, 4; "Temple Israel," *Advocate*, 9 November 1916; "Speaking at Twentieth Century Club, Dr. Eichler Hails Founding of Jewish State and Rabbi Levi Not in Accord With the Zionist Program," *Advocate*, 3 January 1918. Rabbis Schindler, Fleischer, and Levi were against the Zionist movement, but Schindler and Levi came to support Zionism later in life. See Braverman, "Emergence of a Unified Community," 81–82; Mann, *Growth and Achievement*, 97; Mark A. Raider, "Pioneers and Pacesetters: Boston Jews and American Zionism," in Sarna, Smith, and Kosofsky, *Jews of Boston*, 167–168.

20. *Advocate*, 7 May 1915. Quotation from Brandeis, "The Rebirth of the Jewish Nation," circa 1914–1915, excerpt in Jacob de Haas, *Louis D. Brandeis: A Biographical Sketch* (New York: Bloch Publishing, 1929), 163. Brandeis also spoke at a Temple Israel Sisterhood meeting in 1914, where he reiterated the idea ("Brandeis Speaks to Sisterhood," *Advocate*, 4 December 1914). For World War I, see "Urges Jews to Work for Their Religion and Not for a National Homeland," *Boston Herald*, 22 May 1919; Leon A. Jick, "From Margin to Mainstream, 1917–1967," in Sarna, Smith, and Kosofsky, *Jews of Boston*, 87–88; Raider, "Pioneers and Pacesetters," 260–262. Temple Israel was the only Boston synagogue that did not sign a petition to President Woodrow Wilson urging recognition of a Zionist state at the Versailles peace conference ("Zionist Petition Rapidly Circulating," *Advocate*, 16 January 1919).

21. For members' German identity, see Marjorie Loeb Edenfeld, interview by Frances Godine, 31 October 1997, transcript, WWLSC. For flag-raising, see "Temple Israel," *Advo-*

cate, 5 April 1917; "Raised at Temple Israel," *Globe*, 2 April 1917; "National Flags Unfurled Before Temple Israel," unidentified newspaper clipping, undated, TI Archives. "More Than Two Hundred Jewish Young Men Left for Ayer Sunday. Levi Gives Farewell Address at Common," *Advocate*, 27 September 1917; "Temple Israel," *Advocate*, 22 November 1917; *TI Bulletin*, June 1918. For Levi's speech, see "Temple Israel," *Advocate*, 26 April 1917.

22. *TI Bulletin*, June 1918. "Roll of Honor. Temple Israel Members in Army & Navy," *Advocate*, 14 March 1918. "The Lost Battalion of World War I," www.homestead.com/prosites-johnrcotter/lost_battalion_heroes.html (accessed 25 August 2005). "Adath Israel Subscribes for $2500 in Liberty Bonds," *Advocate*, 31 May 1917. "Food Conservation Exhibits Well Attended," *Advocate*, 14 June 1917. "Navy Night at Temple Israel," *Advocate*, 20 December 1917; "Outings for Soldiers and Sailors," *Advocate*, 8 August 1918. *TI Bulletin*, June 1918.

23. "Report to Temple Israel Board of Trustees," 2 March 1924, Levi Papers; Ida Mae Kahn, interview by Betsy Friedman Abrams and Bobbie Burstein, 11 July 1997, transcript, WWLSC; "Report to Temple Israel Board of Trustees," 2 March 1924. Levi, *1919 Sunday Service*, in TI Archives. Anna Segal Castleman, interview by Frances Godine, 17 December 1996, transcript, WWLSC.

24. Mann, *Growth and Achievement*, 89. Hulda Phillips Tischler Gittelsohn, interview by Betsy Friedman Abrams and Bobbie Burstein, 20 June 1997, transcript, WWLSC. Levi Scrapbook, 16 November 1919.

25. For membership figures, see Levi Scrapbook, 25 January 1920, 3 October 1920, 18 December 1923. For Cohen, see U.S. Census (1920). Castleman, interview, WWLSC.

26. For geographic mobility, see Levi, Annual Address to the Congregation, *TI Bulletin*, June 1920; Cohn, interview, WWLSC. For school's growth, see Levi Scrapbook, 28 January 1917, 7 November 1917; Obst, *Story of Adath Israel*, 27; Levi Scrapbook, 1924–1929.

27. Levi Scrapbook, 15 February 1922, 17 February 1925; Rabbi Samuel Wolk, "Report of Activities," 14 November 1926, Rabbi Samuel Wolk Files, Papers of the Assistant Rabbis, TI Archives; *TI Bulletin*, 27 March 1929. For college activities, see Levi Scrapbook, 5 May 1920, 9 November 1920, 15 October 1922, 6 December 1924. Hirsh and Nanette Sharf, interview by Joan Shilder, 3 June 1983, transcript, Oral History Collection, TI Archives.

28. Levi Scrapbook, 25 March 1927, 16 October 1927. Fannie Barnett Linsky, "The Booklovers," *TI Bulletin*, 9 April 1930.

29. Levi, "The War and the Future of Liberal Judaism," quoted in "Temple Israel," *Advocate*, 5 December 1918. "Asks Christian, Jewish Accord. Rabbi Levi Pleads for Tolerance in B.U. Lecture," unidentified newspaper clipping, 6 December 1932, in Levi Papers. Morris Morse to Felix Vorenberg, in Board Minutes, 4 January 1924.

30. "Rabbi's Report," 2 March 1924, Levi Papers; "Rabbi Levi to be Paid Honor. Head of Temple Israel Hailed as Jewry's Good-Will Ambassador to All Christendom," *Boston Traveler*, 24 January 1932. Levi, quoted in "Asks Christian, Jewish Accord." Harvard president A. Lawrence Lowell's 1922 proposal to restrict Jewish admissions had a strong effect

on Boston's Jewish population. See Marcia Graham Synnott, *The Half-Opened Door: Discrimination and Admissions at Harvard, Yale, and Princeton, 1900–1970* (Westport, Conn.: Greenwood Press, 1979). "Rabbi Levi Denounces Harvard, Deplorable, He Says, to See College Fall to Illiberalism," *Boston Sunday Post*, 24 September 1922.

31. For responses to Levi, see *TI Bulletin*, 26 January 1926, 13 February 1924. For Levi's response, see "Rabbi's Report," 3 February 1924, Levi Papers. "Rabbi Levi Says Radio 'Blessing,'" *Boston Traveler*, 13 March 1925; Donna Halper, "John Shepard—Boston's Showman," April 2001, www.oldradio.com/archives/people/Shepard.htm (accessed 12 August 2005). For mixed reactions to increased attendance, see Levi Scrapbook, 1924. Mann, *Growth and Achievement*, 35; Barbara Frank Cole, interview by Rachel Alexander, 20 August 1997, transcript, WWLSC; President's Message, Board Minutes, 1 March 1925.

32. Rabbi Levi had urged the temple to address this issue as early as 1913, when he suggested that seats in the sanctuary be filled when the balcony was overcrowded (Board Minutes, 2 February 1913). "Temple Israel May Adopt New Pew System," *Advocate*, 17 February 1921. Levi Scrapbook, 27 February 1921; Levi to Kenneth J. Roman, 22 February 1921, Correspondence Files, Levi Papers. Letter to the President from the Unassigned Pew Committee, Board Minutes, 5 January 1921, 4 February 1923.

33. Board Minutes, 29 January 1922, 6 February 1922. Board Minutes, 4 February 1923, 27 April 1924. Mrs. Liebmann, who frequently was absent from board meetings, soon resigned to be replaced by Mrs. Nathan Gordon.

34. "Bessie Ruth Berman, 104, Secretary to Rabbis," *Globe*, 7 October 2002, Bessie Berman, interview by Betsy Friedman Abrams, 10 December 1996, transcript, WWLSC. For Rabbi Wolk, see Board Minutes, 6 February 1922; Wolk, Reports to the Board, in Wolk Files, 1923–1927. Rabbi Lawrence W. Schwartz succeeded him, followed by Rabbi Beryl Cohon in 1930.

35. Administrative Files, 1920s, TI Archives. Board Minutes, 5 January 1930.

36. For increasing numbers, see Levi Scrapbook, 1923–4; "Special Bulletin re Annual Meeting, 24 November 1919," Board Minutes, 25 January 1920. For building plan, see William Coblenz, "Jewish Building Plans Extensive," *Boston Sunday Post*, 5 October 1924.

37. For more on the synagogue center concept and Temple Israel's building project, see Kaufman, *Shul With a Pool*, 261–274.

38. Only one other site (on Audubon Road) was seriously considered. See Board Minutes, 3 February 1924 and 25 April 1924.

39. Report of the Membership Committee, Board Minutes, 10 January 1926. *TI Bulletin*, 7 November 1928 and 28 May 1929.

CHAPTER 4. THE "MENACE OF THESE TRAGIC TIMES," 1928–1953
(pp. 78–102)

1. "Rabbi Levi's History, 1910–1939," Levi Scrapbook, 14 June 1929, Levi Papers. *TI Bulletin*, 2 April 1930; Membership figures for January 1929, Membership Committee Report, Board Minutes, 26 January 1930.

2. *TI Bulletin*, January 1929 and June 1929. For dues increases, see Treasurer's Report, Board Minutes, 31 December 1930. Rabbi Levi's Report, Board Minutes, 15 February 1931.

3. Treasurer's Report, Board Minutes, 6 November 1932; Membership Committee Report, Board Minutes, 1 March 1931, 28 January 1933, 7 May 1933; Treasurer's Report, Board Minutes, 6 November 1932, 24 January 1932, 23 July 1933, 13 September 1938; Rabbi Levi's Report, Board Minutes, 5 March 1933. The temple removed the architectural drawing of the complex from the *TI Bulletin*'s masthead in 1938 (*TI Bulletin*, 7 December 1938).

4. Board Minutes, 5 April 1931. Report of Rabbi Harry Levi, Board Minutes, 1 May 1932.

5. Rabbi Beryl D. Cohon, "The Philosophy of Our Religious School Curriculum," in *TI Bulletin*, 14 January 1931. Staff figures for the 1931–1932 school year state that Temple Israel educated a total of nine hundred children in the morning, afternoon, and branch schools, and graduated its first high school class (see Board Minutes, 6 March, 27 May 1932; *TI Bulletin*, 14 January 1931). For scholarships, see School Committee Report, Board Minutes, 5 April 1936, 30 January 1938; *TI Bulletin*, 27 March 1929. For budget cuts and enrollment restrictions discussion, see Board Minutes, 6 March 1932, 10 April 1932, 27 May 1932.

6. School Committee Report, Board Minutes, 15 February 1931; Levi Scrapbook, 14 June 1929. *TI Bulletin*, 13 March 1929. Youth Commission Report, Board Minutes, 10 October 1948.

7. Education Department Report, Board Minutes, 6 March 1932, 28 January 1933, 8 April 1933, 5 April 1936, 30 January 1938.

8. For Brotherhood, see *TI Bulletin*, 26 January 1938; "We Must Get Back," *Brotherhood News*, April 1933. Hirsh and Nanette Sharf, interview by Joan Shilder, 3 June 1983, transcript, Oral History Collection, TI Archives. Dr. Julius Aisner Biographical File, TI Archives. We are grateful to Ruth Aisner for this information.

9. President's Report, Board Minutes, 2 January 1938. *Sisterhood Bulletin*, December 1931, Exchange Report to Sisterhood, 1937, Sisterhood Collection; *TI Bulletin*, 1 October 1930.

10. For antisemitism in Boston, see Thomas H. O'Connor, "The Jewish-Christian Experience," in Sarna, Smith, and Kosofsky, *Jews of Boston*, 335; James M. O'Toole, *Militant and Triumphant: William Henry O'Connell and the Catholic Church in Boston, 1859–1944* (Notre Dame, Ind.: University of Notre Dame Press, 1992), 137–138, 148; Alan Brinkley, *Voices of Protest: Huey Long, Father Coughlin, and the Great Depression* (New York: Vintage Books, 1983); Nat Hentoff, *Boston Boy* (New York: Alfred A. Knopf, 1986); Robert Stack, *International Conflict in an American City: Boston's Irish, Italians and Jews, 1935–1944* (Westport, Conn.: Greenwood Press, 1979); Jenny Goldstein, "Transcending Boundaries: Boston's Catholics and Jews, 1929–1965" (senior thesis, Brandeis University, 2001), published by the Center for Christian–Jewish Learning, Boston College, http://www.bc.edu/research/cjl/meta-elements/texts/cjrelations/resources/articles/goldstein.htm (accessed 10 June 2008). For Friedman, see President's Report, Board Minutes, 26 January 1936.

11. For Levi's presence in Boston, see "Rabbi Levi to be Paid Honor," *Boston Traveler*, 24 January 1932; Mann, *Growth and Achievement*, 97. For Levi and Zionism, see Douglas

A. Haber, "The Burden of the Witness: The Response of Boston's Jews to the Holocaust, 1941–1945" (senior honors thesis, Middlebury College, 2004), 13; Raider, "Pioneers and Pacesetters," 167–168; Harry Levi, *A Rabbi Speaks* (Boston: Chapple Publishing, 1930), 31. For Levi's retirement, see Mann, *Growth and Achievement*, 97; Rabbi Levi's Report, Board Minutes, 9 October 1938; Board Minutes, 6 November 1938; *TI Bulletin*, 30 November 1938. Rabbi Levi died in 1944. One example of Levi's attempts to bring attention to antisemitism occurred in 1936, when he encouraged two local Jewish Harvard track stars to boycott the Berlin Olympics. See "American Boycotters—Milton Green," in "The Nazi Olympics, Berlin 1936," U.S. Holocaust Memorial Museum, http://www.ushmm.org/museum/exhibit/online/olympics/detail.php?content=american_boycotters_milton_green&lang=en (accessed 26 August 2008).

12. For Cohon's achievements, see Board Minutes, 7 March 1937. Education Department Report, Board Minutes, 6 March 1932, 28 January 1933, 8 April 1933, 30 January 1938. Report of the Special Committee to Reorganize the Rabbinate, Board Minutes, 27 June 1938; Board Minutes, 16 November 1938. Rabbi Cohon's Report, Board Minutes, 11 December 1938; Abramson, "Social History of Temple Israel," 36. For Cohon's modern Reform ideas, see Rabbi Levi to Albert Ehrenfried, 4 October 1938, in Ehrenfried Papers.

13. Music Committee Report, Board Minutes, 24 December 1938; Rabbi Cohon's Report, Board Minutes, 8 January 1939. Albert Ehrenfried to the Temple Israel Board of Trustees, undated, in Ehrenfried Papers; Board Minutes, 4 June 1939.

14. Board Minutes, 28 and 16 May 1939. Board Minutes, 4 June 1939. "History of Temple Sinai," www.sinaibrookline.org/page.php/id/122 (accessed 21 September 2005); Board Minutes, 9 July 1939, 3 December 1939; Justin L. Wyner, "Personal Reminiscences," Remarks at Temple Israel Sesquicentennial Finale, 20 May 2005.

15. Joseph Reimer, "Passionate Visions in Contest," 297. Rabbi Liebman's Report, Board Minutes, 15 October, 3 December 1939. Abramson, "Social History of Temple Israel," 36; Rabbi Liebman's Report, Board Minutes, 28 June 1939.

16. Sarna, *American Judaism*, 258, 288–289. Rabbi Liebman's Report, Board Minutes, 28 June 1939, Board Minutes, 9 July 1939.

17. Rabbi Liebman to Rabbi Jacob Weinstein, Temple K.A.M., Chicago, 31 May 1940, in Rabbi Joshua Loth Liebman Papers, TI Archives; Rudolph Wyner, interview by Genevieve Wyner, 29 June 1981, transcript, Oral History Collection, TI Archives. Rabbi Liebman's Report, Board Minutes, 5 November 1939.

18. Rabbi Liebman's Report, Board Minutes, 9 July 1939. Rabbi Liebman's Report, Board Minutes, 15 October 1939. Liebman to Ann Smith of Chicago, 20 December 1939; Liebman to Rabbi Jacob Weinstein, Temple K.A.M., Chicago, 31 May 1940; Marine Private Howard H. Heiman to Liebman, 6 May 1942; all in Liebman Papers, TI Archives.

19. Board Minutes, 15 October 1939, 3 December 1939, 7 January 1940, 4 May 1941; for Oneg Shabbat, see Board Minutes, 27 January 1942; *TI Bulletin*, January 1942.

20. Abramson, "Social History of Temple Israel," 43. Liebman, speech given to Temple Israel religious school teachers, 21 August 1939, in Liebman Papers, TI Archives.

21. Ida Mae Kahn, speech, "Program Honoring the Retirement of Samuel A. Nemzoff," 9 June 1974, audiotape, Audio/Visual Collection, TI Library.

22. Rabbi Liebman's Report, Board Minutes, 10 March 1940, 15 October 1939.

23. Board Minutes, 5 November 1939; Liebman Report, Board Minutes, 3 November 1940. Nemzoff to Liebman, 29 January 1943, in Liebman Papers, TI Archives.

24. Rabbi Liebman's Report, Board Minutes, 5 November 1939, 9 June 1940.

25. Reimer, "Passionate Visions in Contest," 297. Membership Committee Report, Board Minutes, 9 November 1941; *TI Bulletin*, 3 January 1940. Members hired private tutors to prepare their sons for bar mitzvah elsewhere. See Sharf, interview, Oral History Collection and Justin L. Wyner, interview by Susan L. Porter, 10 and 13 October 2006, audiotape, Oral History Collection, TI Archives.

26. For membership strategies, see Gertrude S. Tichell, Clerk, to Judge A. K. Cohen, Board Trustee, Board Minutes, 18 October 1939; Liebman Report, Board Minutes, 3 December 1939; Liebman to Rabbi Maurice Eisendrath, Holy Blossom Temple, Toronto, 10 and 17 February 1941, in Liebman Papers, TI Archives. For increased membership, see Board Minutes, 15 October 1939; Liebman to Rabbi Solomon Goldman, Anshe Emet Synagogue, Chicago, 9 October 1941 and Liebman to Dr. Tobias Schanfarber of Chicago, 17 October 1941, in Liebman Papers, TI Archives; Board Minutes, 7 December 1941.

27. President Joseph H. Cohen, Annual Report, 1954; *TI Bulletin*, 28 October 1955.

28. Board Minutes, 15 October 1939; Liebman to Lee M. Friedman, 30 April 1942, in Liebman Papers, TI Archives. Goldstein to Rabbi Wolk, 7 May 1945, in Goldstein Papers, AJA. Rabbi Liebman's Report, Board Minutes, 12 April 1942. "Rabbi Joshua Loth Liebman of Temple Israel, Boston," on "Message of Israel," NBC, 2 September 1939, in Liebman Papers, TI Archives.

29. *Boston Evening Transcript*, 24 June 1939; Stephen H. Norwood, "Marauding Youths and the Christian Front: Antisemitic Violence in Boston and New York During World War II," *American Jewish History* 91, no. 2 (June 2003): 233–267; Katherine Donovan and Paul Murphy, *He Brought "Peace of Mind to Millions"* (Boston: Hearst Newspapers, 1948), [17–20].

30. "Full Support of Labor and Landsleit Groups Pledged for 1941 Combined Appeal," *Advocate*, 3 October 1941.

31. Board Minutes, 8 February 1942, 6 March 1942.

32. For wartime activities, see *TI Bulletin*, 1942–1945; *G.I. News*, 1942–1945, in Brotherhood Collection, TI Archives. Board Minutes, 8 February 1942; *G.I. News*, July 1944.

33. *Advocate*, 4 December 1942, 4; Dr. Joshua Loth Liebman, "'How Can I Believe in God Now?' An Address Broadcast over Station WNAC," 7 February 1943, and on "Message of Israel," NBC, 2 October 1943, Liebman Papers, TI Archives.

34. "Fate of European Jewry Rests Upon Defeat of Nazis," *Advocate*, 7 May 1943. Jick, "From Margin to Mainstream," 94–96; "Says Jews Claim Huge Reparations," *New York Times*, 23 November 1941.

35. *Advocate*, 30 November 1944; Jacob Kaplan, Associated Jewish Philanthropies president, quoted in Haber, "Burden of Witness," 95.

36. Donovan and Murphy, *He Brought "Peace of Mind*," [1]. Isaiah 40:1; Liebman, "What Shall We Do with the Germans and Ourselves?" 20 May 1945.

37. Andrew R. Heinze, *"Peace of Mind* (1946): Judaism and the Therapeutic Polemics of Postwar America," *Religion and American Culture* 12, no. 1 (Winter 2002): 35–40; Mann, *Growth and Achievement*, 105. Donovan and Murphy, *He Brought "Peace of Mind*," [11].

38. Sarna, *American Judaism*, 272–273, Heinze, *"Peace of Mind"* (1946), 45. For reader mail, see Liebman Papers, TI Archives and Rabbi Joshua Loth Liebman and Fan Loth Liebman Collection, The Howard Gotlieb Archival Research Center, Boston University.

39. Board Minutes, 7, 15, 28 September 1947; 6, 19 October 1947.

40. John Morse, Treasurer's Report, Annual Meeting, Board Minutes, 25 January 1953. Reimer, "Passionate Visions in Contest," 295–297. Samuel Nemzoff, interview by Genevieve Wyner, 14 July 1981, transcript, Oral History Collection, TI Archives. For postwar American religious education, see Sarna, *American Judaism*, 279–280.

41. Nemzoff, interview, Oral History Collection; President Joseph D. Cohen's Annual Report, 1954; *Torchbearer* (1947), 2.

42. Board Minutes, 14 March, 9 May, 5 December 1948; *TI Bulletin*, 25 March 1958. For Garden Club, see Garden Club Collection, TI Archives. Emmanuel Kurland, Supper Club Chairman, Board Minutes, 13 November 1949.

43. *Advocate*, 12 June 1948, 5. *Herald*, 12 June 1948.

44. Board Minutes, 10 October 1948; Board Minutes, 20 June 1948, 26 July 1948, 5 December 1948.

45. Board Minutes, 1 May 1949.

46. Board Minutes, 24 April 1949. "Abraham Klausner, 92, Dies; Aided Holocaust Survivors," *New York Times*, 30 June 2007. Alex Grobman, *Rekindling The Flame: American Jewish Chaplains and the Survivors of European Jewry, 1944–1948* (Detroit, Mich.: Wayne State University, 1993).

47. Rabbi Leon Jick, quoted in Abramson, "Social History of Temple Israel," 56. Board Minutes, 24 April 1949, 1 May 1949. "Personal and Confidential Data as Requested by Mr. Joseph Schneider," Board Minutes, January 5, 1953. Rabbi Klausner's Address, Board Minutes, 1 May 1949.

48. Judith Rothman, interview by Meaghan Dwyer, 13 July 2007, audiotape, Oral History Collection, TI Archives. *Torchbearer* (1948), 5. *Sisterhood Bulletin*, November 1951. Abramson, "Social History of Temple Israel," 61, 57. Emmanuel Kurland, Supper Club Chairman, Board Minutes, 13 November 1949. *TI Bulletin*, 23 September 1952.

49. For communal attempts to establish suburban congregations, see Rabbi Levi's Report, Board Minutes, 10 April 1932; Board Minutes, 21 June 1947; Sarna, *American Judaism*, 282–284. Abramson, "Social History of Temple Israel," 57–59; "Report of the Trustees Concerning Termination of the Rabbi's Tenure," 5 January 1953. For music services, see Herbert Fromm Papers, TI Archives.

50. "Report of the Trustees Concerning Termination of the Rabbi's Tenure," Board Minutes, 5 January 1953. Rabbi Klausner's Address, Board Minutes, 25 January 1953.

51. "Abraham Klausner, 92, Dies," *New York Times*, 30 June 2007. Jick, quoted in Abramson, "Social History of Temple Israel," 52.

CHAPTER 5. PROPHETIC JUDAISM AND THE "SYMPHONY OF AMERICAN LIFE," 1953–1973 (pp. 103–124)

1. Jonathan Sarna, *American Judaism*, 272–282. See also Will Herberg, *Protestant, Catholic, Jew* (Garden City, N.Y.: Anchor Books, 1960).

2. Board Minutes, 1 March 1953. Gladys Damon, "A Celebration of the Life of Rabbi Joshua Loth Liebman," *Advocate*, 28 April 1988; Jick, quoted in Abramson, "Social History of Temple Israel," 65.

3. Board Minutes, 19 May 1953; Rabbi Roland B. Gittelsohn, interview by Justin L. Wyner, 15 June 1987, transcript, Oral History Collection, TI Archives. Board Minutes, 10 June 1953.

4. Gittelsohn, interview, Oral History Collection; Board Minutes, 15 November 1953; *TI Bulletin*, 30 October 1953.

5. For temple atmosphere, see Wyner, "Personal Reminiscences." For notable members, see Membership Records, TI Archives; Justin Wyner, interview, Oral History Collection.

6. Mann, *Growth and Achievement*, 121–126.

7. Abramson, "Social History of Temple Israel," 70; Kahn, interview, WWLSC. See also Sarna, *American Judaism*, 277, 289.

8. *TI Bulletin*, 1 September 1956; Temple Committee Report, Annual Meeting, Board Minutes, 9 December 1956; Temple Committee Minutes, Board Minutes, 17 September 1957; Special Meeting regarding Pew Ownership, 11 May 1958; Gittelsohn, interview, Oral History Collection; *TI Bulletin*, 1 September 1956. Gittelsohn was aided by Board President John Morse, a third-generation member.

9. *TI Bulletin*, 17 December 1954, 2 March 1955, 17 March 1957.

10. For membership figures, see Board Minutes, 31 August 1953, 13 December 1953, 17 September 1968. For garage and other transportation issues, see Board Minutes, 22 November 1959, 22 September 1956, 24 April 1960, and 1 June 1960. Charles Goldman, Vice Chairman of the Legal Committee, to Temple Israel Board, 22 April 1960, Board Minutes, 17 May 1960; Board Minutes, 1 June 1960, 14 June 1960.

11. Long Range Planning Committee Report, Board Minutes, 23 November 1958. Board Minutes, 23 October 1955; *TI Bulletin*, 3 October 1956, 24 December 1957, 10 October 1961. Board Minutes, 18 October 1960; Annual Education Report, Board Minutes, 14 June 1961. Member Merle I. Locke, an engineer and contractor, supervised the project.

12. Board Minutes, 29 June 1954; Nemzoff, interview, Oral History Collection; Rudolph Wyner, interview, Oral History Collection; *Torchbearer* (1954), 9; Board Minutes, 1 June 1960, 18 October 1960; Annual Education Report, Board Minutes, 14 June 1961.

13. *TI Bulletin*, 1 September 1961, Board Minutes, 29 June 1954, *TI Religious School Parents' Handbook* (1956); Nemzoff, interview, Oral History Collection.

14. *TI Bulletin*, 1 September 1956. *TI Religious School Parents' Handbook* (1956). Board Minutes, 13 November 1955; *TI Bulletin*, 2 March 1956, 12 September 1956. Board Minutes, 7 November 1956. See also Lois Isenman, "Breaking Ground: My Bat Mitzvah," 1 January 2007, in TI Archives.

15. Board Minutes, 29 June 1954; *TI Religious School Parents' Handbook* (1956). Ruth Scheinwald Cowin, interview by Joan Rachlin, 13 and 25 February 1997, transcript, WWLSC; Selma Gross Finstein, interview by Betsy Friedman Abrams and Bobbie Burnstein, 30 September 1997, transcript, WWLSC; Board Minutes, 11 April 1954, 29 June 1954.

16. Finstein, interview, WWLSC. Nemzoff, interview, Oral History Collection. Helen Fine, interview by Emily Mehlman, 1991, audiotape, Oral History Collection, TI Archives. Syril Stone, "An Interview with Mr. Reuben Lurie," *Torchbearer* (1950), 63.

17. *Torchbearer* (1954), 57; *TI Bulletin*, 8 September 1954, 11 November 1954, 3 October 1956. Finstein, interview, WWLSC; *TI Bulletin*, 11 November 1958, Board Minutes, 1953–1964, passim. *TI Bulletin*, 29 October 1956, 26 December 1956.

18. Nemzoff, interview, Oral History Collection. *TI Bulletin*, 13 May 1958. Youth Committee Report, Board Minutes, 18 October 1960; *TI Bulletin*, 23 January 1962, 27 February 1962.

19. Board Minutes, 11 April 1954, 12 November 1954; Finstein, interview, WWLSC. *TI Bulletin*, 31 October 1961. Board Minutes, 23 October 1955, 19 March 1961. For more regarding school activities, see *Torchbearer*, 1950–1969, in TI Archives.

20. "From Iwo Jima to Zion," *Reform Judaism* 12, no. 2 (Winter 1983), 18. For sermon examples, see "Israel and World Peace," 9 November 1956; "Golda Meir — A Modern Esther. A Pre-Purim Sermon Evaluating the Career of Israel's Foreign Minister," 8 March 1957; "Common Misconceptions About the State of Israel," 29 March 1957; "What Israel Means to the World," 28 November 1958, in Rabbi Roland B. Gittelsohn Papers, Sermons Files, TI Archives. For Israel trips, see *TI Bulletin*, 7 October 1958; Board Minutes, 13 December 1959; *TI Bulletin*, 8 April 1958. *TI Bulletin*, 1 September 1964. For Gittelsohn quote, see "What Israel Means to American Jews," 5 April 1959, in Gittelsohn Papers, Sermons Files.

21. Jack Wertheimer, *A People Divided*, quoted in Sarna, *American Judaism*, 318. "Temple Israel Follows Generous Tradition," *Boston Traveler*, 16 June 1967. *TI Bulletin*, 17 February 1970; correspondence and fliers, 1969–1980, in Israel Committee Collection, TI Archives.

22. Education Report, Board Minutes, 24 April 1960; *TI Bulletin*, 17 October 1961. "Clergy Corner," *TI Bulletin*, 25 November 1955; Sarna, *American Judaism*, 277. *TI Bulletin*, 13 November 1953, 1 September 1956; Board Minutes, 9 December 1956, 13 December 1959. The temple also switched to Sephardic pronunciation (see Temple and Education Committee Reports, Board Minutes, 17 May 1960, 14 June 1960; *TI Bulletin*, 23 January 1962).

23. *TI Bulletin*, 16 February 1955; Board Minutes, 18 October 1960.

24. Quote from Edenfeld, interview, WWLSC. Kahn, interview, WWLSC; Board Minutes, 18 October 1960; *TI Sisterhood News*, 1950–1960.

25. Frank L. Kozol to Charles Goldman, 26 January 1956, in Board Minutes, 19 February 1956; Sarna, *American Judaism*, 288; Board Minutes, 13 November 1955.

26. Robert Levi, quoted in *TI Bulletin*, 13 March 1957. For Brotherhood activities, see *Brotherhood News*, 1950–1968; *TI Bulletin*, 2 February 1965.

27. President Frank P. Cohen, Board Minutes, 8 May 1949, 20 January 1957; Sarna, *American Judaism*, 307–310. *TI Bulletin*, 1 May 1957, 28 August 1953, 1 October 1954, 2 February 1955.

28. *TI Bulletin*, 17 December 1957; 7 January, 14 February, and 15 April 1958; Joseph W. Copel, MD, "Temple Israel — Boston Social Action Group Statement of Purpose," 6 October, 1959, Social Action Committee Files, Box 1, TI Archives.

29. Mann, *Growth and Achievement*, 124; Sarna, *American Judaism*, 308. Copel, "Social Action Group Statement of Purpose." *TI Bulletin*, 1 September 1961. Board Minutes, 13 December 1959; *TI Bulletin*, 16 February 1960.

30. Quote from Anne Jackson, interview by Fran Putnoi and Pam Goodman, 4 February and 19 May 1997, transcript, WWLSC. For activities, see *TI Bulletin*, 26 December 1961, 9 January 1962, 17 April 1962, 3 September 1963, 9 March 1965.

31. *TI Bulletin*, 3 December 1963, 7 January 1964, 17 March 1964, 5 October 1965, 16 June 1966.

32. *TI Bulletin*, 6 April 1965. Gittelsohn was scheduled to march but cancelled because of illness (Gittelsohn, interview, Oral History Collection). Louis Grossman, "March on Montgomery," *Torchbearer* (1965), 22. King's visit was not well documented; he spoke without notes. See *TI Bulletin*, 20 and 27 April 1965; Helaine Klein, "Dr. King at Temple Israel," *Torchbearer* (1965), 22.

33. "The Legion Bars Award to Rabbi Who Backed March," *New York Times*, 4 December 1965; *TI Bulletin*, 21 December 1965. *TI Bulletin*, 7 December 1965, 28 December 1965.

34. Gittelsohn, "From Iwo Jima to Zion," 33; *TI Bulletin*, 7 and 28 December 1965. Gittelsohn, interview, Oral History Collection.

35. Gittelsohn, interview, Oral History Collection; Board Minutes, 12 April 1977.

36. Benjamin Altman, Maintenance Committee Chair, to Hirsh Sharf, 1 April 1963, in Long Range Planning Committee Summary [LRPC] Report, in Board Minutes, 25 January 1968.

37. For a discussion of the various options, see LRPC Report. For the final decision, see LRPC Meeting Minutes, 22 October 1963, in LRPC Report, Appendix 2, page 7. For synagogues moving to the suburbs, see Gamm, *Urban Exodus*.

38. For the decision to remain in Boston, see Wyner, "Personal Reminiscences;" LRPC Meeting Minutes, 22 October 1963, in LRPC Report, Appendix 2, page 3. For quote, see Altman to Lloyd D. Tarlin, 15 May 1964, in LRPC Meeting Minutes, 1 June 1964, in LRPC Report, Appendix 3, page 5. Lease between Boston University and Temple Israel, 27 February 1968, in Commonwealth Avenue Files, Buildings Collection; Board Minutes, 24 March 1968; Abramson, "Social History of Temple Israel," 71.

39. "Temple Israel Lays Cornerstone for New Sanctuary," *Advocate*, 5 October 1972, "Temple Israel's New Home," *Advocate*, 1 November 1973. "Sky Covenant" has been called the "largest and most important outdoor sculpture" by Nevelson in America.

CHAPTER 6. "A HOME FOR EVERY CONSTITUENCY," 1973–1988
(pp. 125–160)

1. Rabbi Roland B. Gittelsohn, "Speech at the Dedication of Temple Israel's New Sanctuary," 21 September 1973, audiotape, Audio/Visual Collection, TI Library. Sarna, *American Judaism*, 318–325. See also Dana Evan Kaplan, *American Reform Judaism: An Introduction* (New Brunswick, N.J.: Rutgers University Press, 2003); Fred Rosenbaum, *Visions of Reform: Congregation Emanu-El and the Jews of San Francisco, 1849–1999* (Berkeley, Calif.: Judah L. Magnes Museum, 2000).

2. *TI Bulletin*, 5 September 1973; Frances Putnoi, interview by Susan L. Porter and Lisa Fagin Davis, 10 and 20 November 2006 and 11 December 2006, audiotape, Oral History Collection.

3. Membership Committee Reports, Board Minutes, 25 October 1973, 16 September 1975, 28 May 1976. For religious school figures, see Board Minutes, 14 October 1975. 1957 was the peak birth year for baby boomers. Sarna, *American Judaism*, 319–323; Abramson, "Social History of Temple Israel," 71–77; Evaluation Committee Report, Board Minutes, 17 December 1974; Rabbi Bernard Mehlman and Emily S. Mehlman, interview by Meaghan Dwyer, 10 December 2004 and 4 March 2005, audiotape, Oral History Collection; Frances Godine, interview by Meaghan Dwyer, 25 February 2005, audiotape, Oral History Collection. For comparable changes at other American synagogues, see Jick, "The Reform Synagogue," 104–107; Rosenbaum, *Visions of Reform*, 251–295.

4. Sarna, *American Judaism*, 328.

5. For the endowment fund, see Board Minutes, 6 December 1959. For deficit numbers, see Budget and Treasurer Reports, 1971–1979, TI Archives. The 1971–1972 projected budget deficit was $4,645; the final figure was $16,791 (Board Minutes, 15 June 1971). In 1973, the temple owed $1,350,000 (*TI Bulletin*, 19 June 1973; Budget Report, Board Minutes, 11 December 1973). For financial strategies, see Board Minutes, 11 December 1973, 14 February 1974, 14 January 1975, 14 October 1975, 16 December 1975. Report of the Special Committee on the Rabbinate, 17 December 1974, TI Archives.

6. Samuel Nemzoff, Religious School Report, 10 April 1970, Board Minutes, 26 April 1970; Joan Schilder, PTA Report, Board Minutes, 19 May 1970; *TI Religious School Handbook* (1972), Religious School Files; Board Minutes, 22 May 1973. Board Minutes, 16 September 1975. Saturday sessions were eliminated in 1975.

7. Evaluation Committee Report, Board Minutes, 17 December 1974. Forty-four percent of congregants responded to the initial letter. Of that number, 60 percent were interviewed; the remainder felt their comments were of little importance or they had already left the congregation.

8. Evaluation Committee Report, 17 December 1974.

9. Ibid.

10. Ibid. For members' opinions about Gittelsohn, see Gittelsohn, interview, Oral History Collection. Board Minutes, 18 December 1953. Marion Eisenman, interview by Emily Mehlman, 19 May 1997, transcript, WWLSC. See also Cowin, interview, WWLSC.

11. Rudolph Wyner, interview, Oral History Collection. UAHC and CCAR Guidelines, "The Rabbi and His Congregation," *Synagogue Service*, January 1958. For Levi campaign, see Board Minutes, 13 August 1964; Justin Wyner, interview, Oral History Collection.

12. For *The Jewish Catalog*, see Sarna, *American Judaism*, 319–322. Rabbi Citrin, "The Rabbis' Corner," *TI Bulletin*, 27 December 1977. For havurot, see Lawrence Levinson, quoted in *TI Bulletin*, 9 January 1978. Board Minutes, 12 April 1977, 16 December 1975, 18 January 1977, 15 March 1977. Citrin, "The Rabbis' Corner," *TI Bulletin*, 3 October 1977. For family services, see *TI Bulletin*, 16 March 1971.

13. Anita Bender, interview by Lesley Schoenfeld, 11 November 2005, audiotape, Oral History Collection; Roberta Burstein, interview by Peggy Morrison, 11 November 2005, audiotape, Oral History Collection.

14. Sylvia Cooper, interview by Barbara Burg, 2 and 30 December 2005, audiotape, Oral History Collection.

15. Burstein, interview, Oral History Collection; Mehlmans, interview, Oral History Collection. For bylaws changes, see Board Minutes, 11 July 1977, 6 November 1977; President's Address, Annual Meeting, Board Minutes, 12 November 1978; *TI Bulletin*, 4 December 1978. In November 1979, there were 3,000 voting members.

16. Cooper, interview, Oral History Collection; Gittelsohn to Mrs. Harold Drachman, 4 May 1979, in Gittelsohn Papers, Correspondence A–K, Box 16, Folder 2, TI Archives; Hulda Gittelsohn, interview, WWLSC; Putnoi, interview, Oral History Collection.

17. "Report of Outgoing President Milton Linden, Annual Meeting," 4 November 1979, in *TI Bulletin*, 19 November 1979; Gittelsohn to the Congregation, 29 October 1976, Board Minutes, 13 October 1976; Board Minutes, 21 September 1976; Advisory Committee Report, Board Minutes, 30 September 1976; Board Minutes, 7 November 1976. Max I. Dimont to Gittelsohn, 12 October 1979, in Gittelsohn Papers, Correspondence A–K, Box 16, Folder 2, TI Archives.

18. "Report of Outgoing President Milton Linden." Search Committee Report, 11 July 1977. Board Minutes, 11 July 1977; Board Minutes, 2 August 1977.

19. For comparisons of rabbinic styles, see Sarna, *American Judaism*, 324. For Mehlman, see Curriculum Vitae of Rabbi Bernard Mehlman, in Board Minutes, 11 July 1977. Search Committee Report, 11 July 1977; Temple Committee Minutes, 18 June 1985. Board Minutes, 2 August 1977.

20. For Mehlman's opinion of the temple, see Search Committee Report, 11 July 1977; Board Minutes, 2 August 1977. For Mehlman's goals, see Temple Committee Minutes, 18 June 1985; Board Minutes, 2 August 1977; Mehlman, Curriculum Vitae; *TI Bulletin*, 4 December 1978. See also Mehlmans, interview, Oral History Collection and Rabbi Ronne Friedman, interview by Lisa Fagin Davis, 17 August 2007, audiotape, Oral History Collection.

21. For Mehlman's goals, see Board Minutes, 5 April 1978. Mehlmans, interview, Oral History Collection. Three hundred and ten families out of 1,600 enrolled children in the school (Board Minutes, 5 April 1978 and 20 September 1977). Budget Analysis, June 1977.

The deficit was $63,000 in 1976–1977; the projected deficit for 1977–1978 was $71,000. For Rabb, see Fiscal Review Committee Report, Board Minutes, 20 June 1978.

22. *TI Bulletin*, 11 June 1979. Membership Committee Report, Board Minutes, 19 September 1978, 17 October 1978. *TI Bulletin*, 19 May 1980. Board Minutes, 29 January 1980, 23 February 1982, 14 October 1982.

23. Board Minutes, 29 January 1980. Conversation with Fran Putnoi, 14 September 2007. See also Temple Israel Files, Wyner Family Papers, Wyner Center of the American Jewish Historical Society [AJHS], Hebrew College, Newton, Massachusetts.

24. *TI Bulletin*, 4 November 1969; the nine were Charlotte Daum, Helen Levenson, Zifre Lurie, Anita Bender, Deborah Hauser, Fran Putnoi, Genevieve Wyner, Laurel Friedman, and Betsy Abrams. For more on female leaders, see Bender, interview, Oral History Collection; Putnoi, interview, Oral History Collection; Genevieve Wyner, interview by Meaghan Dwyer, 10 October 2006, audiotape, Oral History Collection.

25. Board mailing, 8 October 1980, Board Minutes, 23 September 1980. See also Justin Wyner, interview, Oral History Collection.

26. Board Minutes, 11 September 1979; President Wyner's Address, Annual Meeting, Board Minutes, 4 November 1979; President Wyner's Report, Board Minutes, 8 June 1982.

27. Rabbi Mehlman, "The Rabbi: A Definition," Annual Meeting, Board Minutes, 6 November 1977; Mehlman, Curriculum Vitae.

28. Board Minutes, 6 November 1977. Friedman and Mehlman, "Building Community"; Board Minutes, 28 February 1978, 5 April 1978.

29. President Milton Linden's Address, Special Meeting, Board Minutes, 6 November 1977; Rabbi's Report, Board Minutes, 19 September 1978; Dennis Gaffney, "An Old Tongue a New Way: Learning Hebrew by Computer," *The Tab*, 9 November 1983; Board Minutes, 28 October 1980.

30. Religious School Annual Report, Board Minutes, 13 February 1979, 4 November 1979; Mehlmans, interview, Oral History Collection.

31. Board Minutes, 10 April 1979, 28 October 1980.

32. *TI Bulletin*, 6 September 1982, 21 February 1983, 19 December 1983.

33. President Wyner's Address, Annual Meeting, Board Minutes, 17 May 1981; Rabbi Mehlman's Address, Annual Meeting, Board Minutes, 15 June 1982. Louise Freedman, Chair, to the Continuing Education Committee, 28 April 1983, Board Minutes, 26 April 1983. For Friedman's goals for the religious school, see Rabbi Friedman's Address, Annual Meeting, Board Minutes, 12 June 1983; *TI Bulletin*, 13 June 1983. For various statistics, see Board Minutes, 29 November 1983, 31 January 1984; *TI Bulletin*, 21 February 1983.

34. *TI Bulletin*, 18 April 1978; Board Minutes, 20 June 1978, 19 September 1978. Board Minutes, 21 November 1978.

35. Board Minutes, 21 November 1978; *TI Bulletin*, 5 March 1979; Mehlmans, interview, Oral History Collection; *TI Bulletin*, 27 October 1980, 17 September 1979; Board Minutes, 17 December 1979; *TI Bulletin*, 10 November 1980, 22 November 1982.

36. *TI Bulletin*, 31 October 1978.

37. For Purim, see Mehlmans, interview, Oral History Collection; Board Minutes, 5 April 1978; *TI Bulletin*, 6 March 1978, 18 April 1978. For Passover, see *TI Bulletin*, 30 March 1976, 13 April 1976, 5 February 1979.

38. *TI Bulletin*, 6 September 1978, 19 September 1978.

39. Rabbi Mehlman, "The Rabbi: A Definition," Annual Meeting, Board Minutes, 6 November 1977; Janet Richmond and Irving Fisher, quoted in "History and Timeline of Temple Israel, 140th Anniversary Booklet," ed. Betsy Abrams (Boston, 1994).

40. *TI Bulletin*, 20 February 1979.

41. For Reform cantors, see Jeffrey A. Summit, *The Lord's Song in a Strange Land: Music and Identity in Contemporary Jewish Worship* (New York: Oxford University Press, 2000), 53–54. Gittelsohn, interview, Oral History Collection, Board Minutes, 18 December 1953. *TI Bulletin*, 31 October 1977. For Cantor Simon, see Music Committee Report, 24 March 1981; Simon's Statement, 30 November 1982, Board Minutes, 13 December 1982; Mehlmans, interview, Oral History Collection.

42. *TI Bulletin*, 13 June 1983.

43. Temple Committee Meeting Minutes, 23 May 1978. David Brody to Betsy Abrams, 18 May 1982, Temple Committee Files.

44. Marianne Aaron to President Herbert Schilder, 16 January 1983, Temple Committee Files.

45. *TI Bulletin*, 18 October 1982, 20 December 1982. Temple Committee Minutes, 8 February 1982, 1 June 1982, 15 February 1983, 11 October 1983, 14 February 1984. See also Rabbi Mehlman's Speech, Annual Meeting, Board Minutes, 8 June 1999.

46. Temple Committee Minutes, 18 June 1985.

47. Eisenman, interview, and Cowin, interview, WWLSC.

48. Rabbi Mehlman, Speech at Annual Meeting, Board Minutes, 8 June 1989. Board Minutes, 5 April 1978. Rabbi's Report, Board Minutes, 19 September 1978; *TI Bulletin*, 4 October 1978; *TI Bulletin*, 13 June 1983; Rabbi's Address, Annual Meeting, Board Minutes, 14 June 1984.

49. President Wyner's Address, Annual Meeting, Board Minutes, 15 June 1982, 30 March 1982.

50. Mehlmans, interview, Oral History Collection; Board Minutes, 29 January 1980, 2 January 1980. "History of Saturday's/Sunday's Bread," http://www.satsunbread.org/history .html (accessed 5 June 2008).

51. Board Minutes, 29 January 1980; *TI Bulletin*, 26 January 1981; Board Minutes, 22 March 1983; *TI Bulletin*, 23 January 1984, 1 January 1992.

52. Sarna, *American Judaism*, 333.

53. Social Action Committee Report, Board Minutes, 16 September 1975, 14 October 1975. Board Minutes, 12 April 1977. See also Margo Strom, "A Work in Progress," http:// www.facinghistory.org (accessed 7 December 2007).

54. *TI Bulletin*, 31 October 1977, 14 November 1977, 2 September 1977, 6 March 1978,

26 April 1982. Board Minutes, 25 October 1983. *TI Bulletin*, 17 October 1977, 12 June 1978, 3 January 1983; *TI Bulletin*, 14 November 1977; *TI Bulletin*, 13 June 1972.

55. *TI Bulletin*, 15 October 1979; Edie Mueller, quoted in Abrams, ed., "History and Timeline of Temple Israel, 140th Anniversary Booklet"; Board Minutes, 29 January 1980. Board Minutes, 28 May 1985.

56. Sarna, *American Judaism*, 317–318; Mehlmans, interview, Oral History Collection.

57. *TI Bulletin*, 13 November 1978; *TI Bulletin*, 26 January 1981, 31 August 1981; Board Minutes, 13 January 1982. See also Ronya Schwaab, interview by Vicki Gabriner, 18 and 26 January 1997, 3 and 7 February 1997, 18 June 1997, transcript, WWLSC.

58. For more on Soviet Jewry, see *TI Bulletin* and Board Minutes, 1980s–1990s; Mehlmans, interview, Oral History Collection; Rabbi Mehlman's Address, Annual Meeting, Board Minutes, 7 June 1988. Other congregants, including the Wyners, visited the Soviet Union separately.

59. Mehlmans, interview, Oral History Collection. For notices regarding Project Integration, the job databank, and other programs, see *TI Bulletin*, 1988–1992.

CHAPTER 7. "A COMMUNITY OF COMMUNITIES," 1988–2009 (pp. 161–197)

1. For the "big tent" concept, see the "Synagogue 2000" movement led by Lawrence A. Hoffman and Ron Wolfson. Hoffman, "Imagine A Synagogue For the 21st Century," *Reform Judaism* 25, no. 1 (Fall 1996), 21–26. Isa Aron, *Becoming a Congregation of Learners* (Woodstock, Vt.: Jewish Lights, 2000), xiii, quoted in Sarna, *American Judaism*, 365. For the focus on inclusiveness, see "A Statement of Principles for Reform Judaism," Central Conference of American Rabbis (CCAR), Pittsburgh Convention, May 1999, http://ccarnet.org/Articles/index.cfm?id=44&pge_id=1606 (accessed 6 June 2008). Summit, *Lord's Song*, 55.

2. For interfaith programs, see *TI Bulletin*, 21 March 1983, 3 January 1984, 4 September 1989.

3. "Reform Movement's Resolution on Patrilineal Descent: The Status of Children of Mixed Marriages," CCAR, 15 March 1983, http://www.jewishvirtuallibrary.org/jsource/Judaism/patrilineal1.html (accessed 18 March 2008); "The Challenge of Intermarriage," *Advocate*, 16 November 1995; "Interfaith Marriage," *Jewish Educational Ventures*, 31 October 2000; Jonathan Sarna, "Contemporary Reform Judaism: An Historical Analysis," K.A.M. Isaiah Israel, Chicago, 12 February 2008, http://kamiiweinsteinweekend.blogspot.com/search/label/Professor%20Sarna%27s%20address (accessed 18 March 2008).

4. Conversation with Rabbi Ronne Friedman, 20 August 2007; "Gay and Lesbian Havurah at Services," *TI Bulletin*, 1 March 1992; *TI Bulletin*, 1 September 1996.

5. The median membership age was between 60 and 65; 13.5 percent of members were under age 39; 19.4 percent were over 80. See Board Minutes, 22 September 1992.

6. Board Minutes, 5 April 1936; Nursery School Committee Report to the Board, Board Minutes, 26 November 1991. $300,000 had been pledged for the preschool, including

gifts from the Cohens and Jacobsons, as well as $50,000 that was allocated from capital campaign funds to classroom construction to jointly serve the preschool and religious school.

7. Board Minutes, 22 October 1991, 26 November 1991, 18 May 1993; *TI Bulletin*, 1 April, 1 July 1993. President's Column, *TI Bulletin*, 1 July 1994; Kevin Alexander, "Junior Achievers," *Boston Magazine*, September 2007, http://www.bostonmagazine.com/articles/junior _achievers/page4 (accessed 17 October 2007). Cohen taught at Wheelock College and served on the UAHC's Task Force for the Development of Moral and Ethical Education. By 2004, the FJECC had about one hundred students.

8. Pamela Nadell, *Women Who Would Be Rabbis: A History of Women's Ordination, 1889–1985* (Boston: Beacon Press, 1998); Sarna, *American Judaism*, 340–343; Rabbi Elaine Zecher, interview by Lisa Fagin Davis, 15 October 2007, transcript, Oral History Collection.

9. Mehlmans, interview, Oral History Collection; Friedman, interview, Oral History Collection; Zecher, interview, Oral History Collection. Fran Putnoi, Report of the President, 23 January 1990, in Frances Stieber Putnoi Papers, Board Presidents Files, TI Archives.

10. Zecher, interview, Oral History Collection; Matthew S. Robinson, "Sister Act: Unique Pair Discuss Women's Role in Rabbinate," *Advocate*, 28 October 1999, B1. *TI Bulletin*, 1 October 1990; Women's Study Group Files, TI Archives.

11. Zecher, quoted in Summit, *Lord's Song*, 62.

12. For Learner's Minyan, see *TI Bulletin*, 1 October 1990. For healing service, see Board Minutes, 23 October 1990. For Heneinu, see *TI Bulletin*, December 1998.

13. Sumner Rodman, Treasurer's Report to Annual Meeting, 10 June 1986; Mehlman's Report, Board Minutes, 10 June 1986. Capital campaign newsletter, Fall 1989, Development Files, TI Archives; Marvin Grossman, interview by Leslie Schoenfeld, 16 November 2005, audiotape, Oral History Collection.

14. For Mehlman's vision for the renovation, see *TI Bulletin*, 15 January 1990; Maintenance Committee Report, 23 January 1990; *TI Bulletin*, November 1990. Trustees transferred $400,000 from the capital campaign into the general endowment fund (Board Minutes, 31 May 1992).

15. Board Minutes, 26 January 1988; Justin Wyner, interview, Oral History Collection; Board Minutes, 23 August 1989; *TI Bulletin*, 15 January 1990, 1 January 1992.

16. For Mehlman's tenure agreement, see Board Minutes, 10 June 1986. Reimer observed the religious school for two years. See Joseph Reimer, *Succeeding at Jewish Education: How One Synagogue Made it Work* (Philadelphia, Jewish Publication Society, 1997).

17. Rabbi Ronne Friedman, Report on Parlor Meetings Between Members of Board & Rabbis Held During Fall/Winter 1991–2, 20 January 1992, Board Minutes, 25 February 1992. For the "co-rabbinate" proposal, see Board Minutes, 27 November 1990; Report of Ad Hoc Committee on Rabbi Friedman's Contract, 30 April 1991.

18. Board to Rabbi Friedman, 1 July 1991, Board Minutes, 15 February 1992.

19. Irving Rabb, interview by Joan Rachlin, 12 December 2005, 17 January 2006, 22 March 2006, and 26 April 2006, audiotape, Oral History Collection. Rabbi Friedman, Report on Parlor Meetings, Board Minutes, 25 February 1992; Marvin Grossman, interview, Oral History Collection; Justin Wyner, interview, Oral History Collection. Cooper, interview, Oral History Collection; Mehlman to Hoffman, 14 April 1992, Board Minutes, 28 April 1992.

20. For opposition to succession plan, see Eisenman, interview, WWLSC. Rabbi Friedman, Presentation to the Board, Board Minutes, 24 March 1992; Grossman, interview, Oral History Collection; Putnoi, interview, Oral History Collection; Justin Wyner, interview, Oral History Collection. For support for the plan, see Putnoi, interview, Justin Wyner, interview, and Rabb, interview, Oral History Collection.

21. For mailings, see Temple Israel: Governance MASCO to Unity Committee (Box 69), Wyner Family Papers, AJHS. For views on "continuity," see Putnoi, interview, Justin Wyner, interview, and Rabb, interview, Oral History Collection.

22. For final vote, see Annual Meeting Report, Board Minutes, 16 June 1992; "Temple Israel Rejects Rabbinic Succession," *Advocate*, 19 June 1992; "Decision at Temple Israel," *Advocate*, 26 June 1992. Gerald Holtz, "Remarks," and Rabbi Friedman, Address to the Congregation, Board Minutes, 16 June 1992; Robert Israel, "Friedman Resigns after 16 Years at Temple Israel," *Advocate*, 12 May 1994.

23. Putnoi, interview, Oral History Collection. President Robert Hoffman to Congregation, 17 June 1992. Justin Wyner, "Remarks," Report of the Annual Meeting, Board Minutes, 16 June 1992.

24. For committee formation, see Temple Israel: Governance MASCO to Unity Committee (Box 69), in Wyner Family Papers, AJHS; "Temple Israel Rejects Rabbinic Succession," *Advocate*, 19 June 1992; Board Minutes, 10 September 1992. For conclusions, see Temple Israel Unity Commission, 14 December 1992; Summary of Report on Unity Commission, 26 January 1993.

25. Conversation with Rabbi Friedman, 21 August 2007; "Gay and Lesbian Havurah at Services," *TI Bulletin*, 1 March 1992; Irving Levy to Robert Hoffman, 9 September 1992, in Temple Israel: Governance MASCO to Unity Committee (Box 69), in Wyner Family Papers, AJHS; Board Minutes, 22 December 1992. Laurel Friedman and Richard Goldman, "Report Regarding Gay and Lesbian Jews in the Synagogue," Board Minutes, 26 January 1993.

26. *TI Bulletin*, 1 October 1992; Board Minutes, 27 October 1992; *TI Bulletin*, 16 February 1993, 1 July 1993; Board Minutes, 28 September 1993.

27. Genevieve Wyner, interview, Oral History Collection. *TI Bulletin*, 1 January 1994.

28. Preliminary Long-Range Planning Report, Board Minutes, 21 November 1993.

29. Membership Analysis, 11 September 1992, Board Minutes, 22 September 1992; Membership Analysis, Board Minutes, 24 September 1996. Board Minutes, 25 January 1994. For campaign, see Mehlman to Board, Board Minutes, 19 September 1995; Michael Gelbwasser, "Mehlman, Lead Rabbi at Temple Israel," *Advocate*, 2 July 1998; Board Minutes,

27 January 1998. For renovations, see Board Minutes, 28 March and 23 May 2000. Nessel's $2,046,353 gift called for a name change for Plymouth Street to Nessel Way and an inscription on the building (Memo from President Levin, Board Minutes, 9 August 2000).

30. For new worship trends, see Kaplan, *American Reform Judaism*, 92–96; Rosenbaum, *Visions of Reform*, 409–411; Daniel Freelander, Robin Hirsch, Sanford Seltzer, *Emerging Worship and Music Trends in UAHC Congregations*, (UAHC, 1994), 20. Summit, *Lord's Song*, 51–56; Temple Committee Minutes, 1982–85; *TI Bulletin*, 1 October 1992.

31. For service content, see Joint Meeting of Board and Unity Commission, 11 May 1993; Board Minutes, 15 February 1994; *TI Bulletin*, 1 September 1994, 1 January 1995, 1 September 1995. For service times, see Board Minutes, 24 March 1992, 1 March 1997. The number of Qabbalat Shabbat services increased from twenty-six in 1993–1994 to forty in 1994–1995 to fifty-two in 1995–1996 (*TI Bulletins*, 1993–1996).

32. Joint Meeting of Board and Unity Commission, Board Minutes, 11 May 1993; Board Minutes, 15 February 1994; *TI Bulletin*, 1 September 1994, 1 January 1995, 1 September 1995. On services, see Board Minutes, 24 March 1992, 1 March 1997; *TI Bulletin*, 11 June 1998.

33. For quote, see Adult Outlook Report, 20 April 1993, Board Minutes, 15 June 1993. For senior activities, see "Meeting the Spiritual Needs of Jewish Seniors," *Advocate*, 26 October 1995; Board Minutes; 23 April 1991; "A Home for Life: Temple Israel's Palette of Programs for Older Members," *TI Bulletin*, 1 April 1996. For Generational Link, see Board Minutes, 29 September 1994; *TI Bulletin*, 1 February 1995.

34. *TI Bulletin*, June 1998.

35. Long-Range Planning Report, Board Minutes, 21 November 1993; Andrea Downs, "Temple Chooses Annual Themes: New Approach Serves Congregation's Needs," *Allston-Brighton TAB*, 19–25 November 1996.

36. For the family educator position, see Board Minutes, 27 April 1993, 28 September 1993, 26 October 1993; *TI Bulletin*, 1 July 1993, 16 May 1994, September 1997. For Jewish Family Connection, see *TI Bulletin*, September 1998.

37. For Outreach Committee, see "The Challenge of Intermarriage," *Advocate*, 16 November 1995; "Interfaith Marriage," *Jewish Educational Ventures*, 31 October 2000. For task force, see *TI Bulletin*, 17 October 1988, 1 July 1994; Board Minutes, 28 September 1993. For the annual meeting, see *TI Bulletin*, 1 January 1996, 1 May 1997.

38. Michael Gelbwasser, "Mehlman, Lead Rabbi at Temple Israel," *Advocate*, 2 July 1998. Response to CCAR questionnaire, Rabbinic Search Committee Report, 24 August 1998; Robert Hoffman to Search Committee, 11 September 1998 and Statement for Rabbinical Placement Commission, 17 September, 1998, both in Rabbinic Search Committee Files, TI Archives.

39. Fax from Justin Wyner to search committee, 26 January 1999, in F2: General Correspondence, 1998–99, Temple Israel: Governance MASCO to Unity Committee (Box 69), in Wyner Family Papers, AJHS; James W. Segel, Search Committee Chair, to Congregation, 28 January 1999, Rabbinic Search Committee Files. Stephen M. Richmond to Rich-

ard L. Berman, Mitchell H. Shames, James W. Segel, 17 February 1999, Board Minutes, 25 March 1999; *TI Bulletin*, April 1999.

40. For Friedman's acceptance speech, see *TI Bulletin*, April 1999. "Personal Statement," Rabbinic Search Committee Files, 1998–1999; Friedman, interview, Oral History Collection.

41. *TI Bulletin*, July/August 1999, October 2000; Matthew S. Robinson, "Rabbi Returns to Boston's Temple Israel," *Advocate*, 17 February 2000, 2. For meetings, see Susan Levin and Mitchell Shames, Chair of Transition Committee, to Congregation, 2 November 1999.

42. *TI Bulletin*, December 2000. See also Putnoi, interview, Oral History Collection.

43. *TI Bulletin*, March 2001.

44. For Mehlman, see *TI Bulletin*, January 1998. Friedman's criteria include the completion of an "Introduction to Judaism" class, a commitment to maintaining a Jewish household and raising Jewish children, and an understanding that the non-Jewish spouse does not actively practice another religion (Friedman conversation, 21 August 2007). For CCAR inclusiveness policies, see 1999 Pittsburgh Platform (*Globe*, 24 May 1999, A1).

45. Board Minutes, 6 June 2002.

46. *TI Bulletin*, 1 February 1995, 12 September 2000, 28 November 2000, 9 January 2001, 1 December 2003; "About Us," http://www.riverwayproject.org/about_us/index.php (accessed 6 June 2008).

47. Board Minutes, 24 March 1992.

48. For GBIO, see Board Minutes, 23 March 1999, 28 September 1999; "Our Mission," http://gbio.org/ (accessed 16 July 2007). For Pesner, see *TI Bulletin*, July/August 1999.

49. *TI Bulletin*, February 2002; "Social Justice — Ohel Tzedek," http://tisrael.org/caring _action/index.php?id=37&page=37 (accessed 18 March 2008).

50. Rabbi Jonah Pesner, "We Will Go — Our Young and Our Old," Shabbat sermon, 30 January 2004, http://www.tisrael.org/uploads/1191JPJan302004.pdf (accessed 6 June 2008); Shayndi Raice, "Synagogue in Boston a Model for Social Action," *Advocate*, 17 February 2006. "Just Congregations: About Us," http://urj.org/justcongregations/staff/ (accessed 6 June 2008).

51. Ann Green, "Forum Gives Jewish Perspective on Same-Sex Marriage," *Advocate*, 4 July 2002, 20. Kay Longscope, "Religious Leaders, Gay Groups Back Bill to Redefine 'Family,'" *Globe*, 16 May 1991. Friedman, quoted by Religious Coalition for the Freedom to Marry, "Religious Leaders Support Civil Marriage Effort: Call on Legislators to Reject Religious Arguments," 5 June 2003, http://archive.uua.org/news/2003/030605b.html (accessed 5 June 2006); Batia Charpak, "Program Details Need to Lift Ban on Same-Sex Marriages," *Advocate*, 10 April 2003. For marriages, see Friedman, interview, Oral History Collection.

52. *TI Bulletin*, November 2001; "Boston Interfaith Dialogue Center Profile," http:// www.pluralism.org/research/profiles/display.php?profile=73214 (accessed 1 August 2007). Temple Israel and Bethel AME Church held an annual joint celebration on Martin Luther King Day for many years.

53. Kaplan, *American Reform Judaism*, 126–131; For Or Hadash and Seeds of Peace, see http://tisrael.org/about_us/clergy.php (accessed 15 March 2008).

54. Sesquicentennial Planning Files, Anniversaries Collection, TI Archives; Barbara Rabinovitz, "At Age 150, Boston's Temple Israel Marks Milestone as 'New Beginning,'" *Advocate*, 8–14 July 2005, 1.

55. Friedman, interview, Oral History Collection.

56. TI Annual Report, 2007–08.

57. Ibid. For renovations, see "From Dream to Reality: The Work Begins," http://www .tisrael.org/about_us/giving.php?page=16716. Information regarding renovations courtesy of John Snow, facilities manager.

58. Statistics from mid-2008, courtesy of Chris George, information technology manager. For TILLI, see TI Annual Report, 2007–08.

59. Quote from Kaplan, *American Reform Judaism*, 112.

page 9 Hazan Sachs sidebar: Albert Ehrenfried, *A Chronicle of Boston Jewry* (Boston, 1963), 374; Stephen S. Birmingham, *"Our Crowd": The Great Jewish Families of New York* (New York: Harper and Row, 1967), 52, 244; U.S. Census (1860), Schedule 1 (Population).

page 10 Torah image: *American Israelite*, 12 May 1856.

page 12 Wakefield cemetery images: Blanche Linden-Ward, *Silent City on a Hill: Landscapes of Memory and Boston's Mount Auburn Cemetery* (Columbus: Ohio State University Press, 1989); Temple Israel Necrology, Temple Israel Archives, Boston, Mass. [hereafter TI Archives].

page 14 Lincoln assassination minutes image: Temple Israel, Board of Trustees Minutes [hereafter Board Minutes], 18 April 1865; Jonathan D. Sarna, *American Judaism: A History* (New Haven, Conn.: Yale University Press, 2004), 122.

page 15 Hazan Shoninger sidebar: Ehrenfried, *Chronicle of Boston Jewry*, 374–375; U.S. Census (1870, 1910); "Golden Gifts for Them," *Boston Globe* [hereafter *Globe*], 30 November 1904; "Aged Rabbi is Dead," *Globe*, 23 May 1910. For Shoninger's position on reforms, see Board Minutes, 29 March 1863. The board was divided over reforms, and rehired Shoninger on a yearly basis. By 1870, the majority was pressing for reforms, and the board

advertised the hazan position yearly until Solomon Schindler was hired in 1874. Between 1871 and 1874, Shoninger instituted some changes at the board's behest. See, for example, Board Minutes, 26 August 1866, 11 October 1868, 31 July 1870, 14 April 1872, 22 March 1874.

page 17 Rosenfeld family and school report images: U.S. Census (1870, 1880, 1900, 1910, 1920, 1930); Vital Records, 1862, Massachusetts State Archives, Boston, Mass.; "Annual Report, Comprising the Attendance, the Deportment, and the Industry of Every Pupil of the Sabbath School, Temple Adath Israel, from Nov. 1, 1878 till June 1, 1879," Religious School Files, TI Archives; Cemetery Records, TI Archives; Sarna, *American Judaism*, 122.

page 21 Rabbi Schindler sidebar: Annual Meeting, Board Minutes, 1 March 1908; "Boston Mourns: Sudden Death of Rabbi Solomon Schindler," [Boston] *Jewish Advocate* [hereafter *Advocate*], 7 May 1915. American Jewish Committee, *American Jewish Yearbook* (Philadelphia: Jewish Publication Society of America, 1899), 273.

page 24 Festival images: Sarna, *American Judaism*, 136–137, Solomon Schindler, "Chanukah Celebrations in Boston," *Advocate*, 18 December 1914.

page 29 Columbus Avenue synagogue image: David A. Kaufman, "Temples in the American Athens: A History of the Synagogues of Boston," in *The Jews of Boston*, 2nd edition, ed. Jonathan D. Sarna, Ellen Smith, and Scott-Martin Kosofsky (New Haven, Conn.: Yale University Press, 2005), 183–185; Gerald Gamm, *Urban Exodus: Why the Jews Left Boston and the Catholics Stayed* (Cambridge, Mass.: Harvard University Press, 1999), 135.

page 31 Holyoke Street images: U.S. Census (1880); Temple Israel Necrology, 1860–1890s; Membership List, 1880, 1885; G. W. Bromley, *Atlas of the City of Boston*, 1883.

page 32 Jacob and Lina Hecht sidebar: U.S. Census (1870, 1880). Allon Gal, *Brandeis of Boston* (Cambridge, Mass.: Harvard University Press, 1980), 16–17, 34; *New York Times Saturday Review*, 27 May 1899; Barbara Miller Solomon, *Pioneers in Service: The History of the Associated Jewish Philanthropies of Boston* (Boston, 1956), 51. For Schindler's reference to Lina, see *Jewish Chronicle*, 29 January 1892. For the Hechts' charitable work, see Gerald H. Gamm, "In Search of Suburbs: Boston's Jewish Districts, 1843–1994," in Sarna, Smith, and Kosofsky, *Jews of Boston*, 142; Susan Ebert, "Community and Philanthropy," in Sarna, Smith, and Kosofsky, *Jews of Boston*, 223; Solomon Schindler, *Israelites in Boston: A Tale Describing the Development of Judaism in Boston* (Boston: Berwick and Smith, 1889), chap. 5. "Hebrew Industrial School," *Boston Advocate*, 11 August 1905.

page 37 Edward and Theresa Goulston sidebar: "Honor Mrs. Goulston on 70th Anniversary," *Advocate*, 14 February 1918. Board Minutes, 12 October 1880. The other female trustee was Hennie F. Liebmann (see Board Minutes, 27 April 1924). For Edward's quote, see Jonathan D. Sarna, "Jews of Boston in Historical Perspective," in Sarna, Smith, and Kosofsky, *Jews of Boston*, 6. "When Mercy Seasons Justice," *Advocate*, 8 May 1919. Their daughter, Aimee, married a Chicago architect; the other son, Ernest, ran a building company (see U.S. Census [1920], World War I Draft Registration Cards, 1917–1918).

page 41 Rabbi Fleischer sidebar: Arthur Mann, ed., *Growth and Achievement: Temple Israel, 1854–1954* (Boston: Congregation Adath Israel, 1954), 65–69; Mann, "Charles Fleischer's Religion of Democracy," *Commentary* (June 1954): 557–565. American Jewish Committee, *American Jewish Yearbook* (Philadelphia: Jewish Publication Society of America, 1903), 54; "Dr. Chas. Fleischer, Editor and Lecturer," *New York Times*, 3 July 1942.

page 42 Purim Ball image: "Purim Ball a Brilliant Spectacle," *Globe*, 9 February 1900.

page 44 Red Sox poster image: Roger I. Abrams, *The First World Series and the Baseball Fanatics of 1903* (Boston: Northeastern University Press, 2003), 18. Fleischer also contributed to the inaugural issue of *Baseball Magazine*, edited by sports writer and congregant Jake Morse. See Charles Fleischer, "A Bit of Baseball Biography," *Baseball Magazine*, vol. 1, no. 2, June 1908, 35–36.

page 47 Commonwealth Avenue temple image: Clarence H. Blackall, "The

Symbolism of Temple Adath Israel,"
typescript, in Commonwealth Avenue
Files, Buildings Collection, TI
Archives.

page 56 Rabbi Levi sidebar: Harriet
Segal Cohn, interview by Helene
Bailen, 9 and 16 January 1997;
transcript, Women Whose Lives Span
the Century Oral History Project,
sponsored by Temple Israel and the
Jewish Women's Archives, in Temple
Israel Archives [WWLSC]. "Elected to
Succeed Fleischer," *Advocate*, 2 March
1911, 1; "Rabbi Harry Levi," *Advocate*,
1 September 1911, 8; Mann, *Growth and
Achievement*, 87–88; Board Minutes,
29 November 1947.

page 57 Jacob Morse and cornet images:
Schindler, *Israelites in Boston*, chap. 1;
Board Minutes, 29 January 1911. The
cornet was made by Boston Musical
Manufacturers (estab. 1869), located on
Sudbury Street in Boston. By the 1900s,
the cornet may have been used instead
of a shofar, as this was then common
in Reform congregations. See Leon
A. Jick, "The Reform Synagogue," in
*The American Synagogue: A Sanctuary
Transformed*, ed. Jack Wertheimer
(Cambridge: Cambridge University
Press, 1987), 104.

page 61 YPSOTAI images: Information
compiled from YPSOTAI programs,
U. S. Census (1910, 1920, 1930),
TI membership lists, 1912, 1924, and
TI Confirmation Programs, 1912–1924,
TI Archives.

page 62 Sisterhood program image:
Address of Mrs. Rose Frank,
30 November 1913, Sisterhood
Collection, TI Archives.

page 63 Hebrew Industrial School image:
It became the Boys & Girls Club of
Allston-Brighton. Gamm, "In Search
of Suburbs," 142; "American Principles
Taught," *Globe*, 28 January 1900, 22.

page 64 Model Citizens sidebar:
Ehrenfried, *Chronicle*, 628–631.
William Alan Braverman, "Ascent
of Boston's Jews, 1630–1918" (Ph.D.
diss., Harvard University, 1990) 118,
93–94, 100. "A. C. 'Cap' Ratshesky,"
http://www.grantsmanagement.com/
acrfhistory.html (accessed 5 August
2006). Ebert, "Community and
Philanthropy," 235–236. "Abraham
Ratshesky, Banker, Diplomat, 78,"
New York Times, 17 March 1943.
"Felix Vorenberg, Boston Merchant,"
New York Times, 11 August 1943;
George Berkeley, *The Filenes* (Boston:
International Pocket Library, 1998),
158.

page 71 Segal sisters image: Cohn,
interview, WWLSC.

pages 74–75 Women and Jewish Culture
sidebar: Finding Aid, Fanny Goldstein
Papers, American Jewish Archives,
Cincinnati, Ohio [herafter AJA].
Education Department Report, Board
Minutes, 30 January 1938; Rabbi Levi,
Annual Address, Board Minutes, 6
November 1932; Fannie Barnett Linsky,
"The Booklovers," *TI Bulletin*, 9 April
1930. *New York Times*, 24 November
1941, 23 May 1946. See also Fanny
Goldstein Papers, Special Collections,
Boston Public Library. Goldstein's
works include *The Jewish Child in
Bookland: A Selected Bibliography of
Juveniles for the Jewish Child's Own
Bookshelf* (New York: Jewish Book

Council of America, 1947). U.S. Census (1900, 1920, 1930); "Social Happenings," *Advocate*, 28 June 1912.

page 85 Waterman Library images: Board Minutes, 7 June 1931; Ehrenfried to Board, Board Minutes, n.d.; Rabbi Cohon to Board, Board Minutes, 31 July 1939.

page 87 Rabbi Liebman sidebar: Mann, *Growth and Achievement*, 100–106. Katherine Donovan and Paul Murphy, *He Brought "Peace of Mind" to Millions: An Intimate Biography of Joshua Loth Liebman, 1907–1948* (Boston: Hearst Newspapers, 1948); Liebman, "Statement on Visit to Palestine," Box 1, Folder 16, in Rabbi Joshua Loth Liebman and Fan Loth Liebman Collection, Howard Gotlieb Archival Research Center, Boston University. David Davidson and Hilde Abel, "Meet an American Rabbi and His Family," *Ladies Home Journal*, January 1948, 123ff. See also Andrew R. Heinze, *Jews and the American Soul: Human Nature in the Twentieth Century* (Princeton, N.J.: Princeton University Press, 2004), 195–240.

page 100 Rabbi Klausner sidebar: "Abraham Klausner, 92, Dies," *New York Times*, 30 June 2007. "Abraham Klausner, Shoah Survivors' Advocate," *Jewish Daily Forward*, 11 July 2007. Alex Grobman, "An Unassuming Hero Who Made A Difference," *Jewish Press*, 11 July 2007. Susan Abramson, "The Social History of Temple Adath Israel 1911–Present" (unpublished paper, 1973, Temple Israel Library), 51–63; Judith Rothman, interview by Meaghan Dwyer, 13 July 2007, audiotape, Oral

History Collection, TI Archives. For Klausner's experiences with displaced persons, see Abraham J. Klausner, *A Letter to My Children from the Edge of the Holocaust* (San Francisco, Calif.: Holocaust Center of Northern California, 2002). The seder's accompanying *Survivor's Haggadah*, with its stark, moving woodcut illustrations and preface by Rabbi Klausner, explicitly linked the ancient story of the exodus from Egypt with the modern Holocaust and liberation. See Saul Touster, ed., *A Survivor's Haggadah* (Philadelphia: Jewish Publication Society, 2000), 77.

page 105 Rabbi Gittelsohn sidebar: Roland B. Gittelsohn, interview by Justin L. Wyner, 15 June 1987, transcript, Oral History Collection; Tom Long, "Rabbi Roland Gittelsohn, 85; Activist Who Led Boston Temple," *Globe*, 15 December 1995; David Stout, "Roland Gittelsohn, 85, Rabbi and a Marine Chaplain on Iwo Jima," *New York Times*, 15 December 1995; "Ruth Gittelsohn, 70; Was Active in Jewish Affairs," *Globe*, 8 December 1980.

page 107 Centennial banquet image: *TI Bulletin*, 5 March 1954; Jay Gotland, "Observe Century of Temple Israel," *Advocate*, 17 June 1954; Sisterhood Report, in Board Minutes, 11 April 1954.

page 123 Sanctuary exterior image: Louise Nevelson, "Speech at the Dedication of 'Sky Covenant,'" 16 December 1973, audiotape, Audio/Visual Collection, TI Library; Roland B. Gittelsohn, *Sermons in Steel, Stone and Thread* (Boston: Temple Israel, n.d.), 10–11.

page 131 Services images: Liturgy booklets, in Publications Collection, TI Archives. For Debbie Friedman, see TI Bulletin, 10 April 1973; http://www.debbiefriedman.com/ (accessed 16 July 2008).

page 134 Garden images: "Biblical Garden of Temple Israel Boston," Garden Club Files, TI Archives.

page 136 Tapestry image: Board Minutes, 23 September 1980; *TI Bulletin*, 13 October 1980.

page 138 Rabbi Mehlman sidebar: Rabbi Mehlman, Curriculum Vitae, Board Minutes, 11 July 1977; Rabbi Bernard and Emily S. Mehlman, interview by Meaghan Dwyer, 10 December 2004 and 4 March 2005, audiotape, Oral History Collection; Rabbi Ronne Friedman and Rabbi Bernard Mehlman, "Building Community: Preserving our Memories, Enriching Our Lives, Ensuring Our Dreams," Burstein Scholar in Residence Program, 6 November 1988, Lecture Series Files, TI Archives. Program, "Honor Our Clergy by Building Our Future" event, 21 May 2008, 8, in TI Archives.

page 140 Family Kallah image: Leslie Ann Dropkin, "Family Kallah Revisited," *TI Bulletin*, 2 September 1980.

pages 150–151 Sound of Music sidebar: Jeffrey A. Summit, *The Lord's Song in a Strange Land: Music and Identity in Contemporary Jewish Worship* (New York: Oxford University Press, 2000), 4. For Gideon, see Music Collection, TI Archives; *Advocate*, 17 March 1927, 1; "Guide to the Miriam Gideon Papers," Music Division, New York Public Library, New York, http://www.nypl.org/research/manuscripts/music/musgideo.xml (accessed 6 June 2008). For Fromm, see "Herbert Fromm," http://www.milkenarchive.org/artists/artists.taf?artistid=83 (accessed 20 May 2008); Herbert Fromm Collection, Library of the Jewish Theological Seminary, New York. Books include *Hymns and Songs for the Synagogue* (New York: Sacred Music Press, 1961), *The Key of See: Travel Journals of a Composer* (Boston: Plowshare Press, 1967), and *On Jewish Music: A Composer's View* (New York: Bloch, 1978). For Cantor Simon, see *TI Bulletin*, 31 October 1977; "Professional Staff," http://www.thejewishcenter.org/about/staff.asp (accessed 6 June 2008). For Cantor Einhorn, see *TI Bulletin*, 13 June 1983; Program, "Honor Our Clergy," 6; Cantor Roy Einhorn Papers, TI Archives. Einhorn and Jodi Sufrin, cantor at Temple Beth Elohim in Wellesley, Massachusetts, were the first married cantorial couple to graduate together from HUC–JIR.

page 165 Rabbi Abramson image: Rabbi Susan Abramson, conversation with Susan L. Porter, 15 April 2008. Abramson is also the author, with her son, Aaron Dvorkin, of the *Rabbi Rocketpower* children's book series.

page 167 Rabbi Zecher sidebar: *TI Bulletin*, 21 May 1990; Program, "Honor Our Clergy," 7; Elaine Zecher, interview by Lisa Fagin Davis, 15 October 2007, transcript, Oral History Collection.

page 179 Wyner Museum images: "History of the Wyner Museum," Wyner Museum Files, TI Archives.

page 185 Rabbi Friedman sidebar: Rabbi Ronne Friedman, Curriculum Vitae, Rabbinic Search Files, 1998–99; Ronne Friedman, interview by Lisa Fagin Davis, 17 August 2007, audiotape, Oral History Collection; Program, "Honor Our Clergy," 5.

page 191 Passport to Israel images: "Boston Teens Save for Passport to Israel," *Advocate*, 29 August 1991, 13; Board Minutes, 27 April 1993; *TI Bulletin*, 1 July 1993; Temple Israel Brotherhood Annual Report, 1992–1993, Board Minutes, 28 September 1993; *TI Bulletin*, 1 June 1995.

BIBLIOGRAPHY

MANUSCRIPT COLLECTIONS

American Jewish Archives, Cincinnati, Ohio
    Albert Ehrenfried Papers
    Fanny Goldstein Papers
    Rabbi Roland B. Gittelsohn Papers
    Rabbi Solomon Schindler Papers
American Jewish Historical Society, Hebrew College, Newton, Massachusetts
    Boston New Century Club
    Boston YMHA–Hecht House
    Combined Jewish Philanthropies
    Congregation Mishkan Israel
    Congregation Beth Israel
    Congregation Kenesseth Israel
    Congregation Ohabei Shalom
    Louisa May Alcott Club, Boston
    Abraham C. Ratshesky Papers
    United Hebrew Benevolent Association, Boston
    Wyner Family Papers
Boston Public Library, Special Collections, Boston, Massachusetts
    Fanny Goldstein Papers
Boston University, Howard Gotlieb Archival Research Center, Boston, Massachusetts
    Rabbi Joshua Loth Liebman and Fan Loth Liebman Collection
National Archives and Records Administration (accessed via Ancestry.com)
    Boston Passenger Lists, 1820–1943
    U.S. Federal Census, Schedule 1 (Population); 1840–1930
    U.S. Naturalization Records Indexes, 1794–1972
    U.S. Passport Applications, 1795–1957
    World War I Draft Registration Cards, 1917–1918
University of New Orleans, Louisiana and Special Collections Department, Earl K. Long
    Library, New Orleans, Louisiana
    Moses Ehrlich, President, v. Mendez Kursheedt and others, 1856. State of Louisiana,
    Second District Court of New Orleans. Supreme Court of Louisiana Legal Archives
    (Mss 106), New Orleans, 1846–1861, Docket 4604
Temple Israel Archives, Temple Israel, Boston, Massachusetts
    Assistant Rabbis Papers
    Audio/Visual Collection [Temple Israel Library]
    Board of Trustees Minutes, 1863–2008

Board Presidents Papers
Brotherhood Collection
Buildings Collection
Herbert Fromm Papers
Membership Records
Oral History Collection
Rabbi Charles Fleischer Papers
Rabbi Roland B. Gittelsohn Papers
Rabbi Harry Levi Papers
Rabbi Joshua Loth Liebman Papers
Rabbi Solomon Schindler Papers
Religious School Files
Sisterhood Collection
Social Action Committee Files
Temple Israel Bulletin, 1907–2008
Wakefield Cemetery Collection
Women Whose Lives Span the Century Oral History Project
Wyner Museum Files

PUBLISHED WORKS AND OTHER MATERIALS

Abrams, Betsy, ed. "History and Timeline of Temple Israel, 140th Anniversary Booklet."
    Boston, 1994.
Abrams, Roger I. *The First World Series and the Baseball Fanatics of 1903*. Boston:
    Northeastern University Press, 2003.
Abramson, Susan. "History of Temple Adath Israel As Seen Through the Evolution of the
    Worship Experience." Senior honors thesis. Brandeis University, 1976.
———. "The Social History of Temple Adath Israel, 1911–Present." Unpublished paper,
    1973. Temple Israel Library.
Antin, Mary. *The Promised Land*. Boston: Houghton Mifflin Co., 1912.
Aron, Isa. *Becoming a Congregation of Learners*. Woodstock, Vt.: Jewish Lights, 2000.
Baltzell, E. Digby, Allen Glicksman, and Jacquelyn Litt. "The Jewish Communities of
    Philadelphia and Boston: A Tale of Two Cities." In *Jewish Life in Philadelphia 1830–
    1940*, ed. Murray Friedman, 290–313. Philadelphia: ISHI Publications, 1983.
Berkeley, George. *The Filenes*. Boston: International Pocket Library, 1998.
Birmingham, Stephen S. *"Our Crowd": The Great Jewish Families of New York*. New York:
    Harper and Row, 1967.
Boston Globe. Boston, Mass., 1874–2008.
Boston Hebrew Observer. Boston, Mass., 1883–1886.
Boston Herald. Boston, Mass., 1863–2008.
[Boston] *Jewish Advocate*. Boston, Mass., 1905–2008.
Boston Jewish Herald. Boston, Mass., 1893–1894.

Braverman, William Alan. "The Ascent of Boston's Jews, 1630–1918." Ph.D. diss. Harvard University, 1990.

Brinkley, Alan. *Voices of Protest: Huey Long, Father Coughlin, and the Great Depression.* New York: Vintage Books, 1983.

Connolly, James J. *The Triumph of Ethnic Progressivism: Urban Political Culture in Boston, 1900–1925.* Cambridge, Mass.: Harvard University Press, 1998.

Davidson, David, and Hilde Abel. "Meet an American Rabbi and His Family," *Ladies Home Journal,* January 1948, 123ff.

De Haas, Jacob. *Louis D. Brandeis: A Biographical Sketch.* New York: Bloch Publishing, 1929.

Deutsch, Sarah. *Women and the City: Gender, Space, and Power in Boston, 1870–1940.* New York: Oxford University Press, 2000.

Donovan, Katherine, and Paul Murphy. *He Brought "Peace of Mind" to Millions: An Intimate Biography of Joshua Loth Liebman, 1907–1948.* Boston: Hearst Newspapers, 1948.

Ehrenfried, Albert. *A Chronicle of Boston Jewry.* Boston, 1963.

Eisenstadt, Peter. *Affirming the Covenant, A History of Temple B'rith Kodesh Rochester, New York, 1848–1998.* Rochester, N.Y.: Temple B'rith Kodesh, 1999.

Fleischer, Charles. "A Bit of Baseball Biography," *Baseball Magazine* 1, no. 2 (June 1908): 35–36.

Flower, B. O. *Progressive Men, Women, and Movements of the Past Twenty-five Years.* Boston: New Arena, 1914.

Free Religious Association. *Proceedings at the Twenty-ninth Anniversary.* New Bedford: Free Religious Association, 1896.

———. *Proceedings at the Thirty-third Annual Meeting.* Boston: Free Religious Association, 1900.

Friesel, Evyatar. "The Americanization of American Jewry: Old Concept, New Meanings" *American Jewish History* 81, nos. 3–4 (1994): 321–330.

Fromm, Herbert. *Hymns and Songs for the Synagogue.* New York: Sacred Music Press, 1961.

———. *The Key of See: Travel Journals of a Composer.* Boston: Plowshare Press, 1967.

———. *On Jewish Music: A Composer's View.* New York: Bloch, 1978.

Gal, Allon. *Brandeis of Boston.* Cambridge, Mass.: Harvard University Press, 1980.

Gamm, Gerald. *Urban Exodus: Why the Jews Left Boston and the Catholics Stayed.* Cambridge, Mass.: Harvard University Press, 1999.

Gittelsohn, Roland B. *Sermons in Steel, Stone and Thread.* Boston: Temple Israel, n.d.

———. "From Iwo Jima to Zion," *Reform Judaism* 12, no. 2 (Winter 1983): 18ff.

Goldman, Karla M. *Beyond the Synagogue Gallery: Finding a Place for Women in American Judaism.* Cambridge, Mass.: Harvard University Press, 2000.

Goldstein, Fanny. *The Jewish Child in Bookland: A Selected Bibliography of Juveniles for the Jewish Child's Own Bookshelf.* New York: Jewish Book Council of America, 1947.

Goldstein, Jenny. "Transcending Boundaries: Boston's Catholics and Jews, 1929–1965." Senior thesis. Brandeis University, 2001.

Grobman, Alex. *Rekindling The Flame: American Jewish Chaplains and the Survivors of European Jewry 1944–1948*. Detroit, Mich.: Wayne State University, 1993.

Haber, Douglas A. "The Burden of the Witness: The Response of Boston's Jews to the Holocaust, 1941–1945." Senior honors thesis. Middlebury College, 2004.

Halper, Donna. "John Shepard—Boston's Showman." April 2001. www.oldradio.com/archives/people/Shepard.htm (accessed 12 August 2005).

Handlin, Oscar. *Boston's Immigrants: A Study in Acculturation*. Cambridge, Mass.: Harvard University Press, 1941.

Heinze, Andrew R. *Jews and the American Soul: Human Nature in the Twentieth Century*. Princeton, N.J.: Princeton University Press, 2004.

———. "*Peace of Mind* (1946): Judaism and the Therapeutic Polemics of Postwar America," *Religion and American Culture* 12, no. 1 (Winter 2002): 31–58.

Hentoff, Nat. *Boston Boy*. New York: Alfred A. Knopf, 1986.

Herberg, Will. *Protestant, Catholic, Jew*. New York: Anchor Books, 1960.

Higham, John. *Strangers in the Land: Patterns of American Nativism, 1860–1925*. New Brunswick, N.J.: Rutgers University Press, 1955.

Hoffman, Lawrence A. "Imagine a Synagogue for the 21st Century," *Reform Judaism* 25, no. 1 (Fall 1996), 21–26.

Jewish Chronicle. Boston, Mass., 1891–1893.

Jick, Leon. *The Americanization of the Synagogue*. Waltham, Mass.: Brandeis University Press, 1992.

Kaplan, Dana Evan. *American Reform Judaism: An Introduction*. New Brunswick, N.J.: Rutgers University Press, 2003.

Kaufman, David. *Shul With a Pool: The "Synagogue-Center" in American Jewish History*. Waltham, Mass.: Brandeis University Press, 1999.

Klausner, Abraham J. *A Letter to My Children from the Edge of the Holocaust*. San Francisco, Calif.: Holocaust Center of Northern California, 2002.

Kliman, Burton Samuel. "The Jewish Brahmins of Boston: A Study of the German Jewish Immigrant Experience, 1860–1900." Senior honors thesis. Brandeis University, 1978.

Levi, Harry. *1919 Sunday Service*. Boston: Temple Israel, 1919.

———. *A Rabbi Speaks*. Boston: Chapple Publishing Co., 1930.

Linden-Ward, Blanche. *Silent City on a Hill: Landscapes of Memory and Boston's Mount Auburn Cemetery*. Columbus: Ohio State University Press, 1989.

Mann, Arthur. "Charles Fleischer's Religion of Democracy: An Experiment in American Faith," *Commentary* (June 1954): 557–565.

———. *Yankee Reformers in an Urban Age*. Cambridge, Mass.: Belknap Press of Harvard University Press, 1954.

———, ed. *Growth and Achievement: Temple Israel 1854–1954*. Boston: Congregation Adath Israel, 1954.

Meyer, Michael A. *Response to Modernity, A History of the Reform Movement*. New York: Oxford University Press, 1988.

Mostov, Stephen G. "A Sociological Portrait of German Jewish Immigrants in Boston: 1845–1861." In *American Jewish History, Vol. 2. Central European Jews in America, 1840–1880: Migration and Advancement*, ed. Jeffrey S. Gurock, 243–274. New York: Routledge, 1998.

Nadell, Pamela. *Women Who Would Be Rabbis: A History of Women's Ordination, 1889–1985*. Boston: Beacon Press, 1998.

New York Times, New York, N.Y., 1863–2008.

Nizel, Jeannette S., and Abraham E. Nizel. *Congregation Ohabei Shalom: Pioneers of the Boston Jewish Community. An Historical Perspective of the First One Hundred and Forty Years, 1842–1982*. Boston, 1982.

Norwood, Stephen H. "Marauding Youths and the Christian Front: Antisemitic Violence in Boston and New York During World War II," *American Jewish History* 91, no. 2 (June 2003): 233–267.

Obst, Stella. *The Story of Adath Israel*. Boston, 1917.

O'Connor, Thomas H. *Bibles, Brahmins and Bosses: A Short History of Boston*. Boston: Trustees of the Public Library of the City of Boston, 1991.

Olitzky, Kerry M. "The Sunday-Sabbath Movement in American Reform Judaism: Strategy or Evolution?" In *American Jewish History, Vol. 5. The History of Judaism in America: Transplantations, Transformations, and Reconciliations, Part Two*, ed. Jeffrey S. Gurock, 769–782. New York: Routledge, 1998.

O'Toole, James M. *Militant and Triumphant: William Henry O'Connell and the Catholic Church in Boston, 1859–1944*. Notre Dame, Ind.: University of Notre Dame Press, 1992.

Reimer, Joseph. *Succeeding at Jewish Education: How One Synagogue Made it Work*. Philadelphia, Jewish Publication Society, 1997.

Rosenbaum, Fred. *Visions of Reform: Congregation Emanu-El and the Jews of San Francisco, 1849–1999*. Berkeley, Calif.: Judah L. Magnes Museum, 2000.

Sanford, M. Bourchier. "In Favor of the Jew," *North American Review* 152 (January–June 1891): 126–128.

Sarna, Jonathan D. *American Judaism: A History*. New Haven, Conn.: Yale University Press, 2004.

———. "The Debate Over Mixed Seating in the American Synagogue." In *American Jewish History, Vol. 5. The History of Judaism in America: Transplantations, Transformations, and Reconciliations, Part Two*, ed. Jeffrey S. Gurock, 737–768. New York: Routledge, 1998.

———. "The Evolution of the American Synagogue." In *The Americanization of the Jews*, eds. Robert M. Seltzer and Norman J. Cohen, 215–229. New York: New York University Press, 1995.

Sarna, Jonathan D., Ellen Smith, and Scott-Martin Kosofsky, eds. *The Jews of Boston*, 2nd edition. New Haven, Conn.: Yale University Press, 2005.

Schappes, Morris, ed. *A Documentary History of the Jews in the United States, 1654–1875.* New York: Citadel Press, 1971.

Schindler, Solomon. *Dissolving Views in the History of Judaism.* Boston: Lee and Shepard, 1888.

———. *Israelites in Boston. A Tale Describing the Development of Judaism in Boston, Preceded by the Jewish Calendar for the Next Decade.* Boston: Berwick and Smith, 1889.

———. *Messianic Expectations and Modern Judaism. Lectures Delivered by Solomon Schindler, of the Temple Adath Israel, in Boston. With an Introduction by Minot J. Savage.* Boston: S.E. Cassino and Co., 1886.

Seltzer, Robert M., and Norman J. Cohen, eds. *The Americanization of the Jews.* New York: New York University Press, 1995.

Seltzer, Sanford. *Emerging Worship and Music Trends in UAHC Congregations.* New York: Union of American Reform Congregations, 1994.

Shay, Felix. "The Church of Citizenship," *Roycroft* 2, no. 2 (April 1918): 62–63.

Silverstein, Alan. *Alternatives to Assimilation, The Response of Reform Judaism to American Culture.* Waltham, Mass.: Brandeis University Press, 1994.

Simmons, S[imon]. *The History of Temple Ohabei Shalom, Principal Events from Its Organization in 1843, to the Fiftieth Anniversary Celebration on February 26th, 1893.* Boston, 1893.

Solomon, Barbara Miller. *Ancestors and Immigrants: A Changing New England Tradition.* Cambridge, Mass.: Harvard University Press, 1956.

———. *Pioneers in Service: The History of the Associated Jewish Philanthropies of Boston.* Boston, 1956.

Stack, Robert. *International Conflict in an American City: Boston's Irish, Italians and Jews, 1935–1944.* Westport, Conn.: Greenwood Press, 1979.

Summit, Jeffrey A. *The Lord's Song in a Strange Land: Music and Identity in Contemporary Jewish Worship.* New York: Oxford University Press, 2000.

Synnott, Marcia Graham. *The Half-Opened Door: Discrimination and Admissions at Harvard, Yale, and Princeton, 1900–1970.* Westport, Conn.: Greenwood Press, 1979.

Touster, Saul, ed. *A Survivor's Haggadah.* Philadelphia: Jewish Publication Society, 2000.

Wertheimer, Jack, ed. *The American Synagogue: A Sanctuary Transformed.* Cambridge: Cambridge University Press, 1987.

Wieder, Arnold A. *The Early Jewish Community of Boston's North End.* Waltham, Mass.: Brandeis University Press, 1962.

INDEX

5, 38, 44, 50; as choir singers, 20;
and liberal Christian philosophy,
34–36, 37–38, 44–45, 51; philanthropic
organizations of, as models, 13–14,
27, 33; proselytizing, 10, 33; social
intermingling with Jews, 32, 42. *See
also* Antisemitism; Interfaith relations
Purim, 25, 33, 42, 45, 65, 113, 147, 149, 181
Purim Association, 42
Putnoi, Deborah, 189, 223n2
Putnoi, Donald, 159, 168
Putnoi, Frances Stieber, 135, 140–141, 158,
162, 165, 171, 178–179, 191, 200, 225n24

Qabbalat Shabbat services (1978), 152–154,
159, 166, 176–177, 184, 230n31

Rabb, Irving, 104, 123, 139, 229n19, 229n20,
229n21
Rabb, Norman, 104
Rabb, Sidney, 104
Rabbi Harry Levi Auditorium (1947),
56, 77, 79; renovation of (Leers,
Weinzapfel, 2008), 192, 194–195.
See also Riverway campus
Rabbi Joshua Loth Liebman Education
wing addition (Merle I. Locke, 1957),
108–109, 121. *See also* Riverway campus
Rachlin, Joy, 147
"Radio Rabbi." *See* Levi, Rabbi Harry
Radio/television sermon broadcasts, 56,
71–72, 78, 83, 85, 91–92, 101, 104, 137
Ratshesky, Abraham C., 64, 76
Red Cross, 64, 68, 92
Reform Judaism, 24–25, 29, 41, 54, 56,
90–91, 150–151, 172, 186–187; classical, 40, 47, 54, 55–57, 68–69, 106, 172,
184; debate over adopting, 14–18,
19–20, 22–23; early ritual changes of,
16, 20, 22, 33, 35, 36–39, 40, 47–49,
204n31, 205n2, 205n6; festivals and

life-cycle events of, 24, 28; gender-
neutral language, adoption of, 165;
Messianism, rejection of, 20, 34, 205n3;
and mixed seating/family pews, 18, 19,
22, 29, 68–69, 72, 106, 205n1; modern,
86, 87, 104–106, 131, 138–139, 148–149,
153–154, 161, 176; and music, 16, 18–20,
22, 204n31; new American, 125–126,
128, 163–166, 171, 175–176, 197–198;
and Pittsburgh Platform, (1885) 34,
40; scientific rationalism, connection
to, 19, 34–36, 49–51, 54; and Sephardic
Hebrew pronunciation, adoption of
(1961), 115, 221n22; Sunday Sabbath,
debate over, 36, 44–45, 210n56. *See also*
Bar/bat mitzvah; Confirmation; Friday
evening services; Sunday worship
services
Reform Youth Federation of Temple Israel
(RYFTI), 145
Refusniks, 121, 135, 158–159, 185, 227n58
Reimer, Joseph, 171, 228n16
Religious school, 23–25, 40–42, 69–71, 99,
108–113, 139, 142–147, 156–158, 188–189,
199–200, 223n6; at branch schools,
65–67, 70, 73, 80; college-level classes,
128, 130; curriculum of, 10–11, 23,
33–35, 57–58, 65, 78–81, 88–89, 108–109,
128–129, 143–145; and Education
Committee, 25, 37, 80, 88, 110–111,
135; enrollment in, 17, 59, 70, 126, 145,
195, 216n5, 224n21; facilities, 22–23,
29, 47, 73, 76–77, 107–109; family, 145,
180–181; Hebrew language study, 10,
23, 33–34, 58, 88–89, 99, 108–110, 143,
184–186; kindergarten (1950), 99,
108, 145; Monday night school (1979),
143, 145; peak years of, 73, 78, 96, 108;
post-confirmation classes, 23, 59,
99, 108–109, 112, 128, 143; preschool,
162–164, 195, 227n6, 228n7; staff,

258 *Index*

ABOUT THE AUTHORS

MEAGHAN DWYER-RYAN is a Ph.D. candidate in American history at Boston College, specializing in immigration and ethnicity. Her forthcoming dissertation is entitled, "Ethnic Patriotism in Boston's Irish and Jewish Communities, 1880–1929." She has contributed articles to such publications as *The Encyclopedia on U.S. Immigration and Ethnic History*, *New York Irish History*, *Foilsiú*, *The Encyclopedia of Ireland*, and the *Dictionary of American History*. A graduate of New York University's Archives and Public History Program, she has been the archivist at Temple Israel since 2002.

SUSAN L. PORTER, a historian who specializes in American social history, is a scholar at the Brandeis University Women's Studies Research Center, a faculty member in Museum Studies at the Harvard Extension School, and a research consultant. After earning her Ph.D. at Boston University, she taught history for many years at Boston-area colleges, including Simmons College (1990–1997). From 2000 to 2005, she was the research manager at Historic New England (formerly the Society for the Preservation of New England Antiquities). She is the editor of *Women of the Commonwealth: Work, Family, and Social Change in Nineteenth-Century Massachusetts* (University of Massachusetts Press, 1996) and the *Pierce House Historic Property Report* (Historic New England, 2005), and the author of *Gendered Benevolence: Orphan Asylums in Antebellum America* (Johns Hopkins University Press, forthcoming). She has also published essays on the history of child welfare, adoption, and work and curated several exhibitions.

LISA FAGIN DAVIS is a medieval bibliographer and manuscript consultant in the Boston area; her Ph.D. is from Yale University. Published works include *The Gottschalk Antiphonary: Music and Liturgy in Twelfth-Century Lambach* (Cambridge University Press, 2000), *Pre-1600 Manuscripts in the United States and Canada: A Directory of Current Repositories and a Record of Dispersed Collections from the Census and Supplement* (Bibliographical Society of America, forthcoming) with Melissa Conway, and *La Chronique Anonyme Universelle jusqu'à la mort de Charles VII* (Brepols Publishers, forthcoming).